Praise for Author Gary Eldred

"Donald Trump and I have created Trump University to offer the highest quality, success-driven education available. Our one goal is to help professionals build their careers, businesses, and wealth. That's why we selected Gary Eldred to help us develop our first courses in real estate investing. His books stand out for their knowledge-packed content and success-driven advice."

—*Michael W. Sexton, CEO*
Trump University

"Gary has established himself as a wise and insightful real estate author. His teachings educate and inspire."

—*Mark Victor Hansen, Coauthor,*
Chicken Soup for the Soul

"I just finished reading your book *Investing in Real Estate, 4th Edition.* This is the best real estate investment book that I have read so far. Thanks for sharing your knowledge about real estate investment."

—*Gwan Kang*

"I really enjoyed your book, *Investing in Real Estate.* I believe it's one of the most well-written books on real estate investing currently on the market."

—*Josh Lowry*
Bellevue, WA
President of Lowry Properties

"I just purchased about $140 worth of books on real estate and yours is the first one I finished reading because of the high reviews it got. I certainly wasn't let down. Your book has shed light on so many things that I didn't even consider. Your writing style is excellent. Thanks again."

—*Rick Reumann*

"I am currently enjoying and learning a lot from your book *Investing in Real Estate.* Indeed it's a powerful book."

—*Douglas M. Mutavi*

"Thanks so much for your valuable book. I read it cover to cover. I'm a tough audience, but you've made a fan here. Your writing is coherent, simple, and clean. You are generous to offer the benefits of your years of experience to those starting out in this venture."

—*Lara Ewing*

The 106 Common Mistakes Homebuyers Make (and How to Avoid Them)

FOURTH EDITION

GARY W. ELDRED, PhD

WILEY

John Wiley & Sons, Inc.

Published by John Wiley & Sons, Inc., Hoboken, New Jersey.
Published simultaneously in Canada.

Limit of Liability/Disclaimer of Warranty: While the publisher and author have used their best efforts in preparing this book, they make no representations or warranties with respect to the accuracy or completeness of the contents of this book and specifically disclaim any implied warranties of merchantability or fitness for a particular purpose. No warranty may be created or extended by sales representatives or written sales materials. The advice and strategies contained herein may not be suitable for your situation. You should consult with a professional where appropriate. Neither the publisher nor author shall be liable for any loss of profit or any other commercial damages, including but not limited to special, incidental, consequential, or other damages.

For general information on our other products and services or for technical support, please contact our Customer Care Department within the United States at (800) 762-2974, outside the United States at (317) 572-3993 or fax (317) 572-4002.

Wiley also publishes its books in a variety of electronic formats. Some content that appears in print may not be available in electronic books. For more information about Wiley products, visit our web site at www.wiley.com.

Library of Congress Cataloging-in-Publication Data:

Eldred, Gary W.
    The 106 common mistakes homebuyers make : and how to avoid them / Gary W.
Eldred.--4th ed.
        p. cm.
    Includes index.
    ISBN-13 978-0-471-75123-6 (pbk.)
    ISBN-10 0-471-75123-5 (pbk.)
    1. House buying. I. Title: One hundred six common mistakes homebuyers make. II.
Title: Common mistakes homebuyers make. III. Title.

    HD1379.E43   2005
    643'.12--dc22   2005047505

Printed in the United States of America.

10 9 8 7 6 5 4 3 2 1

Preface to the Fourth Edition

Successful sales for the three previous editions of *106 Mistakes* proved that this unique guide to mistake-free homebuying will give you the heads-up knowledge you need. Indeed, I greatly appreciate the positive comments that readers have sent me (via e-mail: gary@garyeldred.com) as well as favorable media reviews (a special thanks to Robert Bruss). In addition, *106 Mistakes* has been condensed by *Reader's Digest* and cited in many leading publications such as *Business Week, Money Magazine, Your Money, Bottom Line,* and *Kiplinger's Personal Finance.*

Now, this new fourth edition keeps everything that past readers have found helpful, but it also presents the latest developments in the fields of homebuying and mortgage lending. Plus, we've added examples and information that show you how to:

1. Identify homes that will appreciate the fastest.
2. Qualify and secure lower cost financing.
3. Work profitably with your real estate agent and loan broker.
4. Understand the ins and outs of credit-scoring.
5. Write and negotiate your purchase offers.
6. Gain valuable information from the Internet.

Because failing to buy remains the number-one mistake of renters, this fourth edition includes an expanded Chapter 11, "How to Afford the Home You Want." This chapter leads you through the mortgage qualifying process and shows you how to shape up your finances and strengthen your borrower profile. Because many homebuyers still mistakenly accept without question the so-called standard purchase contract form, Chapter 12, "Writing Your Offer," explains the pitfalls of such contracts and tells how to rewrite them to achieve a win-win agreement.

For homebuyers who wish to use the web, I've included within each chapter various web sites where you can research topics such as home values and sales prices, neighborhood data, mortgage loans and costs, financial calculators, consumer information, environmental hazards, bargain-priced properties, credit scores, credit records, and school rankings. For your convenience, I've also listed these web sites in an Internet Appendix. You'll find a comprehensive homebuyer checklist that integrates with the topics covered in this new edition at the web site, www. stoprentingnow.com.

I've written this fourth edition of *106 Mistakes* to guide you through a satisfying and profitable homebuying adventure. I wish you the best as you move toward your cherished goal of home ownership.

Special Note for Investors

Although I originally wrote *106 Mistakes* to guide homebuyers, investors (both new and experienced) have told me that the examples in this book have helped them avoid buying the wrong property. Condo investors especially appreciate the tips on how to read markets and forecast price increases.[1] So, whether you buy a home or an investment property, *106 Mistakes* will guide you to a better choice. Indeed, when you follow this advice, your home will almost certainly prove to be your best investment.

Acknowledgments

For their valuable help in preparing this fourth edition, I thank my secretary Barbara Smerage and assistant Mohsen Mofid.

---

[1]See also, Gary W. Eldred, *Make Money with Condominiums and Townhouses*, 2004 (Wiley).

Contents

3   Home Ownership: How to Make It Your Best Investment   40

4   How to Find a Good Buy   69

5   Locate a Great Neighborhood   **95**

6 Is This Home for You? 124

9   **Become a Satisfied Homeowner**   **221**

10 The Biggest Mistakes of All   **249**

11 How to Afford the Home You Want   **257**

12 Draft Your Offer   **280**

Internet Appendix   **301**

Index   **304**

CHAPTER 1

Profit from the Mistakes of Others

Thinking about buying a home? Good for you. You're about to make one of the best personal and financial decisions of your life—if you do it right. And that's just what this book will help you do.

As you read through the eye-opening stories—sometimes funny, sometimes sad—you will see how to steer clear of potential pitfalls. Even better, you will learn to profit from the opportunities that you discover (or create) along the way. You will gain not only from the knowledge I've accumulated from dozens of my own property transactions, but also from the experiences of hundreds of homebuyers, real estate agents, mortgage loan officers, and home inspectors.

Here are some of the fears, mistakes, and pitfalls you'll learn how to handle:

1. Getting turned down for a mortgage
2. Paying too much for mortgage interest, fees, and costs
3. Overpaying for your house
4. Discovering that a house or neighborhood comes with hidden and unwelcome surprises
5. Being taken advantage of by a real estate agent, loan officer, or lawyer
6. Buying too little, too much, or the wrong kind of insurance
7. Suffering discrimination

8. Buying a house whose value doesn't appreciate much
9. Running into problems at (or on the way to) closing
10. Buying a house that doesn't meet your needs, wants, or budget

Unlike other books on homebuying, the discussions here don't merely present general principles, simplistic questions, or a "homebuying process." Instead, *106 Mistakes* illustrates what you need to know through dozens of real-life examples. Through these examples, you'll see how to conquer your confusion, become more confident, and make the right homebuying decision.

The Origin of This Book

Throughout the past 20 years I've taught graduate and undergraduate college courses in real estate; professional education programs for Realtors®, home builders, and mortgage loan officers; and STOP RENTING NOW!™ seminars that are directed especially toward first-time homebuyers. In these courses, one of the most favored classroom topics has been "How to prevent mistakes in homebuying."

Although just about everyone knows that real estate, particularly home ownership, stands out as one of the best ways to build personal wealth, a growing number of people also realize that successful homebuying doesn't occur easily. It requires education. Shopping for a home, negotiating, arranging financing, and qualifying to buy have become much more complex. There are many ways to get bamboozled. Naturally, then, learning about the mistakes of others has proved to be a good prescription for a happy and profitable homebuying experience.

When I first began to discuss mistakes in homebuying with my classes, I relied on many of my own experiences (and mistakes). Over time, though, students were eager to broaden their knowledge and learn firsthand about the mishaps, misfortunes, and mistakes suffered by others. As a result, I incorporated "interview papers" into class assignments. To carry out these assignments, students interviewed Realtors, home builders, loan officers, recent homebuyers, and other people involved in homebuying and financing.

The students asked their interviewees to describe in concrete detail the homebuying mistakes that the interviewees had made themselves or had seen others make. Next, the students wrote up their conversations and we scheduled a class session or two to discuss what they had learned.

These classroom discussions became quite popular. As a result, many students suggested that they would like to see the most common (and costly) mistakes I've collected brought together in a book. Fortunately, John Wiley & Sons, Inc., and senior editor Michael Hamilton agreed. In this book we've aimed to help you benefit from the experiences of hundreds of people who have been involved in homebuying. Read through these stories and apply the lessons to your own situation. You'll enjoy a more profitable and more satisfying homebuying adventure.

---

[1]To protect the privacy of individuals, in many instances I've changed names and specific identifying facts. But all told, these experiences are real.

CHAPTER 2

Explore Possibilities, Set Priorities

As you search for a home, you'll run up against many choices, confusions, and contradictions. You may face discouragement. In fact, some potential homebuyers give up on the challenges they encounter. They then make the biggest mistake of all: They needlessly continue to rent.

As you go through this chapter you will see that, regardless of your present situation, the power of knowledge, motivation, and goals can move you into the home you want.

You also will see why you can profit when you explore various neighborhoods, price ranges, types of homes, and home features. Even if you think you can describe (and afford) the perfect home, the mistakes in this chapter show you why you should still broaden your knowledge of the market. Greater knowledge will encourage you to rethink your priorities and discover better alternatives for you at this stage of your life.

MISTAKE # **1**

We want to own, but we pay less to rent.

LESSON: *Over time, you will pay far more to rent than to own. Plus, homeowners gain the wealth-building power of home equity.*

Do you believe that you'll pay more to own than to rent? If so, you're experiencing the same confusion that troubles many of the renters who attend my STOP RENTING NOW!™ seminars. They want to own, but they hesitate because they think owning costs too much. Undoubtedly, the recent increase in home prices has made this myth even more prevalent.

But here are the facts you need to know: After you weigh in income tax deductions, personal freedom, long-term rent increases, and the accumulation of wealth through growing home equity, you will see why it actually costs much more to rent. In addition, renters stand to lose tens (and often hundreds) of thousands in net worth.

Benefit from Tax Deductions

As a homeowner, you can deduct most of your monthly mortgage payments from your taxable income. As a result, your actual out-of-pocket home costs may fall—depending on your combined federal, state, and local marginal income tax rate (MTR)—to 20 to 40 percent less than the actual check you write each month to your mortgage lender.

Say your house payment (principal, interest, property taxes, and insurance) will cost $1,000 a month. Chances are, after counting the tax benefits of owning, that $1,000 may cost you only $700. A $2,000-per-month mortgage payment may cost you around $1,400 a month. Or to look at it in terms of rent, if you're paying your landlord $600 a month, you may be able to afford $750 to $800 a month for your own home. If you're now paying $1,800 per month in rent, you might be able to go up to $2,500 a month for your mortgage payment. To get a general idea of your potential savings, see Table 2.1.

Your personal rent-versus-own cost figures will differ from those listed. But this point is true: Don't assume that monthly mortgage payments will

Table 2.1 **Rent-Equivalent Mortgage Payments after Benefit of Tax Deduction**

	Marginal Tax Bracket (After-Tax Costs)			
Monthly Rent($)	.15 (MTR)	.25 (MTR)	.33 (MTR)	.40 (MTR)
450	530	600	672	750
600	706	800	896	1,000
750	882	1,000	1,119	1,250
900	1,058	1,200	1,343	1,500
1,200	1,412	1,600	1,791	2,000
1,500	1,765	2,000	2,239	2,500
2,000	2,667	3,200	2,985	3,333

cost more than renting. Talk with a loan representative and tax advisor. Run through specific figures. In today's world of home finance, lenders offer multiple ways to obtain lower monthly payments. Quite likely, you'll be pleasantly surprised to learn how advantageous it is to own.

Escape from Renter's Jail

After buying her own home, Yolanda Jones told me, "I can't believe it. Not only am I saving money each month and building equity, but I feel like I've escaped from renter's jail." When I asked her what she meant by "renter's jail," Yolanda explained, "For the first time in my life I feel free. No more landlords to tell me how I can decorate, who I can have over, or whether I can get a dog. This is my home now. I'm free to do with it what I want. Even if it costs me more it'd be worth it."

Yolanda brings out a point many renters overlook. When you own, you don't just buy a home, you gain freedom. You escape from renter's jail. If you're like Yolanda, the personal benefits of owning will far surpass those of renting. When figuring your rent-versus-own cost comparisons, keep in mind those great feelings of freedom and security that owning will bring you.

Think Long Term: Rents Will Go Up

We've all heard dozens of times how America's corporate management focuses on the short term instead of the long term. Renters commit a similar error. In some high-cost areas of the country even after allowing for tax deductions and owner benefits, your monthly mortgage costs still may look higher than the costs of renting. If that's your situation, think long term. In fact, no matter where you live, the most important reason to buy a home is not to save money today. It's to save hundreds of thousands of dollars over the rest of your life.

Say you pay $1,000 a month to rent. Assume that after tax deductions, owning will cost you $1,500 a month out-of-pocket. Renting sure looks cheaper. But wait—don't fall into this trap. Think: If you've got a fixed-rate mortgage, your monthly mortgage payments won't go up— and if at some later date you can refinance at lower interest rates, your monthly costs of owning actually will go down.

In stark contrast, over the longer term, you can only expect your rent to increase. Even at relatively modest rates of inflation, rent levels will head up to the stratosphere. Table 2.2 provides several examples of how rents will increase at rates of four, six, and eight percent a year.

Some of those future rent figures look absurdly large. But consider the rent levels of the 1940s and 1950s. In most parts of the country, you could rent a nice house for $25 to $75 a month. Average house payments were $40 to $60 a month. Today's rent and mortgage payments often run 20 to 40 times higher than the amounts of those earlier years. Likewise, you can safely bet that over the next 20 or 30 years, people in the future will be talking about the ridiculously low rents of the early 2000s.

Fortunately, today's homebuyers will still enjoy mortgage payments at those "ridiculously" low early 2000s prices (and interest rates) decades into the twenty-first century. Those who didn't buy will be paying (if they can afford them) rents 3 to 10 times higher. And if we get years of double-digit inflation similar to previous years, rents could even shoot past the figures in Table 2.2. Over time, owning costs far less than renting—and the benefits are far greater.

When it comes to buying a home, think long term. Pay no attention to how high home prices are today compared to where they sat 5, 10, or 20 years ago. Instead, think how *low* today's prices are compared to where they'll be perched 5, 10, or 20 years from now.

Table 2.2 **Escalating Rents**

Future Monthly Rents with Annual Increases of 4%

Today's Monthly Rent	10	20	30	40
$500	$740	$1,095	$1,620	$2,400
750	1,100	1,642	2,430	3,600
1,000	1,480	2,190	3,240	4,800
2,000	2,960	4,382	6,487	9,602

Future Monthly Rents with Annual Increases of 6%

Today's Monthly Rent	10	20	30	40
$500	$895	$1,600	$2,891	$ 5,140
750	1,342	2,400	4,308	7,715
1,000	1,790	3,200	5,743	10,285
2,000	3,582	6,414	11,487	20,571

Future Monthly Rents with Annual Increases of 8%

Today's Monthly Rent	10	20	30	40
$500	$1,075	$2,330	$ 5,000	$10,862
750	1,612	3,495	7,500	16,293
1,000	2,150	4,666	10,000	21,725
2,000	4,318	9,322	20,125	43,449

Homeowners Build Wealth

We will talk more about the investment benefits of home ownership in Chapter 3. For now, notice the great wealth-building power of home ownership—even in periods of relatively low inflation. True, throughout our country's 200-year history, home prices have proved cyclical: sometimes fast appreciation, sometimes slow; sometimes recession, sometimes depression. Yet, over time, homeowners have always built more wealth than renters.

As you make your monthly mortgage payments, your outstanding loan balance steadily falls—slowly at first, then more rapidly. Even if your home doesn't appreciate much (which is unlikely), at the end of your mortgage term (15, 20, 25, 30, or 40 years) you will own a valuable property free and clear. But at rates of appreciation of say three, five, or seven percent, your home equity will grow to hundreds of thousands of dollars (see Figure 2.1).

As renters become poorer through rising rents, you will become richer through growing home equity. Without a doubt (and in more ways than one), continuing to rent will cost you dearly.

MISTAKE # **2**

We want to own, but we don't have enough for a down payment.

LESSON: *You don't need much savings for a down payment. You may not even need a down payment.*

I was listening to a talk-radio show recently. The subject discussed was "no-money-down" home financing. Just as I tuned in I heard an agent angrily say, "I've been selling real estate for 25 years, and I've never seen a nothing-down deal." This agent went on to complain about the "hucksters" pushing nothing-down seminars, books, and tapes who had gotten rich deceiving the public. "People who attend these seminars and watch too much late-night television just waste my time," this sales agent said. "I tell 'em when they call me, 'If you don't have the money to buy, go bother someone else.' "

Work with Agents or Lenders Who Understand Possibility Analysis

Now contrast this agent's attitude to that of Realtor Joan Evans. "Anytime someone comes into our office seeking a rental," Joan says, "the first thing I do is ask them, 'Do you really want to rent? Or would you rather own?' More often than not, they say, 'Sure, we would like to own, but we don't have enough for a down payment.' When I hear that, that's when I go to work. One of the best parts of my job is to take renters who think that they don't have enough money to own and then figure out ways to turn them into homeowners. Granted, it's not a piece of cake; sometimes it takes six months or more. But I've found many of these

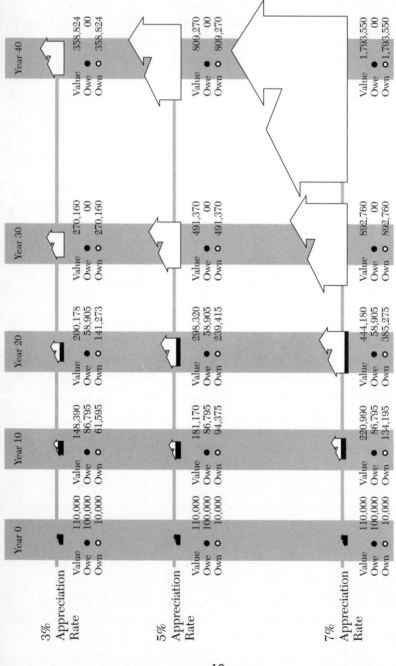

Figure 2.1 Building Home Equity. (To calculate your future equity with a higher-priced home, multiply the figures shown above by a factors of 2, 3, 4, or other multipliers that might apply to your purchase relative to the modest $110,000 in this example.)

buyers become my most loyal clients and a great source of referrals and repeat business."

If you are short on cash, look for a Realtor like Joan Evans. Quickly drop run-of-the-mill agents who show a don't-bother-me attitude to any-one with less than a five-figure bank account.

For the past several years, mortgage lenders, homebuilders, not-for-profit housing groups, and government agencies have been reaching out to cash-short renters who would like to become homeowners. You now have dozens of little- or nothing-down home finance plans to choose from:

- FHA (Federal Housing Administration) 203(b)
- FHA 203(k)
- FHA assumables
- HUD (Department of Housing and Urban Development) fore-closed homes
- Fannie 97
- Freddie Mac Discover the Gold
- Neighborhood Housing Services
- Central city mortgages
- Community Reinvestment Act programs
- Rural Economic Development Programs (formerly Farmers Home Administration)
- Lease-options
- Lease-purchase
- Sweat equity
- State mortgage bond programs
- Land contracts
- Seller "trust deeds"
- Seller seconds
- VA (Department of Veterans Affairs) mortgages
- VA assumables
- State VA programs
- Habitat for Humanity homes
- New home builder grants
- Economic opportunity programs

- Private mortgage insurance
- Pledged collateral
- Gift letters
- Family loans
- Fannie Mae rehab loans
- Fannie Mae and Freddie Mac zero down
- Wrap arounds
- Self-contracting
- Shared equity
- City down payment assistance
- County down payment assistance
- Co-ownership
- Create value/fixers
- Not-for-profit grants
- Employer assistance
- Government grants
- Neighborhood Advantage Mortgage
- Community Homebuyer Programs
- First-time buyer programs
- Coborrowers
- Cosigners
- Blanket mortgages
- REOs (real estate owned by lenders after it's gone through fore-closure)
- Manufactured home financing

We'll look at little- or nothing-down financing in more depth in Chapter 8. For more home-financing possibilities, read my book *106 Mortgage Secrets All Homebuyers Must Learn—But Lenders Don't Tell*, 2003 (Wiley).

To discover ways to buy cash-short in your area, closely read the real estate sections and real estate ads in your local newspapers. Over the course of a month or two, you're likely to see many properties or finance plans that are available with little or no money down.

Buying when you're cash poor may not prove easy. But loan reps and real estate pros who know all the homebuying possibilities will be able to help you locate, develop, and qualify for the financing you need to become a homeowner.

MISTAKE # **3**

We can't afford to buy; the monthly payments are too high.

LESSON: *If you can afford to rent, you can afford to own.*

Before you convince yourself you can't afford to buy, make sure you compare your rent and mortgage payments on an *after-tax* basis (see Mistake #1). But if monthly payments still look too high, don't give up. There are many ways to get over the "unaffordable" monthly payment hurdle. Here's how Doreen Bierbrier did it.

At the time she bought her first home, Doreen says, "I was earning a modest salary (by Washington, D.C., standards) as a government worker…. The only way I could buy a house in a good neighborhood was to find one large enough to accommodate a couple of housemates who paid rent. If everything worked out, the rental income would cover more than half my house payment and two-thirds of the utilities. Adding in tax advantages and appreciation, I figured I would actually make money. Further, when the loan on the house was paid off, I would own a valuable asset free and clear."

As time has proven, Doreen had the right idea. While many moderately paid singles and couples have mistakenly pleaded "not enough income" to buy (see also Mistake #5), others like Doreen have acted creatively and figured out ways to bridge the gap between their current earnings and affordability. Other than taking in housemates, you might also:

- Create an accessory apartment in your home (sometimes called a mother-in-law suite) by converting a garage, attic, or den.
- Reduce your monthly payments with an adjustable-rate mortgage.
- Reduce your monthly payments with a graduated-payment mortgage.

- Reduce your monthly payments by using a balloon mortgage.
- Buy a duplex, triplex, or other type of home that's already producing income that will help cover the monthly mortgage payments.
- See if your area offers a mortgage credit certificate (MCC) program. Through MCCs, the federal government gives you a mortgage subsidy of up to $2,000 a year.
- Take up a part-time job.
- Ask your employer for a raise or housing assistance.
- Buy with someone else.
- Secure an interest rate buy down (discussed in Chapter 8).
- Assume a low-interest FHA or VA loan.
- Assume a low-equity adjustable-rate mortgage.

Generally, these techniques either reduce your monthly payments or increase your available income. But to really boost your borrowing/buying power, prioritize your spending (and savings!).

Match Your Spending to Your Goals

Whenever renters say they can't afford to own, I ask them to list all of their typical monthly expenses. Nine times out of 10, their list reveals spending patterns that wildly deviate from these renters' professed priorities. In other words, they nearly all say that they value home ownership highly. Yet, they spend much of their money on such things as upscale rentals, new cars, boats, jet skis, travel, entertainment, furniture, vacations, electronics, eating out, and many other fleeting pleasures.

Before you complain about affordability, fill in the blanks below. Find out where your money really goes each month:

Rent $_____
Electricity $_____
Gas $_____
Cable TV $_____
Internet charges $_____
Online charges $_____
Telephone(s) $_____

Car payment no. 1	$_____
Car payment no. 2	$_____
Gasoline	$_____
Automobile insurance	$_____
Groceries	$_____
Child care	$_____
Clothing	$_____
Electronics	$_____
Lunches	$_____
Dining out	$_____
Entertainment	$_____
Tobacco	$_____
Beer, wine, liquor	$_____
Other vices	$_____
Health club	$_____
Magazines	$_____
Newspapers	$_____
Furniture	$_____
Appliances	$_____
School expenses	$_____
Health insurance	$_____
Weekend trips	$_____
Vacations	$_____
Housekeepers	$_____
Personal care	$_____
Credit card interest	$_____
Other	$_____
Other	$_____
Other	$_____
Other	$_____
Total	$_____

Now, compare your spending to your priorities. I'll bet you'll find many ways to eliminate (or reduce) wasteful expenses so you can put more money toward your long-term wealth and well-being: home ownership.

Summing Up

At first glance—especially if you live in San Diego or Boston—it's too easy to conclude that you can't afford the monthly payments on the home you want. But first consider the tax benefits of owning. Then look for creative ways to increase your income, cut your expenses, or use some type of affordable, low payment home finance plan. The successful homebuying experiences of millions of moderate-income renters prove that if you can afford to rent, you can afford to buy.

MISTAKE # **4**

No bank will give us a mortgage.

LESSON: Many banks and mortgage lenders have special programs for hard-to-finance buyers. Even better, you may not need bank financing.

When Mary and Joe Cortez filed for bankruptcy, they thought they had lost their chance to become homeowners. They were wrong. Just a little more than a year later, this couple successfully bought their first home with a low-down-payment FHA loan. "We couldn't believe it," says Mary. "Friends told us we wouldn't be able to get credit for years."

No doubt, lenders prefer borrowers whose credit scores top the charts. But the good news is that mortgage lenders need to make loans. And with thousands of potential mortgage lenders, if you're willing and able to make your mortgage payments on time, you can probably find the loan you need to buy a home.

As long as your past financial difficulties do not carry forward into the present, many lenders will give you a chance. Either convince a lender that your blemished credit occurred for reasons outside your control (plant closing, medical bills, business failure, divorce, unemployment) or show persuasive evidence that you've mended your borrow-and-spend ways. Even homebuyers with terrible past credit can qualify for a mortgage—but it does require planning, preparation, and sincere efforts. (Also see Mistake #93.)

Hopefully, you haven't filed for bankruptcy or faced serious credit problems. Nevertheless, you may mistakenly believe that other kinds of problems will block you from getting a loan. Maybe you're self-employed or have been in your current job for less than two years. Maybe you're a college student who works only part-time. Maybe you want to spend 50 percent of your income for a home. Whatever your particular situation, don't assume you can't qualify. Many lenders now specialize in less-than-perfect credit risks with loans graded in B, C, and D categories.

Ask around. Talk to knowledgeable Realtors, mortgage brokers, or even other homebuyers who have faced the same kinds of problems you're facing. In today's mortgage market, nearly everyone can either qualify for some type of home finance plan or place themselves on a path to get qualified within 6 to 24 months. (Beware, through, some sun-prime [predatory] lenders prey on people who have credit problems. See Chapter 8, "Avoid the Sharks or You'll Get Eaten Alive," in my book *106 Mortgage Secrets All Homebuyers Must Learn—But Lenders Don't Tell*).

Look for Owner Financing

When I first started buying houses and small apartment buildings, I was an undergraduate college student. I had no established credit, minimal savings, and only a part-time job. My strategy was to find older people who had tired of managing their rental properties, yet liked the monthly income their properties provided. These types of sellers proved to be great candidates for owner-will-carry (OWC) financing.

By selling their properties to someone who was young and ambitious, they got rid of the hassles of wayward tenants, stopped-up toilets, and furnace breakdowns. At the same time, the money they earned in interest on their seller mortgages gave them better returns than they could have earned from bank savings accounts or certificates of deposit (and far less risk than stocks).

The great thing about owner financing is that owners are free to lend to whomever they please on whatever terms you negotiate.

If it turns out you really can't get a bank or savings institution to lend you the money you need to buy a home, look for OWC financing. Or just skip the banks to begin with. Many homebuyers and real estate investors never worry about qualifying for a mortgage with a typical lender. They only finance their properties with sellers.

MISTAKE # 5

Our agent told us to get prequalified (or preapproved) by a lender so we would know exactly how much home we could afford

LESSON: *No lender can tell you exactly how much home you can afford. Affordability depends on you, not the lender.*

All across the country, mortgage lenders and real estate agents tell homebuyers to get prequalified so they know exactly how much home they can afford. It's as if getting prequalified for a mortgage were like being measured for a custom-made suit. It isn't. How much home you can afford depends on you.

Can you increase your income? Can you cut your expenses? What type of home finance plan are you willing to use? Are MCC (mortgage credit certificate) programs available in your area? Are first-time buyer programs available? What kinds of special financing incentives are new homebuilders or condo and townhouse developers offering? Do you have friends, relatives, or an employer who can make you a gift or a loan? Are you willing to buy a property that includes an accessory apartment or additional rental unit? How much are you willing to stretch your budget? Would you share your home with housemates? Can you buy jointly with someone else? Can you locate an owner who is willing to carry back financing?

Affordability Is Up to You

How much home you can afford depends on answers to these and many other questions. When you look for a house, find a Realtor or mortgage lender who is skilled in *possibility* analysis. Don't rely on fill-in-the-blank preapproval calculations or instant computer automated underwriting programs. You have dozens (even hundreds) of ways to buy and finance your home. Thousands of mortgage lenders and thousands of property owners stand ready to make financing available.

Prequalifying with a specific lender can give you a general idea of how much you can spend based on your current finances and that lender's (or underwriter's) qualifying standards and loan programs. But it can't reveal all of your possibilities. Only through your own efforts of financial planning and possibility analysis can you really decide how much home you can afford and the type of financing that will work best for your situation.

Prequalification versus Preapproval

With prequalification, a lender tells you how much loan you can qualify for based upon the information you provide. A prequalifying letter doesn't mean that a lender will actually make you a loan.

For that you need a *preapproval.* Many lenders will actually preapprove you for a specific loan amount—even before you've found a home to buy. In fact, Robert Bruss, the respected real estate columnist, repeatedly encourages homebuyers to get preapproved because a preapproval letter tells real estate agents and sellers that you are a serious, no-credit-problem buyer. Once you locate the home you want (that's within your preapproved borrowing limit), the agent and sellers can feel secure. They feel confident that you can obtain the financing you need.

Nevertheless, just like prequalifying, preapproved borrowing power depends on specific lenders, loan programs, interest rates, and how well you've shaped up your financial fitness and credit scores. Preapproval works to your advantage. But don't mistake one lender's loan amount for a full view of your home finance possibilities. Note, too, that even a preapproval letter does not guarantee that the lender will actually grant you the loan. The underwriter must still verify all of your documentation and make sure you and the property satisfy other rules and guidelines.

MISTAKE # **6**

Our agent said not to waste time looking at homes outside our price range.

LESSON: Learn about the market of homes priced above and below your "price range."

This mistake follows from the simplistic notion of prequalifying that's become so popular. Just as no one can tell you exactly how much home you can afford, neither do you necessarily face a tightly defined price range. Your full price range depends on your possibility analysis.

Here's another reason you want to look at homes above and below your price range. You can't know what kind of home and neighborhood to aim for until you widely shop the market. Consider the experience of Sue and Bill Henderson:

Sue and Bill followed their agent's advice and looked only at homes in their price range of $260,000 to $280,000. Then after they bought, they were out driving around and went through some open houses in the $285,000 to $325,000 range.

"Wow," said Sue. "We had no idea $300,000 would buy so much more house than we got for our $265,000. These homes are bigger and nicer. If we had known, we would have stretched our budget and prioritized our finances. Maybe we would have switched to an ARM [adjustable-rate mortgage] instead of using a fixed-rate mortgage. We could have even gotten a better school district."

First, Learn What's on the Menu

Don't let someone pigeonhole you into a narrow price range. Look at a wide selection of homes and neighborhoods. Too many real estate agents will ask you, "How much would you like to spend (invest) in a home?" Now imagine walking into a new restaurant and sitting down at a table. The waiter comes up and asks, "What would you like to order?" You probably say, "I don't know. I haven't seen the menu." Of course, you might also want to know what credit cards the restaurant accepts.

The situation is similar when shopping for a home. Make sure you've thoroughly looked over what's on the menu and what kinds of financing are available. If you don't see what you want, switch to a different neighborhood (just as you might look for another restaurant if you weren't satisfied with the menu or terms of credit). You might find you are willing to pay more than you first thought. Or you might decide to spend less. Maybe $250,000 will give you what you need most for now. Instead of paying $265,000, you can use the money you save for a more comfortable lifestyle, or perhaps other investments.

Don't fix on a home, neighborhood, or price range until you've looked at a varied selection of properties and neighborhoods (within reason, of course). Learn your choices. Compare their relative prices and benefits. Then weigh your trade-offs. You'll make a better homebuying decision—a decision you'll be happy to live with.

MISTAKE # *7*

Sure, we would like to buy our own home someday.

LESSON: *Dreams move on if you wait too long. Put a plan into action now.*

In my seminars, I frequently meet renters in their mid- to late 30s and even early 40s who haven't yet bought their first home. "Why didn't you buy earlier?" I ask them. "Well, we didn't think we could afford it," they often reply.

But this answer doesn't ring true. Why? Because from 20 years of teaching and working in real estate, I know that nearly everyone who wants to own a home can own a home—if they put their minds to it. So I probe further. "What do you mean, you couldn't afford to buy? How many mortgage lenders and savvy real estate agents did you talk to? How many owner-will-carry sellers did you contact? How many books and articles on homebuying did you read? How closely and how frequently did you search through the real estate and home builder ads in your local newspaper?" By asking them questions, I'm not trying to put them on the spot or make them feel bad. Rather, I want them to realize the real reason they didn't buy. It certainly wasn't unaffordability. It was because they failed to set homebuying as a primary goal.

They never educated themselves, planned their finances, or established a time frame to buy. Instead, they procrastinated. Although they knew they wanted to buy, it was always easier to put it off. As long as they told themselves they would buy *someday,* they avoided making the effort and doing the planning that makes homebuying possible.

Sadly, procrastination and limp excuses have cost them tens (sometimes hundreds) of thousands of dollars. You can avoid this mistake. Don't wait for *someday.* Put a homebuying plan into action now. Set up a habit of savings. Guard your credit. Don't spend (or borrow) money for things that are less important than owning your own home. Prioritize with a vengeance.

Whether you want to buy this year, or maybe a year or two down the line, plan now to make sure your dreams come true.

MISTAKE # **8**

I wanted to wait until I got married.

LESSON: *Don't postpone your plan to buy for some indefinite future.*

Some years back, Megin Silver finished her MBA at the University of Virginia and took a good job in Washington, D.C. With one foot in the future, Megin eagerly accepted the challenge of work and career. But with one foot in the past, Megin was uncertain whether a single woman should embark on home ownership. "Anyway," Megin told herself, "I'll probably be married within a few years. It will be better to wait to buy until then."

Years rolled by. Megin was still single. No marriage plans stood on the horizon. Yet, during the time she lived in D.C., Megin watched Washington home prices more than double. She now wishes she had bought earlier. With a refinance at the low interest rates, her mortgage payments would have fallen far below the amount she was paying for rent. Plus, she regrets missing out on years of tax deductions (which in her tax bracket she could certainly have used) and thousands of dollars of equity buildup.

Approximately one of every seven homes sold in the United States is bought by a single person. More than half of these single buyers are women. Just because you're single is no reason to put off buying. And if you can't get the home you want on your own income, close your affordability gap by taking in housemates, buying a property with rental units, or bringing in a cobuyer. Still in doubt? Then consider what these single buyers have said about their successful adventures in home ownership:

- "Most of my friends are getting married and having babies. Home ownership, though, is one milestone that's within my control."
- "With every homebuying challenge I met, I would gain more confidence. Now I feel there's nothing that I can't accomplish."
- "I wanted to move from the suburbs into the city, and it made good financial sense to own. I got a terrific tax break, and if I ever relocated, the place could become an excellent source of rental income."
- "I've lived in apartments all my life and I always wanted to live in a house. When I realized that I could own one for just $400 more a month (before tax deductions) than I was paying in rent, I started looking."
- "Owning a home has grounded me. I used to love going out nights and away on weekends. Now I want to go home and have friends spend the weekend with me."
- "It gave me the confidence to make other investments. I actually opened my first IRA and even got into the stock market this year. After buying a home, I feel ready to tackle any major financial matter."

As you can see from these remarks, singles who buy homes count many benefits from their experience. If you're single, don't postpone homebuying until you get married. And if you're married, don't put it off until you have kids. "Waiting until I get married" or "waiting until we have kids" may sound like a plan. But it isn't. As a practical matter, "waiting for" often proves to be just as indefinite as someday. Don't wait for someday.

MISTAKE # **9**

We were told not to buy unless we planned to stay put for at least four or five years.

LESSON: *Don't wait to buy because you may move within a few years. Instead, execute a short-term ownership strategy.*

Over the years, I've seen dozens of homebuying articles and books tell renters, "Don't buy unless you plan to stay put for at least four or five years." In a simple-minded way, this advice sounds reasonable. When you sell after just two or three years, pay a real estate commission and closing costs, and your home hasn't appreciated much, you could end up losing several thousand dollars.

But what happens if you don't buy? Each year you continue to rent you're losing thousands of dollars in tax deductions (see Mistake #1). As another disadvantage, home prices, mortgage interest rates, or both could jump up quickly, just as they have done in the past. Over time, those increases could cost you tens of thousands of dollars. Although you may incur some risks when you buy, you face even greater risks when you wait to buy.

Develop a Short-Term Ownership Strategy

If you think you might move within a few years, your best bet is to develop a short-term ownership strategy. In her excellent book *Housewise*, Suzanne Brangham tells how she bought and lived in more than a dozen homes over a period of just 15 years. Suzanne explains, "There is no wrong time to buy real estate. Regardless of the market, regardless of interest rates, I've turned a profit on my homes through good times and bad for the past 15 years." To achieve her profits, Suzanne buys homes she can improve. With her talents for redecorating and remodeling, Suzanne adds thousands of dollars in value to the homes she buys.

Buying fixer-uppers isn't the only way to execute a short-term ownership strategy. Reed Povitch boasts, "I make my money when I buy, not when I sell." Reed's strategy is to ferret out bargains. Sometimes he finds highly motivated owners; sometimes he buys at probate or foreclosure sales; on other occasions he buys REOs (real estate owned) from mortgage lenders who have taken back properties from borrowers who haven't made their payments.

Consider a Lease-Option

To Robert Bruss, the highly respected, nationally syndicated real estate columnist, the best short-term buying strategy is the lease-option. "By renting with an option to buy," Bruss advises, "you can establish your credit, build up cash (usually through rent credits) to use as a down payment, and you'll be protected against renewed inflation in housing prices." (You can read the excellent commentary of Robert Bruss at www.inman.com. Bruss has also written a number of helpful booklets on homebuying and investing, including a popular one on lease-options.)

A lease-option gives you another benefit that's often overlooked. If during the option period home prices do go up and you choose not to buy, you can sell the option for a profit to someone else. That person would be able to take advantage of your lower-than-market price and any rent credits you've earned.

Here Are Some Other Short-Term Option Strategies

If you think you may want (or have) to move within a few years, try one of these short-term strategies:

1. Lease-option a home.
2. Assume a low-interest-rate loan that you can get with low amounts of cash and closing costs.
3. Look for a fixer-upper where you can create value for the home.
4. Buy with a low- or no-down-payment assumable FHA or VA loan. When you sell, your buyer can easily take over your financing.

5. Shop for a bargain. (See Chapters 3 and 4 for guidelines.)
6. Buy in a neighborhood that's on the cusp of turnaround and revitalization (fast appreciation).
7. Buy a home that would make a good and profitable rental property. (I've elected this option successfully several times.)
8. Buy into a neighborhood, development, or building where homes are always in short supply and sell fast.

In today's mobile and uncertain world, waiting until you're sure to stay may mean waiting for a lifetime. To put off buying because you might move is generally a mistake. Far better, meet uncertainty with a short-term ownership strategy. If you move in a down market, don't sell. Rent out the home and keep it as an investment until the market heats up again. (For more on the profit potential of rentals, see my book *Investing in Real Estate, 5th Edition,* 2006 [Wiley], and my new book, *The Beginner's Guide to Real Estate Investing,* 2004 [Wiley], and my website, garyeldred.com.)

MISTAKE # **10**

We know exactly what we want.

LESSON: *Maybe. But more than likely you will change your mind. Plus, prepare yourself for trade-offs, compromises, and creativity.*

As noted in Mistake #6, to find a home that best meets your needs, do not commit too early to a specific type of house, price range, or neighborhood. Until you really explore the market, don't narrowly strike houses and areas off your list. Give them a fair chance to prove themselves.

Especially keep an open mind when you work with a real estate agent. Before a real estate agent begins to show you homes, he or she should sit down with you, get to know your feelings, and understand your concerns, likes, dislikes, and financial ability. The best real estate agents don't just sell real estate. They solve problems.

Likewise, when you go to a doctor, you don't walk into the office and say what kind of prescription to write or describe in detail the kind of operation you think you need. Instead, a doctor first asks you a battery of questions and takes some tests. Only after he or she gets to know you does the doctor suggest potential remedies.

As with doctors, real estate agents should practice careful listening and examination. A savvy professional should suggest solutions you may have overlooked. That's what they're really being paid for. (You don't need a chauffeur. You need a thoughtful expert.)

Are Buyers Liars?

Among the less thoughtful agents, there's an old saying, "All buyers are liars." This saying arose because dimwitted and lazy agents see themselves as order takers and chauffeurs, not as problem solvers. When they meet someone who is thinking about buying a home, these agents will ask, "What are you looking for?" or "What price range do you have in mind?"

The buyers might answer, "Well, we'd like a three-bedroom, two-bath ranch, probably in Whitehall or River Ridge." Skipping the preliminaries, this type of agent takes their order and starts showing the couple houses. But as likely as not, the buyers don't buy from that agent. They end up with someone else. Then several weeks later the first agent learns these buyers just had their offer accepted on a duplex in Hyde Park. Over coffee at the nearby Dunkin' Donuts, the agent mutters, "Well, it's happened again. Those folks were just wasting my time. It just proves 'all buyers *are* liars.'"

Knowledge Expands Your Possibilities

Of course, the couple wasn't lying to the agent. They said they wanted a three-bedroom in Whitehall because that's what they thought they wanted. They really hadn't explored their options. After they began to consider the relative advantages and disadvantages of various properties, they changed their minds.

Chances are, you won't buy the type of house you now have in mind. It may not exist. It may cost too much. You might discover other homes you like better. You might decide to trade off some features (property or neighborhood) for other features (fix-up value or investment potential) that you previously hadn't paid much attention to. Maybe through creativity you will overcome the objections to a property (or neighborhood) you originally thought were critical. Or maybe, after all is said and done, you really will find the exact home you think you want. Just don't close your mind too soon to other possibilities.

Features and Goals

Another part of the "we know exactly what we want" mistake is to rank certain home or neighborhood features above your most important priorities. Here's what I mean: When you become a homeowner, you are working toward one or more important goals. "Comfortable place to live" or "the best neighborhood" are two possible goals. But at this stage of your life, maybe you should set other priorities. In other words, take measure of these possible goals:

1. Buy at a bargain price.
2. Buy a home where you can create value through improvements and build equity fast.
3. Buy a home in a neighborhood that is poised to beat the market in appreciation.
4. Buy a home with the price and terms that best match your current budget (better to become a homeowner now than wait until you can afford the home and neighborhood of your dreams).
5. Buy a rental property and live in one of the units.
6. Look for a low-interest-rate assumable mortgage that will reduce your monthly payments.

These goals spell economics rather than lifestyle. By pursuing one or more of these goals, you're saying that the chance to make (or save) money ranks above "comfortable place to live" or "the best neighborhood." Yet, by focusing now on economic advantage as opposed to personal preference, you're really positioning yourself to get a much nicer home in the future.

It's Your Decision

By discussing financial goals, I'm not encouraging you to substitute profits for personal preferences. (In fact, maybe you can figure out a way to achieve both.) But don't tell your agent that you want a three-bedroom, two-bath Craftsman in Cedar Grove until you have explored a range of other possibilities. Who knows? After two or three smart buying decisions over the next several years, you might even be able to afford a Bel-Air or River Oaks type of neighborhood in the not-too-distant future. (Remember Suzanne Brangham. Through a series of renovations over a period of 15 years, she advanced from a $40,000 condo to a $1.5 million estate.)

MISTAKE # **11**

We have to have a pool.

LESSON: *Don't let the tail wag the dog.*

When Carol and Blair Alsop moved from Michigan to Florida, they decided their new home must have a swimming pool. This was the first priority on their list of features. "We only want to look at homes with pools," the Alsops told their Realtor. Even when their Realtor tried to get the couple to consider other homes that would meet most of their other requirements, they refused. "Nope, we've got to have a pool," they emphasized.

As it turned out, not one of the pool homes really excited them. The homes were either too large or too small. They needed repairs. They were located in the "wrong" neighborhoods or school districts. Sometimes they cost too much. Nothing they saw really seemed to click. Finally, their Realtor was able to persuade the couple to at least look at a home that had just come on the market.

Except for the swimming pool, the home had everything the Alsops could hope for. It was the right size, the right neighborhood, and, best of all, the right price. The sellers were even willing to carry back financing at a point less than current bank mortgage rates. The Alsops were tempted. But they said no. "If we're going to live in Florida, we're going to have a pool."

— 29 —

Eventually the Alsops did buy a home. They paid more than they really wanted. The home needed repairs. It was larger than they needed. And the location wasn't their first choice. But it did have a pool.

Unfortunately, shortly after moving into their new home, the Alsops knew they had made a mistake. They didn't use the pool as much as they thought they would. The pool and the house cost too much for maintenance and repairs; and the commute to work was longer than they liked. Within two years after they had bought it, they sold the house and moved. Their new house didn't have a pool.

Keep Features in Perspective

Don't misunderstand. By recounting the Alsops' experience, I'm not advising you to avoid buying a home with a swimming pool. Rather, the Alsops mistakenly insisted that one feature of their home should outweigh the importance of all other features. The Alsops really weren't being true to themselves. They had fixated on an idealized image of Florida living—and to their mind, that type of living included poolside parties, after-work swims for exercise and relaxation, and Saturday morning brunch on the patio.

Nice dream, but their reality differed greatly. The necessities of career ambitions, running a household, and raising a family put considerable distance between their imagined lifestyle and the constraints of their everyday lives.

When you shop for a home, put first things first. Align your goals with your priorities. Anchor your dreams in reality. Then, don't insist on a pool, a third or fourth bedroom, a formal dining room, a formal living room, a den, a fireplace, a two-car garage, a big yard, colonial architecture, a view, or any other features that don't really trump the overall benefits your home and neighborhood must provide. Be willing to trade an idealized image for the way you will actually live.

We all have certain features that we would like in our dream homes. But it's usually a mistake to let these dream features override our better judgment. Try to distinguish clearly your wants from your needs. Don't let the tail wag the dog.

MISTAKE # **12**

We liked the house on Elmwood best, but our furniture wouldn't work there.

LESSON: Buy furniture to fit your new house. Don't buy a new house to fit your old furniture.

Real estate agents say they can tell when buyers get interested in a house. The tape measure is pulled out and the prospective buyers begin to figure whether their furniture will fit in the home. Along this same line, some people will reject a house because "there's no way our furniture will work there." Clearly this is putting the cart before the horse. Present and future needs, not previous decisions you've made about furniture, should govern your choice of a home.

I confess that I almost made this mistake several years ago. At the time, I owned a 3,000-square-foot house and was planning a move to a new area. Upon learning I was single, the agent I was working with suggested several homes she thought I would like in the 1,800- to 2,000-square-foot range. "Oh, my," I said, "those are too small. My furniture wouldn't fit in those houses."

Then I began to recall how I had come to acquire a 3,000-square-foot house. I didn't really want or need such a large home. I had bought it because the house had great views of a lake and was located in a very private setting. After I bought the house, I filled it with furniture.

So here I was ready to reject smaller (and more sensible) houses because my furniture wouldn't fit. Fortunately, after thinking through the ridiculousness of the situation, I sold some furniture and bought an 1,800-square-foot house that I enjoyed much more than I had the larger home.

Like many people, I had almost let a past decision set the course for my future decisions. We are creatures of habit. But a major decision like buying a home should prompt us to reevaluate old habits and old decisions. Whether it's your furniture or some other previous decision, distinguish the way you have lived in the past from how you would like to live in the future. Don't subconsciously let the past phase into prologue.

MISTAKE # **13**

There were so many rules, it was like living under socialism.

LESSON: *When going over your possibilities and priorities, don't just think of home features and neighborhoods. Consider, too, the homeowners' association rules and regulations.*

If you buy into an organized co-op, condo, townhouse, or subdivision development, a homeowners' association will require you to live under its rules and regulations; fine you for violations; put a lien against your home if you don't pay your fines, assessments, or monthly dues; and otherwise make your life unpleasant if you persist in violations of one sort or another.

After Chuck and Michelle Kane bought their new home, they wanted to put in a yard. So Chuck took the first weekend and planted grass seed. Two days later a representative of the homeowners' association stopped by to tell Chuck the bad news. In that subdivision, grass seed was not permitted. To comply with association regulations, the Kanes would have to sod their yard. And to encourage the Kanes to follow all other rules, the association fined the Kanes $200.

Once Chuck and Michelle really started to look over their house rules, they learned:

- Their homeowners' association must approve any exterior design changes or painting they planned for their home.
- Chuck couldn't park his antique Chevy in their driveway while he worked on it.

- The Kanes couldn't put a storage shed in their backyard.
- No outside clotheslines, television antennae, satellite dishes, or basketball hoops were permitted.

What Rules Can You Live With?

When Juanita Maertz bought her townhouse, she knew civil rights laws forced the townhouse development to accept her sons, ages four and six. Except for housing developments restricted to only seniors, neither rental companies nor homeowners' associations may exclude children. But accepting children because of the law and making them welcome are two different issues.

After Juanita moved in, she discovered that no kids could play on the grounds of the development. Parents were supposed to take them to a nearby park. "Sure, we accept kids here," Juanita remembers one disgruntled resident telling her. Then he added, "We just don't tolerate them."

To make her new home livable, Juanita joined her association's board, formed a political coalition with other parents, and eventually got the rules changed to try to create a children-friendly environment. "It was a lot of time and effort," Juanita recalled. "But we had no choice. It's our home, too, and our kids should have the right to play here." Of course, from her viewpoint Juanita is right. But others without children may also feel they have a right to peace and quiet. Unfortunately, there's no easy answer to the question, "What rules and regulations should the association enact and enforce?" Whenever people live together in a large complex or development, they undoubtedly will face some difficult choices. How would you judge rules such as these?

- No more than one pet is allowed per unit. Maximum weight of a pet shall not exceed 15 pounds. (Pets that get fat are evicted.)
- A pet deemed by the board to be noisy or uncontrollable must be disposed of within three days' notice.
- No automobile mechanical work whatsoever will be permitted on the premises.
- Bicycles must be stored in designated areas. They must not be left on the grounds, in hallways, or stored on patios or balconies.

- Personal conduct and attire in the common areas are subject to approval of the board.
- No signs ("for sale" or "for rent") shall be displayed in any manner whatsoever.
- No owner/occupant shall install drapes or curtains within any unit unless such drapes have a white liner visible from outside the unit.
- No entertaining of more than 10 people within a given unit shall be permitted.
- Any owner who wants to offer his or her unit for rent must first obtain the approval of the board. All tenants also must be approved by the board.
- No leases of less than one year are permitted.
- The board retains the right to reject a new purchaser in the development for any lawful reason it deems appropriate.
- No driveway basketball hoops and playing areas are permitted.
- No treehouses may be built.
- No chain-link fences are allowed.

Homeowners' association rules and regulations can touch upon nearly anything you might want to do. Before you choose a development, closely review the restrictions you will live under. Even though it's true that homeowners' associations are run democratically and that most rules and regulations operate to enhance the value and livability of the development, for some homeowners, democratic rule means "tyranny by the majority." The rules imposed are just too socialistic.

MISTAKE # **14**

What! Beans for dinner again?

LESSON: *Put as much money as you can into your home. But first correctly figure necessary living expenses.*

When buying your first home, I believe (generally) that you should stretch your budget and buy as much home as you can. Here's why: Over time, as your earnings go up, your mortgage payments will take a smaller and smaller percentage of your income. Although money might seem tight for a few years, as long as your career progresses, you'll soon move into your comfort zone. Plus, a more expensive house often means that you'll build a larger amount of home equity through appreciation.

What is true generally, however, may not be true specifically. Before you stretch to buy, prepare a realistic (even pessimistic) postpurchase budget. If you're borrowing part of your down payment or planning to spend money to improve your house, allow for these additional expenses. If you are using an adjustable-rate mortgage, figure out how well you could manage financially if the interest rate on your ARM moved up each year to its maximum rate.

After several months of looking for a home, it's tempting to increase your price range. Or maybe you find the perfect house, but it's $40,000 more than you had in mind. You start thinking, "Well, we can borrow $10,000 from Mom and Dad. We can put next summer's vacation on the Visa card. We both will probably be getting raises next year. And even though this house means a longer commute, the extra gas won't cost that much." When thoughts like these start running through your mind, you're not making budget decisions. You're rationalizing.

Before you stretch unwisely, write the figures down and run through the numbers. If you feel satisfied with what you see, go for it. If looking at the numbers makes you feel queasy, ask yourself whether you would be happy on a steady diet of rice, spaghetti, and beans. You *should* own a home. But never put yourself into a position where your home owns you.

MISTAKE # **15**

We bought because we were so tired of looking.

LESSON: *Never buy just to "get the decision over with."*

Homebuying presents a paradox. Planning to buy can give you one of the most exciting times of your life. Most everyone enjoys getting up early Sunday morning, bringing in the newspaper, reading through the homes-for-sale ads, and then later going out to tour neighborhoods, look at open houses, explore possibilities, and imagine what life will be like in a new home.[1] But searching for the right home can also frustrate and depress. At some point, you may reach the let's-forget-the-whole-thing stage. Or you may make a let's-just-buy-something-and-get-it-over-with choice.

If you do begin to feel confused, uncertain, and frustrated, don't let these feelings pull you into an unwise decision. Instead, back up and ask yourself these questions:

- Have we lost touch with our most important feelings, needs, priorities, and goals?
- Do we want to have it all? Are we looking for the perfect home?
- Do we lack confidence in our ability to make a good decision?
- Do our wants or goals lie outside market realities or our financial means?
- Are we buying for ourselves? Or are we worrying about how our friends or relatives will judge our decision?
- Have we really explored a full range of options and possibilities?
- Have we developed a reasonable time schedule for getting to know the market and finding a home?
- Is our ability to choose being unduly influenced by my (our) idealized self-image?
- Can we recast difficulties as opportunities?

By asking these questions, you can probably pinpoint the reasons you're feeling confused, uncertain, or frustrated. More than likely, you're being tugged in different directions because conflicting emotions are pushing and pulling you one way and then another. Decision-making expert Dr. Theodore Rubin calls this type of indecisiveness the chairman-is-missing syndrome. When you think truthfully about the issues raised by these questions, you establish control over your decision mak-

---

[1]Of course, you can now search for your home (e.g., realtor.com, hud.gov), neighborhood, and mortgage on the Internet. For tips about useful web sites, see the Internet Appendix.

ing. You'll pound your gavel. Your inner chairman can then bring your internal confusion to order.

MISTAKE # **16**

We feared that discrimination would limit our possibilities for home ownership.

LESSON: *Mortgage lenders, Realtors, homebuilders, and not-for-profit housing groups are reaching out to all potential homebuyers.*

No one denies that discrimination has thrown obstacles in front of many Americans and immigrants who want to own their own homes. But times have changed. Today, as part of the government's national home ownership policy, fair housing laws—and, most importantly, the never-ending pursuit of higher profits—mortgage lenders, Realtors, and home builders are creating many new home-financing programs that reach out to *all* potential home-buyers, regardless of their race, nationality, ethnicity, or marital status.

In fact, in recent years, homebuying among minorities and immigrants has reached record highs. In Los Angeles, neither Smith nor Jones ranks among the top 10 surnames of homebuyers. More common are names such as Chen, Lee, and Lopez. In 2002, President Bush set a national goal to increase the number of minority homeowners by 5.5 million households prior to 2010. As of 2005, the nation is on track to actually surpass this ambitious goal.

In the past, discrimination did block homebuyers in two possible ways: (1) stereotyping or (2) "neutral" underwriting standards. To better understand the present, let's look at these two types of discrimination.

Stereotyping

In the past, some lenders stereotyped people as bad credit risks simply because of irrelevant characteristics such as race, marital status, or occupation. Today, this type of wide-scale discrimination has virtually been eliminated. No reputable lending institution (realty firm, home builder) willfully discriminates in this way as a matter of company policy.

Undoubtedly, some individual loan reps or real estate sales agents do harbor biases that are reflected in their behavior. But if such biased behavior adversely affects your ability to secure a mortgage or buy a home, the offending individual can suffer civil liability, criminal fines, and loss of professional license. Even though some stereotypical discrimination does exist, severe penalties are making it increasingly rare.

"Neutral" Underwriting Standards

Far more troubling (and less visible) discriminatory practices are so-called neutral loan underwriting standards. Consider traditional mortgage credit criteria such as these:

- No home loans for less than $50,000.
- Two years of steady work at the same job.
- A clean credit history and at least four accounts at banks or retail merchants.
- No "mattress money" (cash for a down payment must come from a verifiable, approved source, e.g., a bank savings account).
- No loans in neighborhoods where more than 40 percent of the homes are occupied by renters.
- Monthly mortgage payments shall not exceed 28 percent of gross monthly earnings.

Superficially, each of these credit standards (and many others like them) seems neutral. None blatantly discriminates against anyone for any illegitimate reason. Yet, upon statistical analysis, these rules create discriminatory effects. And that's where lenders are now directing their attention.

Lenders are reevaluating their traditional lending criteria to see why their turndown rates for some minorities are higher than they should be. As a result, most mortgage lenders are throwing out these traditional loan criteria and rewriting their standards to reflect the realities of life as experienced by low- to middle-income borrowers, minorities, single-parent households, immigrants, and other groups that don't fit the cookie-cutter qualifying standards of earlier years.

Reach-Out Efforts

Frank Raines, former CEO of Fannie Mae, the largest and most influential mortgage lender in the country, has put into place a lending policy such that "every American [or legal immigrant] who wants to get a mortgage [to buy a home] will either have their loan approved, or be put on a path that can lead to approval." In putting these words into action, Fannie Mae pledged $1 trillion in mortgage money and has made a public announcement: "We're looking for millions of missing homeowners. Many are ready now. But they may be intimidated by how the system works; or fearful of discrimination.... The housing industry is urgently addressing these problems. And Fannie Mae is taking the lead. We're building partnerships among lenders, real estate agents, credit counselors, and appraisers.... Together we've created an outreach program to help everyone who wants to own a home." (See Fannie's web site at www.homepath.com.)

These outreach efforts are working. In recent years, record numbers of blacks, Hispanics, immigrants, singles, single-parent households, and other types of traditionally underserved individuals and families bought their own homes. No longer do lenders arbitrarily rule people out of home ownership. Unjust exclusion, whether by stereotyping or so-called neutral underwriting standards, has been tossed into the dustbin of history.

During the past 10 years, home ownership among singles, single parents, blacks, and other minorities has grown much faster than home ownership among whites.

If you want to own your own home, don't mistakenly believe that discrimination limits your possibilities. Today, more and more mortgage lenders are reaching out to help all homebuyers either "get their mortgage approved, or be placed on a path that will lead to approval." (For other helpful web sites, see Freddie Mac's www.homesteps.com and www.hud.gov. Both of these web sites explain a variety of reach-out initiatives.)

CHAPTER 3

Home Ownership: How to Make It Your Best Investment

In her 2000 book *Everything You Know About Money Is Wrong*, the nationally prominent financial advisor Karen Ramsey contradicts prevailing American beliefs about home ownership and presumes to tell her readers, "Your house is a roof over your head. *It is not an investment....* To rent or buy comes down to a lifestyle choice" (HarperCollins, 2000, pp. 38, 49).

Well, on this point, it is Ms. Ramsey who is dead wrong, not "you." Yet, unfortunately, Ms. Ramsey's view represents conventional wisdom among a large number of financial planners and financial journalists. "Buy a home to live in—if you want," they say. "But put your real money in stocks. Over the long terms, stocks have yielded the largest returns of any investment." Likewise, you will see that all of this talk about a "housing bubble" is nothing new. Since 1948, "experts" have been warning that "home prices" have reached their peak. If you've been influenced by any of these stock enthusiasts or financial gurus who don't understand the basic facts of history—not to mention elementary calculations of financial return—you need this chapter. It will give you a much more positive (and accurate) perspective.

However, if (like most Americans) you do realize that home ownership can prove to be your best investment, you, too, need this chapter. For it will not only help you guard against investment mistakes, it will show you how to make sure your home-ownership experience yields the excellent returns you anticipate.

MISTAKE # **17**

We're not planning to buy. Experts say home prices won't appreciate in the future as they have in the past.

LESSON: "Experts" have been saying that home prices have reached their peak for nearly 60 years.

Among all the lessons history teaches, none is more certain than the fact that home prices will go up. Regardless of how high you think prices are today, they will be higher 10 years from now. And they will be much, much higher 20 or 30 years into the future. Don't mistakenly believe home prices have reached their peak. Before you put faith in the naysaying of so-called economic experts, take a quick trip through their faulty predictions from years gone by:

- "The prices of houses seem to have reached a plateau, and there is reasonable expectancy that prices will decline." (*Time,* December 1, 1947)
- "Houses cost too much for the mass market. Today's average price is around $8,000—out of reach for two-thirds of all buyers." (*Science Digest,* April 1948)
- "If you have bought your house since the War … you have made your deal at the top of the market…. The days when you couldn't lose on a house purchase are no longer with us." (*House Beautiful,* November 1948)
- "The goal of owning a home seems to be getting beyond the reach of more and more Americans. The typical new house today costs about $28,000." (*Business Week,* September 4, 1969)
- "Be suspicious of the 'common wisdom' that tells you to 'Buy now … because continuing inflation will force home prices and rents higher and higher.'" (*NEA Journal,* December 1970)
- "The median price of a home today is approaching $50,000…. Housing experts predict that in the future price rises won't be that great." (*Nations Business,* June 1977)

- "The era of easy profits in real estate may be drawing to a close." (*Money*, January 1981)
- "In California … for example, it is not unusual to find families of average means buying $100,000 houses…. I'm confident prices have passed their peak." (John Wesley English and Gray Emerson Cardiff, *The Coming Real Estate Crash*, 1980)
- "The golden-age of risk-free run-ups in home prices is gone." (*Money*, March 1985)
- "If you're looking to buy, be careful. Rising home values are not a sure thing anymore." (*Miami Herald*, October 25, 1985)
- "Most economists agree … [a home] will become little more than a roof and a tax deduction, certainly not the lucrative investment it was through much of the 1980s." (*Money*, April 1986)
- "The baby boomers are all housed now. They are being followed by the baby bust. By 2005, real housing prices will sit 40 percent below where they are today." (Harvard Economist, Gregory Mankiw, "The Baby Boom, the Baby Bust, and the Coming Collapse of Housing Prices," *Journal of Regional Economics*, Fall, 1989)
- "We're starting to go back to the time when you bought a home not for its potential money-making abilities, but rather as a nesting spot." (*Los Angeles Times*, January 31, 1993)
- "Financial planners agree that houses will continue to be a poor investment." (*Kiplinger's Personal Financial Magazine*, November 1993)
- "A home is where the bad investment is." (*San Francisco Examiner*, November 17, 1996)
- "Your house is a roof over your head. It is not an investment." *Everything You Know About Money Is Wrong*, 2000)
- "But the real question is, how will [housing prices] look longer term? As I've said in the past, I do not think that housing values will be higher five to ten years from now." (Yale Economist, Robert Shiller, quoted in *Newsweek*, January 27, 2005)

Fortunately, the actual history of home prices and real estate investment returns has differed greatly from those recurring claims of "the end of real estate" as an investment. During the past 60 years, average home prices have multiplied 5, 10, and, in some areas, 20 times or more.

Don't listen to these so-called economic experts. Since World War II, home prices have frequently jumped by 10 or 20 percent a year. On occasion, they've held steady for as long as three to five years. When cities experience severe downturns in their local economies, prices sometimes fall temporarily. During the early 1970s, for example, large layoffs at Boeing drove Seattle home prices down by 20 to 30 percent. A local billboard went up with the request, "Will the last person to leave Seattle please turn out the lights?" Yet, Seattle recovered. Now prices there are eight times higher than they were in 1971.

Likewise, as our new century continues to unfold, we will undoubtedly look back to today's "high" home prices in cities such as Miami, San Diego, Boston, and New York. We'll say, "Boy, those were the days. Can you believe I could have picked up a three-bedroom, two-bath home in Clairemont for just $400,000?" And no doubt, in *some future years*, we will again hear "experts" tell us, "Buy a home as a comfortable place to live—not to make money. Home prices can't go any higher. Just since the mid 2000s the median price of a home has jumped from $225,000 to $325,000. The days are gone when buying a home for investment was a sure thing."

MISTAKE # **18**

The experts were wrong in the past, but things are different today.

LESSON: *The more things change, the more they remain the same.*

Experts always put forth plausible reasons to support their predictions that home prices have reached their peak. In 1947 housing economist John Dean wrote that large jumps in home prices in the 1940s had occurred because of "rapid population growth, inflation, and housing shortages." Then he added, "None of these is likely to continue."

In fact, what have we seen during the past 60 years? Recurring periods of rapid population growth, inflation, and housing shortages. And what about the future?

Population and Incomes Are Growing

The most recent forecasts of the U.S. Bureau of Census show that during the next 10 years, the U.S. population will grow by 20 to 30 million people. Increasing numbers of births (the echo boom), millions of immigrants, and longer life expectancies are adding record numbers to our population. To house our growing population, people will require around 8 to 15 million new homes and apartments. In addition, we'll need between 5 and 10 million more homes just to replace those that are lost because of fires, abandonment, conversion to commercial uses, and natural disasters (earthquakes, floods, hurricanes, tornadoes).

With these and other facts in view (and in contrast to the pessimists) here's what I forecasted in 1997 while writing the 2nd edition of this book: "It's almost certain that at some point within the next several years, we are going to experience tight housing markets again. As of early 1997, both apartment vacancy rates and inventories of unsold homes are falling."

I am just as sure today that continuing population and income growth will make our "high" prices now look cheap within 5 to 10 years. Sure, we may hit some down periods along the way, but the unstoppable trend is up. If you doubt my forecast, go back and reread the historical facts. When it comes to housing price increases, history does repeat itself.

Have We Seen the End of Inflation?

Recent economic news tells us that inflation has generally been low. "Inflation has been squeezed out of the economy," the headlines tell us. But has it really? Or are we deceiving ourselves? This past year consumer prices increased around three percent. This rate of inflation does seem low compared to the 10 to 13 percent rates experienced in the early 1980s. Over time, though, an average annual inflation rate of three percent is not low.

Throughout the 1950s until the mid-1960s, inflation ranged between one and two percent a year. Between the years 1966 to 1973, annual inflation averaged 4.3 percent. No one at that time, however, thought inflation was low. Most economists were so alarmed about "runaway prices" that in 1973 Herbert Stein, President Nixon's chairman of the Council of Economic Advisors, persuaded the president to impose wage and price controls all across the United States.

Relative to the late 1970s and early 1980s, today's inflation rates are low. Relative to much of our postwar history, they are not low. As Mark Twain might have observed, the death of inflation has been greatly exaggerated.

With a growing population (demand), insufficient building of new homes (limited supply), and continued inflation of two to four percent a year, the same factors that have pushed up home prices in the past will push them up in the future. On top of that, regulatory growth management and environmental restrictions will continue to push up costs by limiting the number and increasing the cost of newly constructed homes. Also, literally millions of families either now own (or plan to buy) a second home.

MISTAKE # *19*

Lower rates of inflation mean lower rates of appreciation for homes.

LESSON: *Reduced rates of inflation can actually lead to higher rates of appreciation.*

Until the late 1990s, "experts" claimed that strong rates of appreciation in home prices depend on high rates of inflation. The logic of this argument seems straightforward: With rapidly rising prices for labor and materials, home builders cut back on their new construction and raise their prices. With higher prices for new homes, many homebuyers switch to the resale market and buy existing homes. With more buyers bidding for existing homes, these home prices go up. Increasing demand and a reduced supply of new and existing homes for sale yield strong rates of appreciation for home values.

High Inflation, High Interest Rates

Although this argument is partially true, it doesn't reveal the full picture. Ask any Realtor or homebuilder who lived through the double-digit rates of inflation of the early 1980s. Contrary to today's recollections, those were not boom times for real estate. Reporting on the Southern California market of 1982, a leading national newspaper wrote, "Not only are asking prices falling, but in some cases people who have bought homes in the last few years are selling them for less than they paid for them.... Now people are buying shelter.... " And recall the *Money* magazine article of January 1981 (see Mistake #17). "The era of easy profits in real estate may be drawing to a close," *Money* told its readers.

Although over time higher rates of inflation will jack up building costs, higher inflation also causes interest rates to rise. As interest rates go up, home affordability goes down. People who might like to buy are blocked from the market. Sooner or later, demand for homes falls because with higher interest rates homebuyers can't qualify for financing. Fewer buyers bring price increases to a *temporary* halt.

Low Inflation, Low Interest Rates

On the other hand, low rates of inflation mean low interest rates. With low mortgage interest, more people can afford to buy. If we do experience low inflation, millions of Americans who would be shut out of the mortgage market with interest rates at 9 to 14 percent—the rates that prevailed throughout much of the 1980s—will be able to own their own homes. More buyers will push prices higher.

In fact, if we look back to the 1980s, it wasn't the high inflation years that brought the steepest home price increases. The greatest rates of appreciation (except for the oil belt; see Mistake #25) occurred between 1985 and 1988.

Then, in 1989, inflation climbed up close to five percent. It was the largest increase in the Consumer Price Index (CPI) since 1982. Mortgage interest rates again went over 10 percent in 1989. Home prices stalled (and even retreated) in many cities. Construction of new homes fell. Defense-related industries suffered cutbacks and layoffs. To become more competitive, firms with large managerial bureaucracies, such as General Motors and IBM, shed employees. The country experienced its seventh post–World War II recession and a slowdown in economic growth.

Then from the mid-1990s through (at least 2005), 30-year interest rates fell to as low as 5.5 percent. Throughout the country, housing markets boomed. Home prices shot up. The cycle continues. So, while it is true that high rates of inflation will lead to increased building costs and eventually higher home prices, low rates of inflation can yield a stable economy, more jobs, low mortgage interest rates, and more home-buyers.

Don't mistakenly believe that a slower upward drift of the CPI means weak appreciation in home prices. Between 1950 and 1970 average home prices tripled ($10,000 to nearly $30,000). During this same 20 years, increases in the CPI averaged less than three percent a year (about the same as now). With or without inflation—as long as our economy and population continue to grow—home prices will continue to set new record highs with every passing decade.

MISTAKE # **20**

We thought we could make higher returns investing in stocks.

LESSON: *Even with "low" rates of appreciation, a home will still prove to be your best investment.*

In 1998, Jason and Cathy Stein announced proudly to a reporter who was interviewing them, "We earn $80,000 a year and don't own a home. We could buy if we wanted to. But we think we can do better investing in stocks. We can make a lot higher returns in the market."

Although the weak performance of stocks since 2000 has shaken the faith of some stock market enthusiasts, financial planners still tell their clients that over the long run returns from stocks will beat home ownership. (For example, see the foolishly written article, "Sleep at Home, but Invest in the Stock Market," *The New York Times*, August 19, 2005.) Fortunately for property owners, the financial planners wrong. Here's why:

1. The stock market is not likely to increase during the next 20 years as much as it has during the past 20 years. Recall that from its peak of 341 in September of 1929, the Dow Jones Industrial Av-

erage (DJIA) took more than 50 years to permanently cross the 1,000 mark (1982). Yet, since 1982, the DJIA has multiplied ten-fold to surpass the 10,000 level. Historically speaking, this gain has far exceeded all previous upward movements of stock prices.

Thus, the laws of statistical probability virtually guarantee that future stock returns will fall substantially as average returns regress to the mean. In other words, outsized returns during several decades of time must be offset by low returns over the decades that follow.

2. Still not convinced? Then consider that with annual gains of "just" 12 percent, within 20 years the DJIA would approach the 100,000 mark. Everyone who invests in stocks would (theoretically) become a multimillionaire. Sounds great. But now weigh in a brisk dose of reality. Our economy (Gross Domestic Product) only grows an average of three percent a year. So while these investors may have accumulated large sums of paper wealth, unfortunately the real economy (i.e., the real goods and services that people want to buy) will have lagged substantially.

In other words, you're looking at a logical impossibility. Over time, stock market wealth and the production of real wealth in terms of cars, houses, restaurants, clothing, travel, and so forth, must move in tandem. As the lyrics to a once-popular song said, "you can't have one without the other." Throughout the 1960s and 1970s, real economic growth outpaced stock prices. Throughout the 1980s and 1990s, stock prices wildly outpaced the economy. Looking to the next two decades means slow growth for stock prices as the real economy tries to catch up.

3. When you invest in a home, you gain the magic wealth-building power of leverage. A three or four percent rate of home appreciation yields investment returns far in excess of these "low" rates.

Low Home Appreciation Yields High Rates of Returns

To illustrate through a simple example, say a couple invests $10,000 in a $100,000 home. They finance their purchase with a 30-year, $90,000 mortgage at 6.75 percent. After eight years they will have paid down their mortgage balance to $79,867. With four percent a year apprecia-

Table 3.1 **Low appreciation Yields High Returns**

Today

Home purchase price	$100,000
Original mortgage	90,000
Cash invested	10,000

Eight Years Later

Market value @ 4% appreciation	$136,860
Mortgage balance	79,867
Home equity	56,992

Equity Growth Rate

$10,000	56,992

0   1   2   3   4   5   6   7   8 years

Annual growth rate of home equity = 24.3%. Of course, even if you paid a higher price, 10% down would still yield a 24.3% return.

tion for eight years, their home's value will have grown to $136,860. If we subtract the balance of $79,867 from the home's appreciated value of $136,860, we find that the couple's original $10,000 investment has increased more than fivefold to $56,992 of homeowners' equity. That result yields an after-tax annual rate of return of around 24.3 percent (see Table 3.1).

Consumption versus Investment

Several of my readers have disputed the return calculations that I show in Table 3.1. These readers do not understand that a home is part consumption (a place to live) and part investment (growth in equity). For example, a reader at Amazon.com offered this critique:

> "Grossly exaggerated!!! ... I am constantly irritated by the author bragging [sic] on how real estate would make money. Based on what? His calculations are seriously flawed to a point that it is not even funny. He assumes one does not need money to maintain his/ her house—no money out.
>
> I did a simple calculation ... [for a $180,000 house that shows] the out-of-pocket money WITH tax break will run you up to $1,100

[a month]. If you add lawn mow, cable, water, electricity, etc., you know what I'm talking about. This is money down the drain. Your house needs to appreciate 9% just to break even. How can the author say 4% appreciation rate would make you money ... [the book] is still a good read on many other topics. I just wish the author would save his sales pitch.

In contrast to this reader's confusion, I did not omit monthly costs due to error. Nor did I omit them to provide a biased "sales pitch."

Renters and Owners Incur Monthly Housing Expenses

Regardless of whether you *rent* or *own*, you will incur monthly housing costs. These costs cover your living expenses (i.e., what economists call consumption or housing services). Your investment is your down payment and your cash returns are the dollars you pocket upon sale (or refinance) of the property.

Although your results will differ from those shown in Table 3.1, the basic principle holds: Relatively low rates of appreciation yield much higher rates of return. That's the magic of leverage. For a more detailed discussion of leverage and rates of return, see my book *Investing in Real Estate, 5th Edition*, 2006 (Wiley).

Also, I invite you to query long-term homeowners (and property investors). Ask them if they regret buying. Ask them if they think their properties have yielded good returns. I think you know now what answers the vast majority will give you.

Technical Errors

Now I do admit that the example in Table 3.1 does err in two technical respects. To keep it simple, I ignored mortgage closing costs at purchase and selling expenses upon sale.

However, I also ignored a far more important benefit. Over time rents go up, but payments on 30-year fixed rate mortgages remain constant (or may actually fall if you're able to refinance into a lower rate). To see this strong benefit of home ownership, see Figure 10.1 (p. 255).

Stocks Typically Yield Lower Results

In contrast, depending on whose numbers you use, stocks have yielded average *pretax* returns of between 9 and 12 percent a year over the longer run. On an *after-tax* basis, a 10-percent-a-year return on stocks is considered very good. In fact, over the long term, fewer than 2 percent of professional fund managers have been able to consistently earn after-tax returns on stocks of more than 10 to 15 percent a year.

Recall that at the end of 1965 the Dow Jones Industrial Average stood at 969.26. At the start of 1982 this index of blue chip companies actually stood lower, at 884.36. During this entire 16-year period, the DJIA closed no higher than 1051.70. And it fell to as low as 577.60 in 1974.

Even if you compare stock gains during the *unprecedented* market boom that ran from 1993 (DJIA at 3,500) to early 2000 (DJIA at 11,700), you'll find home equity multiplying just as fast in many cities throughout the United States. For example, in the relatively slow growth town of Gainesville, Florida, a home bought in 1993 for $100,000 could have been sold in 2005 for $200,000. Assuming a $10,000 down payment, that's a tenfold increase in your investment (not counting mortgage paydown).

If instead, you had put $10,000 or $20,000 into say a home in boomtowns like Boston, San Francisco, Boulder, Sarasota—or any one of dozens of other hot housing market cities—you would have enjoyed a greater increase in your original down payment investment.

Summing Up

All things considered, you can expect your home investment to outperform the stock market. With a home you get the magic benefits of leverage. You invest a relatively small down payment. Yet, you receive returns based on increases in the total value of your home. That's why even a "lowly" four or five percent annual rate of appreciation will nearly always outperform the price gains you might get from stocks. And not only is home ownership far less risky than stocks, stocks won't keep you dry when it rains or warm when the weather is freezing cold.

As you grow older, it's best to diversify your wealth into a variety of investments. But don't substitute other investments for home ownership. Nor should you restrict your other investments to stocks and bonds. At today's prices and returns, you can definitely build more wealth with less risk with investment properties.

Beware of those financial planners who say, "If you own your own home, you've got all the exposure to real estate that you need," or those who ignorantly claim, "Over the long run, stocks have (and will) outperform all other investments." (To learn more about the advantages and profit opportunities in real estate, see my books, *Investing in Real Estate, 5th Edition,* 2006 (Wiley) or *The Beginner's Guide to Real Estate Investing,* 2004 (Wiley).

MISTAKE # **21**

We weren't concerned about our home as an investment; we just wanted a comfortable place to live.

LESSON: *When shopping for a home, you should always factor appreciation gains into your decision.*

With so much financial planner talk about "homes not being investments," too many homebuyers have scratched "investment" off the list of criteria by which they judge a home. This is a mistake. In either hot or cold markets, compare homes and neighborhoods on the basis of profit potential. Don't adopt the attitude, "Well, if it appreciates, great. If not, we still have gained the benefits of living in our own home."

Likewise, though, do not believe that hot markets last forever. Invest for the long term. Do not overextend yourself such that a market slowdown or jump in interest rates will wreck your finances.

Nevertheless, for careful buyers, good profits are always available. Remain savvy and persistent in your homebuying efforts. Even when the overall market is not making headlines with galloping prices, you still have opportunities to beat the market. Create your own appreciation.

Create Your Own Appreciation

Just before California headed into recession in 1989, Beth Rosander got divorced. With two children to raise and no job prospects, Beth decided to make a living buying rundown houses, fixing them up, and then quickly reselling them. If Beth had paid attention to the newspapers, she would have known the California boom in housing prices had stalled. No way could she expect to make money buying and selling homes. Couldn't she see? Homes were no longer a good investment.

Fortunately, Beth ignored the steady drumbeat of bad news. Between the years 1988 and 1993, Beth bought, fixed up, and sold six houses. After each sale, she pocketed between $20,000 and $40,000. Remember, too, that Beth bought these houses without income from a job. Bank loans were out of the question. To solve this problem, Beth obtained seller financing. "The deals are not there with a big red flag," Beth points out. "I had to weed through [literally as well as figuratively, I suspect] a lot of properties and get up to speed on the market" (*San Francisco Examiner*, May 2, 1993).

Find a Bargain or "Hot" Neighborhood

Maybe buying a fixer-upper doesn't fit your idea of fun. But you have many other ways to make your home a good investment. You also can buy at a bargain price. Or you can try to locate neighborhoods that will appreciate faster than average. Nearly every city has "hot" neighborhoods or communities that show more promise than general trends in prices would otherwise indicate. (See my book, *Make Money with Small Income Properties*, 2004 [Wiley]).

How do you locate these promising neighborhoods or communities? Here are eight indicators of emerging hot spots:

1. Anticipate an upward trend in prices when the number of days it takes to sell a home in a given neighborhood is falling. Normally, this shorter selling period signals that price gains are just around the corner.
2. The gap between listing prices and selling prices is narrowing. Normally, homes sell within 5 to 10 percent of their listing price.

If average selling prices climb within less than five percent of their listing prices, sellers are likely to boost their prices.

3. An increasing percentage of the homes are being sold to people moving into the neighborhood from another area of the city or from out of town. This figure shows the "hot" neighborhood or community is gaining in popularity vis-à-vis other areas.

4. The income, education, and occupation levels of the people moving into an area are generally higher than the neighborhood's current residents. (Note: Don't mistakenly assume that changing ethnicity of a neighborhood means property values will fall. Such stereotypical views have been proven false. No matter what its ethnic makeup, experience shows that any neighborhood can achieve substantial gains in desirability and value.)

5. New and existing homeowners in the neighborhood are investing in home remodeling and renovations. Homebuilders are constructing new homes in the area. Typically, increasing investment means that values will head up.

6. The percentage of homes in the neighborhood occupied by owners (as opposed to renters) is increasing. This statistic provides an almost 100 percent indicator of rising home values. Neighborhoods nearly always appreciate strongly when homeowners displace renters and absentee landlords.

7. The accessibility of an area is improving. Better roads, a new bridge, or extension of a mass transit can push property values up dramatically. If your city has any major new (or improved) access routes planned, figure out which neighborhoods and communities stand to gain faster commutes to major job centers.

8. The neighborhood's community or homeowners' association zealously works to protect and enhance living conditions in the area. Such activities may involve anything from Take Pride In Your Home campaigns to school improvement programs to crime prevention measures. An involved neighborhood association shows that people care about their homes and their property values.

Over time, appreciation differences among various homes and neighborhoods can mean tens of thousands of dollars to you. When you choose a home, don't overlook this potential. You may still decide to opt for your "preferred place to live." But when faced with such a choice, make the trade-off—personal versus financial—consciously, not unconsciously.

MISTAKE # **22**

We were told to buy in the best neighborhood we could afford. The best neighborhoods always appreciate the fastest.

LESSON: *Compare neighborhoods according to relative prices and benefits. Never assume a good neighborhood will appreciate faster than an inferior one.*

Few homebuyers investigate and compare neighborhoods for their appreciation potential. Conventional wisdom tells them, "Buy in the best neighborhood you can afford. The best neighborhoods always appreciate fastest." Not true. As a preferred place to live, you might consider only the better neighborhoods, but many times these neighborhoods won't appreciate faster than less desirable areas.

During the early 1990s California recession, the most expensive homes in Beverly Hills temporarily fell in value by 20 to 30 percent. Yet, during this same period, homes in Watts and South Central Los Angeles *increased* in value by 30 percent. Granted, this comparison is extreme. But the general principle holds: Look for the flashing green lights that signal a neighborhood or community is on the move (see Mistake #21). It's quite rare for one neighborhood to consistently appreciate faster than alternative neighborhoods for a long period of time. Here's why.

Forecasting Appreciation

Say most homebuyers prefer Hidden Valley Estates to the Swampy River subdivision. Homes in Hidden Valley sell for an average price of $150,000. Homes in Swampy River go for about $100,000. Homebuyers have favored Hidden Valley because its homes have been appreciating at eight percent a year. In contrast, appreciation in Swampy River has been limping along at just two percent a year. Can you count on this trend to continue? Probably not.

With five more years of eight percent appreciation, home prices in Hidden Valley Estates would climb from $150,000 to $220,000. Those Swampy River homes—at a yearly appreciation rate of two percent— would be worth $110,000. Hidden Valley homes now cost twice as much as homes in Swampy River. After another five years of similar appreciation rates, Hidden Valley homes would cost around $325,000. Swampy River home prices would sit far lower at $121,000.

Compare Relative Prices and Benefits

More than likely, well before 10 years have passed, most would-be buyers are going to be priced out of Hidden Valley. Instead, they'll meander through Swampy River. "Well, this place has possibilities," they might say. Before long, as homebuyers switch from Hidden Valley to Swampy River, Hidden Valley rates of appreciation will begin to fall. Swampy River appreciation rates will begin to rise.

The new Swampy River homeowners will then join with other residents and change the name from Swampy River to River View. They will spruce up their homes. They will organize a Neighborhood Watch program. And they will pass a bond measure to improve the local schools, libraries, and parks. Within a few years, River View (a.k.a. Swampy River) will emerge as one of the fastest-appreciating neighborhoods in the area.

But fast appreciation can't last forever. After five years (more or less), homes in River View may become overpriced relative to other neighborhoods and subdivisions. Price increases there will settle down. Appreciation rates in other areas will pick up. Alert homebuyers will create another "hot" neighborhood.

Price trends among types of homes, neighborhoods, and communities nearly always run in cycles. Past appreciation (slow or fast) may not point to more of the same. Investigate market signals. Compare the *relative* prices, benefits, and features of various homes and areas. Ask Realtors to tell you which neighborhoods and communities are just starting to catch attention, which ones are just beginning to move upscale, which ones seem poised for takeoff. Maybe you can get in on the ground floor of the next Buckhead, South Beach, or South of Market.

MISTAKE # **23**

We were told never to buy the biggest or most expensive house in the neighborhood.

LESSON: Buy the home that offers the best value as measured against your priorities and possibilities.

You've probably heard the common advice, "Don't buy the biggest or most expensive house in the neighborhood." Supposedly, the surrounding smaller, lower-priced homes will hold down the value of the more expensive house. As a result, the large home's appreciation rate won't perform as well as the other smaller homes in the neighborhood. Once you think about it, though, this advice fails to make sense.

Say the smaller homes in a neighborhood appreciate at six percent a year. The largest homes appreciate at two percent. With the passing of years, the smaller houses would come to sell for more than the larger houses—which, of course, is not likely. The rules of compound interest work to invalidate this simplistic advice, just as they prove false the claims that the best neighborhoods always appreciate the fastest (see Mistake #22). Table 3.2 illustrates this impossibility.

Table 3.2 **Simple Comparison of Appreciation Rates**				
	Home Values			
Purchase Price	*2 Years*	*4 Years*	*6 Years*	*8 Years*
$150,000 (6% apprec. for smaller homes)	$168,540	$189,371	$212,777	$239,077
$200,000 (2% apprec. for largest homes)	$208,080	$216,486	$225,232	$234,331

Is it likely that large houses would sell at $234,331 while small homes sold at $239,077? Of course not. Whether, in fact, the biggest house on the block will provide a good buy for you depends on your needs, your objectives, and the home's price *relative* to houses more consistent with the neighborhood. If you're asked to pay 50 percent more for a home that's 50 percent larger, you're probably not getting good value. If you can buy the larger home for just 10 percent more, then you're probably getting a great buy.

Don't avoid the largest or most expensive homes in a neighborhood. Instead, perform a value comparison. Figure out how much more home you're getting for your money. You might discover a real bargain.

Priorities and Possibilities

Just as important, compare the size and features of the larger home to your priorities and possibilities. If you have a large family or need space for a home office or more comfortable living, the largest home in a moderate-priced neighborhood might provide an economical way for you to meet these needs.

Consider, too, the possibilities. Even if you don't need the extra space or features of the more expensive home, can you think of a use? How about an art studio, library, or workspace? Could you rent out a room or two or maybe convert part of the home into an accessory apartment or mother-in-law suite?

Think income potential. Think affordability. You might look at a three-bedroom, two-bath house priced at $250,000. With 10 percent down, the mortgage payments on this home would run around $1,459 a month (6.75 percent, 30 years). Now, say you discover a five-bedroom, three-bath house in the same neighborhood. You can buy this larger house for $285,000. With 10 percent down, payments on the larger house would cost $1,663 a month.

You may not need this extra space or want to stretch your budget to come up with another $204 a month. But what if the larger home is designed (or remodeled) so you could rent out those extra two bedrooms and a bath for $475 a month? With this income, your out-of-pocket monthly mortgage payments would drop down to $1,188. Rather than costing $204 a month more, the larger home would actually cost $271 a month *less* than the smaller house. Yet, you would still enjoy three bedrooms and two baths for your own use. And, over time, you would build up a larger amount of home equity.

Don't *Build* the Biggest and Best

In most instances, it's not wise to newly-construct the biggest and best home in the neighborhood. The prices of the smaller houses will hold down the value of the more expensive home. Yet, the biggest and best house will still cost you proportionately more to construct. So, building and buying pose two different questions. When *building new*, you'll pay roughly 50 percent more to construct a 50-percent bigger and better house. When *buying an existing* bigger and better house (compared to the neighborhood average), you may be able to pay a premium of only 20 to 30 percent. It's the original homeowner (or builder) who paid for this overbuilding.

MISTAKE # **24**

I'd never buy a condominium. They make poor investments.

LESSON: *Properly selected, condominiums can yield good returns.*

Several years back, Paul Maglio bought a two-bedroom condominium located near Boston Harbor. He paid $120,500 for the unit. At the time Paul bought, 200 other potential buyers had put their names on the complex's waiting list. Everyone wanted this surefire investment opportunity. With appreciation rates running at 20 percent a year, condominiums were geese laying golden eggs.

Then, the geese died. Throughout Massachusetts, as well as other areas in New England, New York, much of the Southwest, and Southern California, many condominium (and co-op) prices fell 30 to 70 percent off their peaks. Bruce Hopper, another Bostonian who lost a bundle on his condominium, sadly regrets his decision to buy. "It's too bad," Hopper says, "because condos were the ideal situation for a lot of people—first-time homebuyers who wanted the American dream. But it didn't pan out and now we're stuck."

Upon hearing about experiences like these, many first-time home-buyers hesitate to buy a condominium. They'd rather stay put in their rental apartments than take a chance on getting "stuck" with a condo that can't be sold for anywhere near its purchase price.

Don't Prejudge: Weigh Risks against Potential Rewards

These fears and concerns about condos are justified. But as with all investments, weigh potential risks against potential rewards. To dismiss condos as poor investments without closely looking at a sampling of condo projects and complexes that exist in your area could be a mistake. When compared to the prices of single-family homes in many cities, condos once again appear to offer good value and opportunity for moderate appreciation. Search the market and the odds are at least 50–50 that you can find a condo bargain.

How to Spot a Condo Bargain

In nearly every case, condo buyers who have lost money have bought within a year or two of the top of the market. Longer-term owners nearly always have come out ahead. Condo owners who could see the market softening and sold out near the top often made tens of thousands of dollars.

When you learn the lessons of history, you can judge whether condo prices in your area stand a good chance of going up (or down). To spot opportunity, here are the signs to look for:

1. Nearly everyone is pessimistic about future appreciation rates. (Yes, contrarians frequently do make money.)
2. The monthly after-tax payments for principal, interest, property taxes, insurance, and homeowner fees total less than monthly rentals on comparable apartments. In other words, you can own cheaper than you can rent—right now.
3. The market values of units are substantially below the cost of constructing similar new units (see Mistake #31).
4. Vacancy rates for rental apartments are less than five percent.

5. Local economic indicators (number of people working, retail sales, new car sales, bank deposits, new business starts, etc.) are showing strong positive gains.
6. The condo units that you are considering enjoy some *unique* and *highly desirable* advantages (design, views, location).
7. Very few new apartment or condominium complexes are being built or planned. No major conversions of apartments to condominiums are under way or planned. Government restrictions limit apartment conversions.
8. Compared to single-family homes, condo prices (especially when calculated on a price-per-square-foot basis) sit relatively low.
9. The complex you are looking at is stable: strong financial reserves for repairs and replacements, no pending litigation, very few units occupied by renters (fewer than 20 percent is good, less than 10 percent is excellent), relatively little turnover of owners and residents, well-maintained common areas, and cooperative relations among owners.

On the downside, history shows that, in most cases, a fall in condo prices usually is foreshadowed by some combination of these danger signs:

1. A sharp downturn in local employment.
2. Large numbers of apartments being converted to condos, especially when accompanied by easy-qualifier financing.
3. Large amounts of new condo or apartment construction.
4. The current monthly costs of owning greatly exceed the monthly costs of renting.
5. More than 30 to 40 percent of a condo complex's units are investor owned and are occupied by renters (or even worse, vacant).
6. Everybody "knows" values are going up at least 10 to 15 percent a year. The market runs rampant with speculation. Flipping condos becomes a favorite pastime.

Experience has taught lenders, investors, and overly optimistic homebuyers that a condominium isn't necessarily a printing press for money disguised as a place to live. Yet, keep in mind that owning a condominium protects you against future rent increases (see Mistake #1). Even without appreciation your condominium will yield a good financial return. As you pay down your mortgage balance, you will build up your net worth with home equity. And a condominium can help you escape from renter's jail. Today, in most cities throughout the United States, owning a well-selected condominium definitely beats paying rent on an apartment, which is why condominium prices have shot up just as I predicted they would in the 2001 edition of this book.

MISTAKE # **25**

AT&T never lays anyone off, do they?

LESSON: *Before you buy a home, evaluate the emerging strength (or weakness) of your local economy.*

To forecast the direction of home prices—as well as the prices of other types of investments—maintain a sense of history. When you recognize cycles, you guard yourself against excessive optimism or undue despair. With knowledge of the past, you will understand that some housing markets go through recurring periods of economic boom, stability, and sometimes retrenchment.

Economic Cycles

In 1989, as reports of New England's slide into recession caught national attention, homebuyers in Southern California lined up to buy homes as fast as they came on the market. Multiple offers became commonplace. Eager prospects for new homes even camped at development sites while waiting for the kickoff of the sales campaign. "We were afraid that if we didn't buy now, we'd lose our chance forever," said Theresa Nham at the time of her purchase in May 1989. "Forget New England. Southern California's economy is too diversified to suffer a downturn. Home prices here always go up."

In one sense, of course, the years since 1989 have proved Theresa right. Home prices have shot up. But she should have added "over the longer run." In the short run, home prices can weaken. Layoffs and unemployment can bring home prices down. And such a downturn is more likely when speculation runs amok, as it recently has in Las Vegas, Miami, and Washington, D.C.

Evaluate Your Local Economy (Don't Fall for Dot-Com Mania)

Looking back, it's easy to see that too many homebuyers and real estate investors have focused only on the economic present—or, even worse, carried overly optimistic projections into the future as far as the eye can see. To prevent this mistake, check the strength of your local economy. Is it stable and growing steadily? Does it show signs of weakness? Is it exploding with speculation (as was the NASDAQ in the late 1990s)?

What do the economic signals indicate?

- Are unemployment claims increasing or decreasing?
- Is help-wanted advertising in the local newspapers expanding or contracting?
- Is credit becoming more, or less, available for local businesses?
- Are office building occupancy rates and rents increasing or decreasing?
- Are used car prices (especially for the luxury or more expensive models) increasing or decreasing?
- Are bankruptcies of local businesses decreasing or increasing?
- Are home prices increasing moderately or have they been going up by 12 percent a year or more for the past four or five years? Are home prices falling? Are foreclosures pilling up? What is the market signaling?

During the past 20 years, some areas of the country—rust belt, farm belt, oil belt, sun belt, defense belt—have experienced economic downturn. As we move further into the twenty-first century, each of these areas has made a strong comeback. Their home prices have reached new highs.

But downturns do happen. So don't merely assume your area's economic future. Investigate the facts. Areas go through ups and downs. If the short-term economic outlook for jobs in your area seems shaky, maybe you should focus on finding a soon-to-be hot neighborhood, a bargain-priced home (distresses sellers, foreclosures, REOs), or a home where you can create value through improvements.

MISTAKE # 26

With all the new construction, we thought the economy was really booming. Home prices had to go up.

LESSON: *Large amounts of new construction (homes, apartments, office buildings) often signal boom, then recession.*

When General Motors closed the Buick plant in Flint, Michigan and laid off six thousand autoworkers, you didn't need a Ph.D. in economics to know that home prices in Flint would take a plunge. But even when economic indicators show strength, too much new construction in an area can also temporarily depress home prices. Deceptively, new construction often creates a boom before it creates a downturn.

The Construction Cycle

To see this cycle in action, ask yourself: Why do builders build? To make a profit, right? So as homebuying increases and home prices rise, builders start building more homes and apartments. This construction and sales activity creates more jobs for real estate agents, real estate attorneys, home inspectors, title insurers, environmental specialists, site engineers, architects, electricians, carpenters, plumbers, loan officers, and other people who earn their living from home building and homebuying.

All of this new construction also creates a demand for office space as businesses and professional firms expand. This brings in the developers of office buildings. More construction-related jobs bring in even more demand for housing. Home prices continue to increase. Anticipating higher profits, builders continue to build more homes and offices to meet this growing demand.

But all booms end. Sooner or later, depending on the local levels of wages and employment, builders overshoot their market. Their inventories of unsold homes begin to increase. Office-building vacancies climb. Developers cut back on their building. Workers are laid off. Incomes fall. Demand for homes falls. Builders cut prices or offer incentives.

Newspapers take notice. Journalists talk up the weakening market. They find people to interview who are in financial trouble. They quote media experts who say a home is no longer a good investment. Existing home sales begin to fall. They take longer to sell. Home prices soften. Some potential buyers hold off. They want to wait and see. They ask themselves, "Why buy today if prices will be lower tomorrow? Besides, maybe our jobs and income aren't as secure as we thought." Builders and homebuyers begin to fear uncertainty.

With the market slowdown, homes can no longer be sold for prices high enough to cover the costs required to build them. Many builders see red ink instead of profits. Lenders shut down their credit lines. Acquisition, development, and construction (ADC) loans become more difficult to get. Lenders also tighten their credit standards for homebuyers. The housing boom becomes a bust.

Recovery Begins

Yet, even as this slowdown occurs, the population continues to grow. People get married. Children are born. Workers who have been laid off find new jobs. Recent college graduates begin their careers and start earning a monthly income. Businesses and factories that had closed are reopened by other companies. Entrepreneurs create new businesses. Total employment and wages begin to improve.

These economic upswings occur because people who get hurt by downturns figure out ways to get back on their feet. A more confident outlook means more people buy homes. Prices begin to firm up. Still, builders don't yet rush into new construction, for as economic recovery takes hold, construction costs tend to rise. Land, lumber, and building materials become more expensive. Cities tighten environmental regulations and assess impact fees on new homes to pay the costs of needed roads, schools, parks, and other municipal facilities. Before builders gear up to build large numbers of new homes, they wait for more homebuyers to push prices up. That's the only way builders are able to cover the now-higher costs of land and construction.

As recovery takes hold, it's not just new homes that cost more. Upward pressure is placed on the prices of existing homes. As new homes become more costly to build, the values of existing homes are pulled up along with the higher prices of new construction. When homebuyers, home sellers, and builders regain their confidence in the future, journalists change from pessimists to optimists. They begin to write articles more favorable to homebuying. More renters decide to start visiting open houses and calling Realtors for help. Stories of multiple offers are heard. Waiting lists are required for presales of new home developments. Home prices move up by 8 to 12 percent or more. A new cycle is off and running. In response to low inventories of new homes, increasing construction costs, and pent-up demand by wait-and-see buyers, home prices take off.

Know the Price Cycle

When you understand the timing of this homebuilding price cycle, you avoid the mistake of buying with unrealistic expectations. Even with job growth and land shortages, home prices can't increase at rates of 10, 12, or 15 percent year in and year out. When escalating home prices become the chief topic of conversation at cocktail parties and office get-togethers, you can bet that builders will rush into the market with hopes of easy profits. More building means more homes for sale. Eventually, more homes for sale means a temporary leveling off (or decline) in home prices. During the past several years, Las Vegas has served as a classic example of this cycle.

Buying near the top of the price cycle, though, doesn't necessarily mean you've made a mistake. Over time, history shows that "buying now" typically beats perpetual procrastination.

Too many people who wait for the "best time" delay for years while they watch home prices rise higher and higher. In good times they say prices are too high. In down markets they say the economy's too uncertain. They always find an excuse to avoid commitment. Buying at the top clearly beats perpetual procrastination.

However, if market signals do indicate the market is slowing (or booming excessively), proceed cautiously. Don't use wildly creative financing. Be wary of using lower-rate ARMS that enhance affordability but expose you to payment shock. Do not assume that you can easily sell out if your payments shoot up. Don't base your purchase on the belief that home prices are going to double in four years.

The homebuyers caught by market downturns are those who stretch their finances, inflate their expectations, and buy at a cyclical peak.

MISTAKE # **27**

The newspapers say home prices are decreasing/increasing.

LESSON: *Interpret reports of home price decreases or increases carefully. Often such reports don't mean what they seem to mean.*

Have you seen newspaper articles headlined something like, "Home Prices Fell 8 Percent Last Year," or maybe, "March–June Home Prices Up 15 Percent over Same Period a Year Ago"? If you have, don't put full faith in them. Chances are, neither of these statistics is right.

When most newspapers and magazines report changes in home prices, they incorrectly refer to median price figures. The *median* price, however, tells nothing about the actual appreciation (or depreciation) of home values. The median sets a midpoint: Half the homes sold for more and half the homes sold for less than the median price.

In periods when most homebuyers choose lower-priced homes, the median will fall. In periods when upscale buyers disproportionately pour into the market, the median price goes up. Median-price figures can tell you which price segments of the market are most active. But they won't tell you whether the selling prices of specific homes are moving up or down—or even in the same direction—as the median.

"Prince George's County showed the healthiest appreciation of any market," says the *Washington Post*. "The *median* [emphasis added] price of a single-family house, including townhouses, rose to $348,731." Did homes in Prince George's County really appreciate? If so, did they appreciate by 15 percent? To answer these questions correctly, you would have to compare sale–resale data for the same (or similar) homes. The median won't tell you.

More First-Time Buyers Mean Lower Median Prices

By confusing changes in median prices with appreciation/depreciation rates, many reporters unwittingly mislead their readers. I've often talked with potential homebuyers who believed home prices were falling, when prices were actually increasing. During the early 1990s downturn in the San Diego market, for example, many renters feared buying because they thought home prices had stumbled. At the then higher price levels ($500,000 and up), both prices and sales volume had headed down. Statistically, with slow top-end sales and more first-time buyers, the median selling price of homes also fell. At the then entry-level prices of $125,000 to $175,000, though, home prices held steady and maybe even strengthened a bit. As interest rates fell, savvy first-time buyers kept the low-end market selling reasonably well.

Upscale Buying Pulls Median Prices Up

Evaluate price figures carefully. Home prices can appear to appreciate faster than they really are. At some point along the way to full economic recovery, move-up buyers return to the market. As upscale sales increase, the *median* price could quickly jump 15 to 30 percent. But without looking at sale–resale price data, you could mistakenly conclude that home values had actually jumped that much.

Overall, don't misinterpret median prices. Get specific facts about homes and neighborhoods. Ask your Realtor to show you the actual trends in *selling* prices for specific types of properties. With facts instead of averages, you'll develop a better investment strategy.

CHAPTER 4

How to Find a Good Buy

To make your home pay off as much as possible as an investment, shop for a good buy just as you would shop for neighborhood or property features. To help you achieve this goal, the mistakes in this chapter alert you to principles of valuation. When you apply these principles (along with the knowledge gained from other chapters), you will be able to identify homes that offer outstanding potential for appreciation.

MISTAKE # **28**

We thought we got a real bargain. Our house was *listed* $20,000 below other houses we looked at in the neighborhood.

LESSON: *Don't compare homes on the basis of listing price.*

When shopping for a home, you may tend to rank homes as a "good buy" or "overpriced" according to their *listing* prices. Say a real estate agent shows you three similar homes in a neighborhood. One is listed at $172,000, another at $189,000, and the third at $163,000. Based solely on these listing prices, the home priced at $163,000 looks like a bargain.

You may tell yourself, "We should grab this one. The sellers are way under the competition." But hold on. Before you leap for the apparent bargain, investigate "comp sales."

All Homes May Be Overpriced

All of these sellers may be asking too much. None of their homes may be priced in line with the current market. In fact, some sales agents steer eager buyers to three or four overpriced properties and then show the unsuspecting buyers a home that's priced $10,000, $20,000, or even $50,000 less than the others. "I've been saving the best for last," say these agents. "This house just came on the market. You'd be smart to put a contract in on it right away. Several other agents from the office are showing the home later today. This one will probably go fast."

Before you jump at the chance of a lifetime, verify the "bargain" by checking the most recent *selling* prices of homes in the neighborhood. As markets slow down, many home sellers fail to adjust their listing prices with the new market reality. That's one reason sellers lament, "Homes aren't selling." It's not that buyers aren't ready to buy. Rather, "homes aren't selling" because sellers have listed their homes at prices higher than buyers are willing to pay.

As a result, houses sit unsold for months. A few sellers who are serious about selling eventually become educated about the market (or, realistic) and reduce their listing prices. Others, though, hang on and hope for a miracle. Although you can always find some homes listed at their owners' dream prices, overpricing shows up most during market slowdowns. At these times, take an especially careful look at values (comp sales), not listing (asking) prices.

Sellers Will Sell for Less

Listing price can mislead in another way, too. Most sellers will sell for less than their list price. But how much less? The owner who is asking $162,500 may hold tight to that figure. The owners who have listed their home at $179,800 may become so panicked about the slow market or their need for quick cash that they'll take the first serious offer they get—even when that offer is at $150,000.

If you find an overpriced home you like, don't write it off. Probe the sellers or a real estate agent to learn how flexible (desperate) the sellers might be. Use market facts about the selling prices of neighborhood homes to lead the sellers out of their dreams. At first glance, a home listed at $20,000 less than another may appear to be the best buy. But what if you can get the sellers of the overpriced listing to come down $30,000? In that case, the highest-priced listing may end up as the real bargain.

MISTAKE # **29**

We thought we got a real bargain. We paid $20,000 less than the appraised value.

LESSON: *Never put blind faith in an appraisal.*

Many prospective homebuyers believe the end-all of real estate valuation is an appraisal. To the uninitiated, a property is worth what the appraisal says it's worth—no more, no less.

In their book *Getting the Most for Your Home,* Dan Lieberman and Paul Hoffman tell home sellers, "Americans often believe what they see in writing far more than what they are told. A written appraisal for your home sitting on the dining room table, showing its value as higher than your asking price ... gives you the edge in the logical part of convincing a buyer of the value of your home.... Work the appraisal to your advantage, then sell the house 'below appraised value.' Buyers will feel they are getting a bargain" (p. 242).

On numerous occasions when I've been looking at homes, a seller or real estate agent has used this ploy. "Look at this," the agent says. "We've got this home priced $25,000 below its appraised value. The sellers are moving out of town. To get a quick sale, they're willing to give their house away."

Maybe they are. But maybe, too, they've worked the appraisal to their advantage to make buyers feel like "they are getting a bargain." Should you run into this type of sales presentation, here are several things you should know about appraisals and appraisers.

Appraisals Have Time-Limited Value

Appraisals are like a no-refund airline ticket. They're good for one date only. So, first look at the date the appraisal was performed. If home prices are changing (up or down), an appraisal that's even a month or two old could already be out of touch with the market.

Consider the Comp Sale Dates

More important than the date of the appraisal are the sale dates of the comparable homes listed in the appraisal, or "comps." Every home appraisal is based on the recent selling prices of similar homes in the neighborhood. Ideally, these homes should have sold within the past 90 days. Often, though, in slow markets no comp sales have occurred recently. In these cases, appraisers sometimes go back six months or a year for their sales data. Obviously, stale comps may not indicate today's value.

If appraisers do reach back in time for sales price data, they are supposed to bring the figures up to date with a time adjustment. But without recent sales data, how are they to know how much to adjust the past figures? As a result, they don't. They simply use a PFA (pulled-from-the-air) adjustment. Because of these appraisal difficulties, seriously question any appraisal that relies on out-of-date or time-adjusted market data.

Appraisers Don't Measure Value

An appraisal does not certify value. Nor do appraisers measure or determine a home's worth. An appraisal is one person's *opinion* of the price that buyers will likely pay for a home. Naturally, because appraisals reflect opinions, the appraisals leave wide room for subjective judgments. As an informed buyer, feel free to refute an appraisal. Don't let a seller, sales agent, or appraiser bamboozle you. Rely on an appraisal as one piece of market information—not as the only answer.

Appraisals Omit or Ignore Relevant Facts

Appraisals omit many facts of importance. One appraisal caveat states: "The appraiser assumes there are no hidden or unapparent conditions of the property, subsoil, or structures which would render it more or less valuable. The appraiser assumes no responsibility for such conditions, or for engineering which might be required to discover such factors."

In other words, except for obvious defects, the appraiser values the home as if it were problem-free. If the appraiser can't see the defect, then for the purpose of the appraisal, the defect doesn't exist.

Or sometimes, even when the appraiser can see the defect, he or she may assume it doesn't exist. Some years back I was interested in buying a house in Gainesville, Florida. I was dealing directly with the owner. The house was only four or five years old, well designed, located in a good neighborhood, and only a 10-minute walk from the University of Florida campus. The owner showed me an appraisal on the property that estimated its value as $85,000 to $88,000. Those figures were then typical for the neighborhood.

The Appraisal Ignored Serious Defects

However, a serious problem plagued the house. The lower level, which consisted of a three-car garage and an unfinished home office, had several 18-foot-long cracks in the floor. The cement had buckled up much like large tree roots can buckle a sidewalk. I asked the owner, "What caused those cracks?"

"Oh, those are settling cracks," she said.

Settling cracks? Not likely. I called a home inspector to take a look at the problem. He knew the cause of the cracks right away. "This house is built on clay with an improper foundation," he told me. "Every time it rains heavy, the clay absorbs the water, expands, and literally pushes the house upward. When the clay dries out, it compresses, and the house falls."

Next, I called several soil engineers and building contractors. Repairing the problem would cost anywhere from $10,000 to $40,000. And those costs didn't include a guarantee that the repairs would cure the problem. I told the owner about the diagnosis. (Later, I found out she already knew the real cause of the cracks.) I said, "Let's talk price. Given the serious and indeterminate nature of the necessary repairs, I'm willing to pay $60,000."

She balked. "Sixty thousand dollars? The appraisal says $85,000 to $88,000," she pointed out.

"Yes, but that's not considering the foundation and soil problem," I countered.

"Yes, it does," the owner argued. She then showed me in the small print where the appraiser had commented that the cracks in the floor could cause some buyer resistance. Therefore, a probable selling price would sit closer to $85,000 than $88,000.

I said, "That's nonsense. No one's going to pay $85,000 for this house." I then called the appraiser. "How could you discount the value of a house by $3,000 when the repairs could cost $10,000 to $40,000?"

The appraiser said repair estimates weren't a part of her job. "Besides," she added, "that home inspector you used is too critical." Further talks with the appraiser went nowhere. The owner eventually lowered her price to $80,000. But she did that reluctantly. Again and again she referred to the $85,000 appraised value of the house. "At $80,000," she said, "you're getting a bargain. Plus, I'm willing to offer good terms on the financing." (Of course, she had to carry back financing because no financial institution would have accepted the property as collateral with such glaring defects.)

I passed up the deal. But this experience shows how appraisers can assume that problems don't exist, even when they know about them. Just as important, it shows how an owner can ignore the common sense of the matter in favor of wishful thinking. The owner had an appraisal that said her house was worth $85,000. To her way of thinking, any price less than that would be giving the house away. I just hope that the seller didn't find a naive buyer who failed to understand the limits of an appraisal and, furthermore, the need to get a home's physical condition checked out by a professional inspector.

Verify Facts and Figures

To be safe, also check the arithmetic of an appraiser's calculations and the factual description of the appraised property. With the use of computer-prepared appraisals, appraisers have been able to cut down on their addition, subtraction, and multiplication errors. Still, mistakes do occur. So, make sure the appraiser's numbers add up correctly.

Beyond mathematical errors, appraisals too often fall into the "garbage in, garbage out" trap. When appraisers are busy, they might go through 8 to 12 houses a day. Also, some appraisal firms operate "factory appraisal shops." They use untrained, low-wage employees or trainees to perform property walk-throughs. Back at the office a licensed appraiser accepts what the trainee tells him or her and then fills in the appraisal forms and signs off on the report.

No matter what appraisal procedures are used, many kinds of errors can slip into the process. I recently saw an appraisal that included errors in the following areas: the square footage of the home, the size of the site, neighborhood zoning, the floor plan of the house, and the arithmetic. That was truly a garbage in, garbage out appraisal.

By cautioning you to verify the facts and figures of an appraisal, I do not suggest that most home appraisals are prepared incompetently. Nevertheless, verifying the accuracy provides a low-cost check against error. When you naively accept an appraisal, you are making a mistake. This warning especially applies when a homeowner or real estate agent presents an appraisal as part of a sales pitch.

Beware of Lowball Appraisals

Although most often you must guard against sellers' appraisals that come in too high, sometimes you might find a lender's appraisal that comes in too low to justify the amount of your mortgage loan. Consider the experience of Phil Tortellori.

"We had spent almost a year looking at houses," says Phil. "We liked a lot of them, but for one reason or other nothing quite excited our fancy. Then one Saturday we drove by a house we knew we had to have. It was priced right—or I should say, we thought it was priced right. Unfortunately, less than 10 days before closing, we learned the lender's appraiser had reported a different opinion. Her estimate of the home's value came in $10,000 less than our purchase price.

"To offset this lower appraised value, the lender said we'd have to increase our down payment by $8,000. Or, instead, we could ask the sellers to reduce their price. We had bargained hard as it was, so we didn't think the sellers would agree to come down more. And they wouldn't. As for raising our down payment by $8,000—no way! So, the financing fell through and we had to begin our search all over again."

From time to time, both homebuyers and home sellers have complained of lowball appraisals that killed a sale. In some instances lenders have used low appraisals to turn down loans they didn't want to make. At other times lender appraisers give low appraisals in response to tightened government appraisal regulations. Either way, a lowball appraisal can spoil your homebuying plans.

Prevent Deal-Killer Appraisals

To help prevent this problem, make sure your agent shows you recent sales prices (and terms) of similar homes in the neighborhood. Use these prices to guide your offer. Next, learn the name of the appraiser your lender plans to use. Ask your agent to tell the appraiser the comp sales you relied on to figure your offer. Once the appraisal is complete, get a copy from the lender. (You are entitled to a copy of your appraisal under the 1991 Equal Credit Opportunity Act, various state laws, and regulations put in place by the Federal Reserve Board.) Examine the appraisal according to the checks we are discussing in this chapter.

If your lender turns down your loan because of a low appraisal, you can legitimately back out of your purchase contract and recover your earnest money deposit. Or, if you think the appraiser has lowballed you, schedule a meeting with the appraiser, or write out your objections to the appraisal and give them to your lender.

In response, the appraiser can either accept or reject your comments. If he or she rejects them, you can ask the lender to send out another appraiser. If the lender wants your business, it will probably agree to obtain a second opinion. If the lender doesn't oblige, you must increase your down payment, ask the sellers to reduce their price, or apply for a mortgage somewhere else. (To appease your frustrations with the appraiser, write a complaint to the state licensing board. But that won't help you get the financing you need.)

Lowball appraisals don't seem to be a major problem right now, but it is a practice to stay alert for. In sharply rising markets—at least in the past—watch out for "overappraising." With rapid rates of appreciation, lenders, appraisers, and homebuyers get careless. With eyes focused on the future, no one worries much about the price today, because it's sure to be even higher tomorrow. Indeed, the *Wall Street Journal* recently ran an article that showed many recent examples of overappraising due to pressure from loan representatives who typically get paid only if a loan closes.

Appraisals Don't Include Personal Property
(Seller Concessions)

Appraisers limit their value estimates to the house and lot (i.e., real estate). If your purchase price includes any personal property (antique Oriental rugs, custom-made draperies, furniture) or if your seller has agreed to pay an abnormally large percentage of your mortgage points and/or closing costs, the lender's appraiser can exclude these amounts from his or her appraised value. With this exclusion, you probably won't be able to borrow the full amount that you would like. So, before you write seller concessions directly into your purchase contract, learn your lender's rules. Then, ask your real estate agent (or attorney) to figure out the most advantageous way to both get the loan you need and pay the personal property or settlement expenses. Sometimes you can benefit if you write up a separate agreement to cover these items (see also Mistake # 78).

MISTAKE # **30**

The appraiser didn't tell us home values were going to fall.

LESSON: *More than likely, your appraiser, your lender, and your real estate agent will not warn you that home prices may be softening.*

Maria and Jorge Olson were sitting in the living room of the home they wanted to buy. Five other hopeful buyers sat nearby. The desired home was listed at $390,000. The sales agent for the sellers came into the room. Tension hung in the air. "We're going to start the bidding now," the agent said. Offers started flying. Pandemonium broke lose.

"It was really wild," Maria recalled. "Then, after everyone had had their say and written up their offers, the agent and the owners left the room. When they came back, we just knew we'd won. We were right. The owners accepted our offer of $420,000. We celebrated that evening by going out to dinner at the most expensive restaurant in town. With home values increasing 20 percent a year, we felt that we got a great deal."

Sadly, three years later Maria and Jorge were in divorce court. They needed to sell their home and hired an appraiser. His value estimate came in at $360,000—just about the same as the listing price that several real estate agents had suggested to the Olsons. (Several other agents had estimated much higher.)

Lawsuits against Appraisers Require Proof of Negligence

To say the least, the Olsons were distressed and angry. They wanted someone to blame. They decided to sue their lender, their real estate agent, and the appraisal firm that had appraised the house when they bought it. That appraisal showed a value for the home of $425,000. The Olsons knew the current market was soft. But surely prices couldn't have fallen that much. Their lender's appraiser must have overvalued the home. Or, if prices were really going to fall that much, the Olsons argued, someone should have warned them.

The Olsons lost the court case for two reasons. First, expert testimony showed that the original $425,000 value estimate fit within a reasonable price range for the home at that time. Although one could question the appraiser's judgment on several points, the appraisal itself contained no egregious errors. Second, the court ruled that neither appraisers nor realty agents can be expected to predict the future. Estimates of market value apply only to the date of the appraisal. Neither the Olsons nor any other homebuyers should count on an appraiser, their mortgage lender, or even their real estate agent to tell them whether home prices are headed up or down.

Appraisers Don't Forecast Values

Throughout the United States, the ruling in this case generally holds. With limited exceptions, homebuyers must make their own forecasts. Appraisers only describe the current market. Appraisers might believe, "The market is wild with speculation. Buyers are crazy. Within a year prices are going to fall faster than the NASDAQ crash of 2000." But unless specifically directed, appraisers won't put these kinds of comments in their appraisal reports.

Likewise, when performing a market value appraisal, an appraiser wouldn't comment, "This is the best market for homebuyers we've had in years. Home prices are sure to double within the next five years." You could ask an appraiser (or real estate agent) to give you his or her opinion about where the market is headed over the coming years. But for you to see the future as clearly as possible, look to the market signals discussed in Chapter 3.

Many homebuyers think they are getting a great buy if they purchase their home for less than its current market value. However, that's not all you need to consider. Ask these two questions before you buy: (1) What market signals (or property features) indicate this home will be worth more tomorrow than it is today? And (2) what market signals spell D-A-N-G-E-R? (See Mistakes #24, #25, and #26.)

MISTAKE # **31**

We didn't think to calculate replacement costs.

LESSON: *The cost to rebuild a home at today's prices can give you a good idea where market values are headed.*

When Suzy Wilson and Carrie Sloan bought their townhouse in an overheated Dallas market, they paid $123,000 for an 1,100-square-foot, two-bedroom, three-year-old unit. That price works out to about $112 per square foot. Since the market was booming, Suzy and Carrie's real estate agent had found quite a few comparable townhouse units that had sold recently. Based on the selling price of similar units, these young accountants got a good price.

But Suzy and Carrie focused on the rapidly rising home prices of the past year. In doing so, they ignored two critical market signals: (1) The Texas oil economy was slipping, and (2) townhouses similar to the unit these women bought could be built new at a cost of $85 per square foot (including land). That meant condo developers could build new units, sell them at their market prices (over $100 per square foot), and make a profit (killing) of $20,000 to $30,000 a unit. Naturally, with banks and savings and loans shoveling out construction financing to developers (who often owned the S&Ls), the condo market became glutted with new units. As the oversupply of condos ran head-on into the weakening Texas economy, the previous shortage of homes for sale quickly turned into a surplus. Condo prices crashed.

At the same time, single-family home prices went through a similar boom and bust. First, their market values rose far above their costs of construction (including land). Then, fueled by these rising home prices and increased profits, builders rushed in to build more houses.

You've probably heard the end of this story: a collapse of home prices, tens of thousands of foreclosures, and billion-dollar bailouts for the depositors of failed banks and S&Ls.

This Texas experience was extreme. Yet, episodes of overbuilding run throughout our nation's history. And they probably will again. But you can protect yourself against value losses by talking to builders, contractors, or informed real estate agents. Ask them what it costs to build the type of home you're thinking about buying. Do some calculations. If, after allowing for land (lot) value and home depreciation, your home-to-be is priced too high relative to its construction costs, don't count on short-term appreciation. When home prices are, say, 10 to 20 percent higher than construction costs, you can't expect home values to continue rising.

If, however, market values don't exceed new construction costs, then builders won't build new homes and apartments. As a local economy strengthens, growth in incomes, employment, and population will push existing home prices up.

At any given time, market values can rise above or fall below a home's building costs. In hot markets, speculators rush to put contracts on new homes before construction begins. Then they flip their contracts at a higher price and make a fast profit.

Over time, though, home prices (adjusted for depreciation) tend to track the costs of new construction. Today's costs of construction may not tell you much about today's home values. But, they will signal whether home prices are headed up or down. When builders can't build at a profit, they won't build. Shortages occur and prices are bid up. When excessive profits are expected, too many builders and too many speculators enter the market. These frenzied efforts lead to a surplus of new houses, condominiums, or apartments. Rents and home prices begin to soften.

MISTAKE # **32**

We didn't pay attention to lot value. We wasted $32,000 on remodeling.

LESSON: *Before you buy a home, separate the value of the house from the value of the lot.*

When Jeri and Rod Craig bought their older, slightly rundown home, they had great plans for it. The home was located in a neighborhood where larger and newer homes were valued at $450,000. The Craigs paid just $195,000 for their house.

After moving in, the Craigs performed a top-to-bottom makeover on their home. Doing much of the work themselves, they refinished the hardwood floors, installed tile and fixtures in the bathrooms and kitchen, added a deck, enclosed a porch, and gutted the kitchen's out-of-date cabinets and appliances. Through their renovation, they transformed the kitchen into a chef's delight. Indeed, throughout the home, their pride of workmanship displayed itself in every detail. Admiring the fruits of their labor, the Craigs were confident their six months of toil and $32,000 of expenses would enhance their home's value by at least $60,000 to $75,000. At a price of, say, $250,000, their home's value still came in near the low end of their neighborhood.

Unfortunately, the Craigs got to test their value-added theory sooner than they wanted. Within a year of completing their home's makeover, Jeri received a great job offer from a firm in another city. The Craigs decided to move. They knew the housing market had done well. Sales activity was high. Values were up. Compared to the other (and relatively few) lower-priced homes in the neighborhood, the Craigs' home stood out as the best. Since several of these lesser homes had recently sold for $165,000 to $175,000, the Craigs decided to list their house at $260,000 and go for a quick sale.

But 30 days passed, then 60 days, then 90 days. Several offers came in at around $170,000, but the Craigs felt insulted. They kept pointing to the high quality of their renovation work. Potential buyers agreed but wouldn't increase their bids. Eventually, when the Craigs could delay their sale no longer, they accepted an offer of $175,000—hardly enough to cover the cost of the home and their out-of-pocket expenses, not to mention all the work they had put into it.

Beware of Over (or Under) Improving Your House

Why couldn't the Craigs profit from their home improvements? Because prior to their renovation work, they didn't think about the value of their lot. When they paid $195,000, they didn't really pay for a house. They paid for the land. Three weeks after they moved out of their perfectly modernized 1,400-square-foot bungalow, a bulldozer came in and leveled it. In its place, the new owners began construction of their five-bedroom, four-bath, 4,200-square-foot home. The Craigs had misspent their time and effort on a house that had become obsolete for the neighborhood.

In one sense, the Craigs had underimproved their lot. A small remodeled house was not the highest and best use of the site. In another sense, they had overimproved their house. Since the house no longer fit the neighborhood, remodeling wasted time and money.

Before you buy a home to remodel, figure out whether your remodeled home will fit the neighborhood. You can put too much money into a home if you try to increase its value well beyond other nearby homes. And you can also put too much money into a home that's *undervalued* for its location.

Site Value Is Critical

When a site's value exceeds 60 or 70 percent of the total value of the property, be careful. More than likely, the house is functionally obsolete for its site. Most (or all) of the appreciation potential for the home lies in its lot value. That's not bad from an investment standpoint. But in such cases, you should only improve the house for *personal* reasons. At some point (depending on the strength of the housing market), the house may become a teardown—regardless of its physical condition. In the Kerrisdale section of Vancouver, British Columbia, for example, perfectly good three-bedroom, two-bath houses of 1,600 to 1,800 square feet have been sold for $500,000 to $700,000. Within a year of sale, the "small" homes have been torn down and replaced by new houses of 3,500 to 5,000 square feet with values reaching $1,500,000 or more.

Finding a low-priced house in an upscale neighborhood can be a great way to get started in home ownership. But go cautiously with your plans for improvements. Sometimes, it's your lot that's going to appreciate most—not your remodeled house.

MISTAKE # **33**

Those "comps" weren't really comps.

LESSON: *When relying on an appraisal, verify that the comp houses are really very similar.*

"When I bought my home," says Sergio Cabila, "I looked at the appraisal the owner showed me. I didn't know much about it. It looked okay to me. The comp houses listed on the form sold for about the same price my seller was asking. So, I offered $10,000 less and eventually we compromised. He cut his price by $5,000."

"It was only after I moved in," Sergio continued, "that I learned the comp houses shown in the appraisal were in a better school district. That didn't bother me because I don't have kids. What did make me mad was that houses in the better school district typically sell at a $15,000 to $20,000 premium. I paid the premium but didn't get the school district."

Sergio's experience illustrates one type of a general homebuyer (and appraisal) mistake: The comp houses shown in the appraisal weren't similar in *all* important respects. As a result, the appraised value of his home was misleading.

In theory, the comparable sales approach to value tells appraisers (or homebuyers) to estimate the value of one home by looking at the sales prices of comparable nearby homes that have sold recently. In practice, defining "comparable" and discovering recent sales can prove difficult. Whether you're using the comparable sales approach yourself or are relying on an appraisal, isolate those features that make a distinct difference.

1. Make sure the comparable homes really are located in the same neighborhood. When you're unfamiliar with an area, it's easy to overlook subtle differences in location such as school district, zoning laws, prestige, accessibility, noise level, proposed or planned changes (e.g., street widening, airport expansion, new commercial development), crime rates, insurance costs, and property tax rates. (See Chapter 5 for more on these points.)
2. The homes should be similar in size, architectural style, floor plan, amenities, and condition.
3. The lots of comparable homes should equal each other in size, configuration, and value.
4. Ideally, you (or an appraiser) should find several sales of similar homes slightly inferior to the home you're looking at, and several homes slightly superior. If you can say "This house is clearly worth more than these two houses, and clearly worth less than these other three houses," then you've bracketed a minimum and a maximum value for your home. Avoid using comp sales that all sit on either the high side or the low side. Bracketing can show you a much clearer picture of a home's value. Be wary of appraisals that don't bracket the appraised property between both higher- *and* lower-priced comparables.

Choosing comp sales requires judgment and knowledge. It's not easy to definitely say that one house is inferior and another superior. When it comes to homes, subjective feelings, tastes, lifestyles, and personal preferences all play a part. In addition, what if no truly comparable homes have sold recently?

All of these difficulties make it prudent for you to examine and carefully review any appraised values you make or rely on. There is plenty of room for error as well as for reasonable differences in opinion. Looking at the sales prices of similar homes can help you (or an appraiser) make more informed estimates of value. But since perfect comps seldom exist, you need to carefully answer these three questions:

1. How do these homes differ in size, features, quality, condition, or location?
2. How much are these differences worth?
3. Do these homes differ to such a large degree that they really shouldn't count as comparables?

If you can't answer these questions with satisfaction and confidence, gather more (and better) market sales data. Put your agent to work. Get him or her to comb through more past sales. Look at more properties. To accurately estimate the market values of the homes you're interested in buying, you must weigh and consider every difference that makes a difference.

MISTAKE # 34

We figured the swimming pool added more to the home's value than it really did.

LESSON: *Beware of costly extras, room additions, and other special features.*

When you start looking at houses, you'll soon begin to notice many differences that make a difference. One house has an oversized swimming pool and patio, another a hot tub, and another a paddleball court. The home in Oakridge has a remodeled kitchen, the Fairfield house is larger, but only because the owners converted the garage to a den. The Pine Meadows house includes new Berber carpeting throughout all of its rooms.

How do you figure how much these differences add to the value of these houses? Unfortunately, no firm rules apply. And that exposes you to the mistake of overpaying. If you find a home with a feature that hits your hot button, you may get so excited that you overestimate how much that hot button feature is really worth. Or worse, you buy the feature more than you buy the home. In that case, you may end up with a country kitchen you love and a house you don't like.

Guidelines for Pricing Features

The following guidelines can help you estimate how much to pay for extra features such as room conversions or additions or nice amenities:

1. Learn how much it would cost to replace the feature, and then subtract for depreciation. If a swimming pool and patio could be built for $22,000 and are 10 years old, the pool should add no more than $11,000 to the home's value (assuming 50 percent depreciation).
2. How easily could the feature be added to the home? Adding a swimming pool is a lot of trouble. Adding a hot tub or new wall-to-wall carpeting throughout the house is relatively easy. Pay less for features that anyone could duplicate easily in nearly any home.
3. What is the cost of the feature relative to the price range of the house? Expensive features (such as Berber carpeting or Poggenpohl kitchens) don't add much value to low- to moderate-priced homes. "The owner just spent $28,000 for these new custom-made cabinets and SubZero appliances," says the real estate agent. "Yes, they're very nice," you respond. "But I'd have to pay to have them removed. They're too rich for me."
4. Does the feature preserve the basic style and integrity of the house? Or does it seem out of character? I recently looked at a well-kept late-1940s Craftsman bungalow. The owner (a single man) had remodeled the kitchen along the lines of a 1970s suburban tract home. To make matters worse, he had decorated and designed the master bedroom with mirrors and lighting that suited it more for the exploits of Hugh Hefner. No homebuyer should pay more than 10 or 20 cents on the dollar for out-of-place or excessive cost features. (In fact, such features often decrease the home's value.)
5. Does the feature appeal to most homebuyers in that neighborhood or price range? If not, you shouldn't pay much for it. With-

out wide-based popularity, it's not a selling feature—and may even detract. In other words, you're fortunate if the features you like are in high supply (e.g., most houses have small yards, and you prefer a small yard, while most other buyers want large yards).

6. Estimate site value. Recall the Craigs (Mistake #32). If a house isn't the best use of its site, don't pay a premium for special features or tiptop condition. Be wary of expensively improved soon-to-be teardowns.

Watch Out for PFA Adjustments

In valuing differences that make a difference, appraisers may drive by the comp houses listed in an appraisal report, but they don't typically go inside—or even walk around the house and the yard. When an appraiser says one house is worth $18,000 more than another home because it's in better condition, that figure is a guess.

The same thing is true for all of the adjustment figures used in the comp sales that are shown on an appraisal report. These numbers are either pulled from the air (PFA), based on rule-of-thumb estimates, or "ball parked" from second- or third-hand sources (multiple listing data, property tax records, talks with real estate agents).

On occasion, when faced with an appraisal that includes numerous large dollar adjustments for property differences, I've inspected the comp houses. I've knocked on the doors, told the owners what I would like to do, and in most cases found them cooperative. In fact, they're usually interested to learn what information the appraisal includes about their home and the other houses valued in the appraisal report.

Although you might feel uncomfortable asking strangers to let you into their homes, at least drive by the comp properties. Get an impression of the homes and the surrounding neighborhood. Talk to the real estate agent(s) who handled the sale. (Remember, comp houses are homes that have sold recently.) In fact, because the current owners of a comp property are recent homebuyers, they might willingly share with you the knowledge they gained through their search and purchase efforts.

MISTAKE # **35**

We looked at selling prices but still overpaid.

LESSON: *Discover the facts behind the selling prices.*

"We thought we were getting a really good deal on the house we bought," says Steve Rizzoli. "My brother and I knew the house three doors down had sold for $198,200 six weeks before. Our house was about the same size and looked nicer on the outside. In addition, our house had a fireplace and a peek-a-boo view of the mountains from the upstairs front bedrooms. Based on these things, we were really happy to get ours for $200,000."

Later, though, Steve and his brother learned not all selling prices are created equal. The house three doors down did sell for $198,200. But to get that price the sellers (1) paid most of the buyers' loan closing costs, (2) contributed $4,000 toward an interest-rate buy-down, and (3) escrowed money for roof repairs. Together, these seller concessions were worth around $17,700.

In transactions more typical of the Rizzolis' area, seller concessions ranged between $3,500 and $5,000. Here, the sellers paid $10,000 more than normal. Although the purchase contract showed a price of $198,200, the buyers actually bought the house for a price (less special concessions) of around $185,000. When the Rizzolis compared their home's cost of $200,000 to the $185,000 net price their neighbors actually paid, they felt foolish.

Recent selling prices of comparable nearby homes can give you a good idea of the value of your home. But don't accept these numbers without question. Sometimes there's a story behind a home's sale that has pushed the selling (contract) price above or below the home's market value. Consider these questions:

1. Has either the buyer or seller been pressured by time or other circumstances? Sellers who need money fast may sell below market value. Buyers who need a quick move-in date may pay above market value.

2. Does the sale price include any of the seller's personal property or home furnishings? The sellers may not be willing to part with the $5,000 Tiffany chandelier in the dining room—unless the buyers up their price accordingly. The same thing is true for the custom-made window blinds, the kitchen and laundry appliances, the antique grandfather clock, or the basement workshop fully stocked with tools and equipment. If these items become a part of the sale, they also will become a part of the price.

3. Was the sale at arm's length? Whenever buyers and sellers are friends or relatives, the selling price may not tell the full story. Parents selling to their kids aren't likely to insist on top dollar.

4. Was the transaction handled by real estate agents? Buyers and sellers who rely on real estate agents tend to know more about the market. Their transaction prices will more likely reflect market values. On the other hand, sellers or buyers acting on their own are more likely to sell for too little or pay too much. (In other words, for sale by owner [FSBO] sales show much greater price variance.)

5. Does the sale involve owner financing or other seller concessions? Cash-short buyers may agree to pay more for a house if the sellers help with the financing.

6. When did the sale occur? The sale date recorded in public records or multiple listing files reflects the date of closing. That's the date money changed hands and the home's title transferred to the new owners. But the date the purchase agreement was signed by the buyers and sellers could have taken place months earlier.

   In stable markets, time differences of several months needn't cause much concern. In changing markets, a difference of even two to four months can mislead. As a check, ask your Realtor to tell you the date the contracts were signed for the comparable home prices you're evaluating. Then ask whether the market seems to be changing. Are the inventories of unsold homes growing? Are homes taking longer to sell? Is there an increasing gap between listing prices and offering prices? Has buyer traffic been dropping off at open houses?

When you ask these questions, you guard against buying into a slowing market with unrealistic expectations. When markets are changing, look beyond past selling prices. Past prices do not tell you where future prices are headed. Keep track of other market signals.

MISTAKE # **36**

The sellers named the price, we named the terms.

LESSON: *Never agree to pay more than market value for a home—unless you weigh the risks.*

In crazy housing markets of the past, buyers and sellers have done nearly anything they could to make a sale work. With tight money and high interest rates, many buyers fell short of qualifying for bank financing. That left these buyers and their sellers to work out their own terms. Creative financing became the norm. Seller seconds, wraparounds, balloons, third and fourth deeds of trust, lease-options, and land contracts became common.

Homebuyers told sellers, "You name the price, we'll name the terms." As long as buyers could handle the cash-down and monthly payments, they didn't care about price. Anticipating high inflation, buyers figured that even if they overpaid, tomorrow's appreciation would bail them out and still leave room for a healthy profit.

As always, though, the tide receded. Home prices stopped their upward flow. Homeowners who tried to refinance to pay off short-term seller financing found they owed more than their homes were worth. Others who had relied on creative financing and lost their jobs couldn't afford to make their monthly payments and they couldn't afford to sell and pay off a mortgage that exceeded their home's market value.

Cash-Short Buyers Meet Overpriced Sellers

Here's how these homebuyers made their mistake: In most (but not all) instances, buyers were cash-short or for some reason couldn't qualify for bank financing. The would-be sellers frequently had priced their homes too high. This combination offered opportunity for a match. The buyers say, "Okay, we will accept your price of $249,000 if you will accept $10,000 down and monthly payments at five percent interest. After the first three years, we'll refinance and pay off the balance we owe you."

The sellers accept. They receive their $249,000 price (for a home actually valued around $230,000). The buyers receive the terms they want. Unfortunately, three years later the home's value has risen to just $240,000 and the buyers can't come up with the money to pay off the sellers. The buyers face foreclosure. The thrill of owning their first home turns into worry, fear, and sleepless nights.

Does this mean that you should never trade a higher price for owner terms? Not necessarily. But if you do, think downside. Don't count on unrealistic appreciation, don't count on mortgage interest rates to fall, and don't figure you're going to put aside more money from your paycheck than you normally save. Do put a clause in your purchase contract that extends your payoff date should the housing market or mortgage market go against you.

Most important, know the cash sale value of the home you're buying. Especially in hot markets, homebuyers may jump into a deal too eagerly. They don't stop to think how much premium they are paying for the sellers' easy terms. Whenever you offer (or a seller offers you) easy terms, know what those terms are costing you. How much of a price premium are you paying? And are you positively sure that your finances will permit you to fulfill the contract—regardless of what happens in the housing and mortgage markets?

MISTAKE # **37**

Everything looked like a bargain.

LESSON: *When moving from a high-cost area to a low-cost area, recalibrate your sights.*

If you are relocating from, say, San Francisco or Boston to Memphis or Orlando, get set for a great surprise. When you first start looking at houses, you won't believe your eyes. "Four bedrooms, three baths, pool, den, and a half-acre lot—all for $299,900. Unbelievable!" You'll begin to think all the sellers have gone crazy. "Better act quick, this house is a steal. The owners must not know what they are doing."

Filled with excitement about bargains everywhere, you lose critical awareness. You compare the houses you're looking at to the prices of houses back in your previous hometown. Relative to your last city, homes in your new locale seem ridiculously cheap. So, you run the danger of overpaying.

Again, to guard against the bargain illusion, get good local market information. Check selling prices, terms of sale, market conditions, and neighborhoods. Put the home prices of Boston or San Francisco out of your mind. Recalibrate your sights. Stay focused on Memphis or Orlando. Work with a real estate agent who's smart, savvy, and motivated— an agent who will educate you on the local market. Dump agents who urge you to make a quick and uninformed buying decision.

MISTAKE # **38**

I didn't buy anything. All the houses were grossly overpriced.

LESSON: When moving from a low-cost area to a high-cost area, recalibrate your sights. Don't pass up a bargain.

If you relocate to (or live in) a high-priced housing market, you may tell yourself, "Home prices here are outrageous. Everything is overpriced." You talk with other people. You read newspaper articles lamenting the housing crisis. You see articles quoting experts who say homes are no longer a good investment. You hear much chatter about "bubbles." Politicians proclaim something must be done: "Only 18 percent of our young families can afford to buy their own home." Even more depressing, you know friends or family in Des Moines who just bought a 2,300 square-foot, three-bedroom, two-bath ranch for $119,500.

With these influences telling you homes are overpriced, it's easy to adopt a negative mind-set. Sure, you would like to own. You might even (sort of) plan to own. Yet each time you meet the high housing costs face to face, you walk away. You think about those housing bargains in Des Moines, Memphis, or Orlando.

You're Surrounded by "Acres of Diamonds"

Around the turn of the century, Russell Conwell, the founder of Temple University, became famous for his speech "Acres of Diamonds." His speech was so powerful, so enduring, and so simple that throughout his life, Conwell was called upon to deliver it 25,000 times.

Conwell would say, "My friends, that mistake is very universally made … I say to you that you do have 'acres of diamonds' right where you now live." By "mistake" Conwell meant focusing on the better conditions that you think exist in other places, while passing up the possibilities (acres of diamonds) that you can find in your own backyard.

A Missed Opportunity

I confess to making this mistake myself—and I've seen it made countless times by others. Some years ago, I moved from low-priced South Carolina to high-priced Vancouver, British Columbia. In South Carolina, I owned a custom-built brick home in a professional neighborhood. That house sold for $51,000 (then a fair price). In Vancouver, $51,000 would buy a small one-bedroom condo. A modest single-family home would cost $90,000. Rather than focus on the great benefits that Vancouver offered, my mind drifted back to South Carolina, where one could own twice the house for half the money. "These prices in Vancouver are ridiculous," I thought. And many others agreed. Since everything looked too expensive, I rented.

One year later, the owner of the rental house said to me, "I've decided to sell. If you'd like to buy before I list with an agent, I'll give you a good price."

"What price do you have in mind?" I asked.

"Eighty-seven thousand," he replied.

"Eighty-seven thousand!" I choked. "No thanks."

To this day, I can recall laughing with a friend about the price the owner had proposed. My friend and I agreed that $87,000 for a one-bedroom house was ridiculous. Someone would be a fool to pay that much.

That fool was soon found. The house sold for $91,000. The new owners completely rebuilt the house into a four-bedroom, three-bath home. Today that home would sell for upwards of $1,000,000. The lot value alone would run over $500,000.

In misjudging this opportunity, my friend (also new to British Columbia) and I had compared the price of the one-bedroom house in Vancouver to home prices in the relatively low-priced cities where we had previously lived. By that yardstick, Vancouver prices looked ridiculous.

The family who bought the home enjoyed a different perspective. They were from Hong Kong. They realized Vancouver ranked highly as a world-class city. Compared to Hong Kong, Tokyo, San Francisco, New York, or London, Vancouver prices (at that time) were a bargain. Even better, this specific house was located just a 5-minute walk to the beach, a 5-minute walk to shopping and restaurants, a 20-minute walk to the campus of the University of British Columbia, and a 10-minute drive to downtown Vancouver and Stanley Park. In addition, the house enjoyed a panoramic daytime view of the mountains and English Bay and a night-time view of the city lights of downtown Vancouver.

Yet, if asked at the time, most people in Vancouver (not just newcomers) would have believed Vancouver homes were priced too high. The press and nearly everyone else complained about the "housing crisis." No one spoke of great opportunities.

But great opportunities existed then, and they exist today. No matter how high home prices have climbed in your area (or the area you're moving to), relative bargains can be found. Compared to major cities throughout the world, American and Canadian home prices compare favorably. In a recent survey of the world's top 10 most expensive cities, not one U.S. or Canadian city made the list.

In every metro area, you can find homes and neighborhoods well-priced relative to others. Most important, in the future, today's home (and lot) prices will be viewed as the good old days. For each of the past six decades, the U.S. population has grown, the economy has grown, total employment has grown, and home prices have grown. The coming decade will surely to yield the same.

CHAPTER 5

Locate a Great Neighborhood

To judge a neighborhood, think about school district, appreciation potential, affordability, demographics, lifestyles, government services (fire, police, waste disposal, libraries), shopping, parks, zoning, aesthetics, and other features.

In choosing a neighborhood, you usually trade off advantages and disadvantages. Think clearly: What features do you value most highly? Which ones are "deal killers?" Many neighborhood characteristics don't jump out and announce themselves. To get the facts, research like a private investigator and develop skills of discovery. Along these lines, with the homebuying experiences in this chapter, you can sharpen your sense of awareness and ferret out the information that will lead you to make the right decision.

MISTAKE # **39**

My agent said this was a good school district.

LESSON: Never accept a real estate agent's opinions at face value. Concentrate on verifiable facts.

"When I started looking for a home," says Lori Pines, "I wanted the Richmond neighborhood. My sister has two kids in Richmond Elementary, and she thinks it's great. Since my own children were ages four and six, a good elementary school was very important to me. Besides, it would have been nice to live near Sandy and Rick.

"But the problem was I really couldn't find a house I liked at a price I wanted to pay. Then, my agent suggested that I look in Brookview. She said I could get more house for the money and that the schools there were just as good as Richmond's. Well, the agent was right about one thing. I found a house I loved in Brookview for about $25,000 less than it would have cost in Richmond. But I got so excited about the house, I forgot to check out the schools."

What Is a Good School District?

"I just accepted my agent's opinions at face value. What a mistake that was. I'm now driving Lisa and Sean halfway across town every morning to a private school. The money I saved on the house, I'm spending for gas and tuition."

Did Lori's agent really mislead her about the quality of the schools in Brookview? Maybe. Maybe not. Could Lori have easily avoided her mistake? Definitely. Lori should have followed this rule: Don't ask your real estate agent for opinions. Ask for facts. Then verify.

When working with an agent—especially one with whom you've developed rapport—it's easy to rapid-fire questions about the neighborhood: "Is this a good location? Is there much crime? How long does it take to get to downtown from here? Is this a good school district?"

Now think for a moment about these questions. What do you mean when you say "good" school district? What is "too much" crime? Going downtown? By what route? To which building? At what time of the day? For answers you can rely on, ask specific questions. In doing so, you push your real estate agent to answer with facts.

Telling you the commute to downtown is a "breeze" doesn't give quite same information as, "Between 7:30 and 9:00 A.M. the commute will normally require 25 to 35 minutes." To an executive used to a 6:00 A.M., 90-minute drive from Long Island to Manhattan, a 25- to 35-minute commute might easily seem like a "breeze." To an Indiana

University professor who can walk to her office in less than 10 minutes, a 25- to 35-minute hassle with traffic every day could bring on ulcers.

As for crime, consider a divorced mother with two children. She's in residency at a hospital. She'll be working long hours at all times of night and day. She plans to ride her bike to work. Compare her definition of "too much" crime to a 6'4" 34-year-old man who is a triathlete and an ex-Golden Gloves boxer. "Let 'em try something with me" might be his attitude.

Facts! Not Opinions

By asking your agent for facts, not opinions, you'll make sure the two of you are on the same wavelength. Career real estate agents want to do the best job they can for their homebuyers and sellers. To earn a living, they need referrals from pleased clients. So, you help them and yourself by asking questions that they can answer with verifiable facts. "The mean SAT score of college-bound seniors last year at Lincoln High was 1,150" tells you much more than "I believe Lincoln High enjoys a very good reputation." Knowing there were 27 house break-ins in the neighborhood during the past six months tells you much more than the subjective claim, "This is a pretty safe neighborhood."

Statements of opinion may be true. But factual statements convey more useful information and leave less room for ambiguity and disappointment.

MISTAKE # **40**

We never saw the railroad tracks.

LESSON: *Ask the sellers and your sales agent to disclose any disturbing noises in the neighborhood.*

"When we bought our house," says Amy Lee, "all we saw in the backyard was an eight-foot-high wooden fence with tall bamboo growing in front of it. We liked the fence and the bamboo because it gave us so much privacy. We never thought to ask what was on the other side. After we moved in, though, we soon found out.

"Twice a night, every night, a loud house-shaking freight train comes roaring through at 2:00 A.M. and 4:00 A.M. The railroad tracks—we now know—lie just on the other side of our backyard fence."

Before buying, Amy forgot to inquire about noise pollution in the neighborhood. Hundreds of thousands of homebuyers have made a similar mistake because it's so easy to make. Even if you visit a house three or four times before you write your offer, how much time are you likely to spend in the home? Three hours? Four hours? Often, you can't learn much about neighborhood noise pollution—trains, buses, trucks, aircraft flight patterns—in such a short amount of time. You must research. Ask the sellers. Ask your Realtor. Talk to neighbors.

The (Un)Quiet Street

I once bought a house located on a small road removed from noisy traffic. At least that's what I thought until I learned teenagers used the street as a shortcut route to and from their high school. Since the house was near an intersection with a stop sign, during the early morning and after-school hours, it often sounded like race trials for the Daytona 500 were being held outside my door.

Like many homebuyers, I looked at houses on the weekends. On Saturday morning the home was perfectly quiet. And this typical practice helps explain why it's easy to miss noise pollution. Visits to a house may occur when noise pollution is least likely to create a noticeable bother.

The timing of your visit can make the difference. Before you buy, if you can't camp out near the home for 24 hours a day for a week or two, do the next best thing. Vary the times and days you visit the home, and ask the sellers, neighbors, and your Realtor to fully describe and disclose any noises that may disrupt neighborhood tranquility.

MISTAKE # **41**

We bought into an upscale development that's moving downscale.

LESSON: Before buying into a new development, find out what type of homes the developer has planned for later phases.

"Several years ago we bought our first home in an upscale new development," says Dorthea Washington. "We paid $250,000 and put five years of savings into our down payment. Now we've been told that the developer plans to build townhouses and smaller homes right next to ours. He intends to sell them for $125,000 to $160,000. We're afraid this will change the character of the development and make our home less valuable. We wouldn't have bought here had we known the subdivision was moving downscale."

Dorthea is describing a not-uncommon complaint. Sometimes developers build the most expensive phase of a development first. These first-phase homes create an upscale image for the project. This initial image makes it easier for the developer to sell the more modest homes that he builds later. Naturally, buyers of these later phases are attracted to a development that's already noted for its fine homes, manicured lawns, safe streets, and driveways stocked with BMWs, Volvos, and SUVs. Just as naturally, though, the BMW crowd may complain about the cheapening of their neighborhood.

How can prospective buyers of early-phase homes guard against surprises that could downscale the neighborhood?

Ask the Developer

The first line of defense is to ask the developer. Usually, later phases of a development are planned before phase-one sales begin. Also, determine whether the developer plans to merge the stages of the development. Will all homeowners share the same common area amenities (tennis courts, pools, parks, trails), or will each area enjoy exclusive use of its own facilities? Will the separate phases share a common entrance to the development? Will the builder market the lower-priced units under new identities—or will the total development share the same name, or maybe something like Windwood I, Windwood II, and Windwood III? Will the separate phases be organized into one combined homeowners' association, or will each community control its own membership roster? Will the phases be visually and physically separated by boundaries such as parks, greenspaces, lakes, creeks, trees, or major streets?

Even when development plans may be proposed for later phases, seldom are they etched in stone. Over time, housing markets change. Move-up homes may sell fast for several years and then the market might slow. Starter homes might gain popularity. In a changing market, plans for $300,000 homes may be scrapped in favor of $150,000 townhouses and maybe even rental apartments.

Look for Legal Restrictions

As a second line of prevention, determine whether the developer can change his plans for future phases at will. Are developer prerogatives limited by zoning laws, deed restrictions, or a vote by members of the phase-one homeowners' association?

For example, in many developments, deed restrictions prohibit lot sizes of less than, say, one acre, or homes of less than 2,400 square feet. Laws or restrictions also limit housing densities—usually stated as so many units to the acre. Developers of condominiums, townhouses, and apartments typically push for densities as high as they can get them. Homebuyers in early phases prefer low densities in later stages.

When you investigate a development, your best protection against downscaling lies with deed restrictions. Deed restrictions are difficult to weaken without a majority vote of all affected homeowners. Government zoning and other land-use laws give you some protection. But they're subject to change depending on the direction of the political winds. Warranties and representations from the developer concerning future plans suffer in effect because most developers won't make written promises—and you should never rely on the oral promises of the developer's marketing staff.

The builder's sales reps may give you a color brochure and show you scale models of how the development will look in 5 or 10 years, but don't pay much attention to this type of promotion unless it's backed up with guarantees. Too many homebuyers rely on glowing visions painted by an enthusiastic sales staff. Then, later, they face disappointment. Relying on oral promises or promotional brochures, disgruntled homebuyers on occasion have won lawsuits against developers to prevent downscaling. But litigation is a last-ditch effort. It costs years of frustration and hundreds of thousands of dollars in legal fees. And your lawyer still might lose the case.

So, realize that development plans and promises can (and do) change. Later phases may not enhance the value of earlier phases. When such an adverse change is important to you, insist on legally enforceable guarantees and deed restrictions.

MISTAKE # **42**

When we bought our house, the land across the street was a cornfield. Now it's a parking lot and shopping center.

LESSON: *Always envision the future within your neighborhood.*

"I remember when we bought," says Aaron Vasko. "The neighborhood was quiet and you had no trouble pulling in and out of the subdivision entrance. Now, since the shopping center's come in, you might have to wait through two or three light changes, especially at commute times or on Saturday when it seems like everybody's out shopping."

No one can anticipate all the changes that might affect a neighborhood. Some possible changes, though, are easier to spot than others—if you know what to look for. As a starting point, look around for vacant or underutilized land. Are croplands beginning to seem out of place? Do wooded areas of private property sit near other tracts that are already being developed? Are roads or streets being widened?

If you're buying into a city neighborhood, find out whether rates of home ownership in the neighborhood are increasing or decreasing. Are growing numbers of property owners renting out rooms or cutting up single-family homes into apartments? Are any of the single-family homes being converted to offices or retail use? Does the government own any nearby land? Does the federal, state, or local government plan to put up any public low-income housing nearby? Are the parks deteriorating? Is graffiti spreading? Is the number of vacant buildings increasing?

Imagine How the Coming Years Will Bring Change to the Neighborhood

When you buy a home, you're buying into the future of the neighborhood and the surrounding areas. As the neighborhood goes, so goes your home's value. But investigating a neighborhood requires more than just looking at what exists today. It means envisioning what it will look like 5, 10, or 15 years from now.

Close your eyes and let your imagination carry forward from the present into the future. What types of buildings will sit on those vacant tracts? Will the streets and roads become more congested? Will property owners have improved their homes and landscaping? Will trees have matured? Have property owners and neighborhood residents joined together to work for revitalization? Or have they been indifferent (or even destructive) to the character and appearance of the area? Relative to other areas, will this neighborhood have moved up or down on the scale of desirability?

Especially think about traffic congestion. Will it get worse? Can the present roads accommodate all of the new development? How will other areas or neighborhoods compare in terms of accessibility and convenience?

Congestion Can Create Opportunity

Some years back, in metro Columbia, South Carolina, the northwest corridor running out along Interstate 26 became the most popular area for new development. Homebuyers were scrambling to get their children out of city schools and into the suburban school districts. Relative to most other areas of Columbia, the northwest corridor was hot.

But each new subdivision created more traffic. During commute times, key interstate exits would back up for half an hour. As a result, many potential homebuyers searched for developments in less-congested areas. Within two years home appreciation in the northwest corridor slowed. Appreciation rates in the less-congested northeast and southeast areas picked up speed. In fact, within three years, home values in one southeast development that found particular favor jumped by 40 percent.

When evaluating neighborhoods, subdivisions, and communities, remember that change is a fact of life. The future won't necessarily look like the present. When you anticipate changes that seem imminent, you avoid unpleasant surprises—and you might even pick a star performer.

MISTAKE # **43**

It didn't occur to me that on weekends the place could turn into a zoo of wild kids and party animals.

LESSON: *Find out if your neighbors' lifestyles are compatible with yours.*

Like many first-time homebuyers, Ann Hennig had thought about investing in a home off and on for a period of years. Yet, indecision and procrastination conspired to keep her renting. Then, when Ann's landlord gave her a 30-day notice that he wanted to move back into the home where she had been living, Ann decided the time was right. She would buy a home of her own.

Pushing herself to act quickly, Ann found a townhouse that was priced right, spacious, and located only five minutes from her office; and it could be bought with a low-down-payment VA mortgage assumption.

Best of all, her mortgage payments (after tax deductions) would cost her less than she'd been paying in rent. Those were the good points.

Unpleasant Surprises

After moving in, Ann discovered a few things she had overlooked: "Children screaming and riding their Hot Wheels, everyone blasting their boom boxes and car stereos, barking dogs, and late-night parties—all these things came as a big surprise to me," says Ann.

How did Ann get herself into this kind of situation? "First of all," Ann continues, "I have to explain my own ignorance. I came from the neighborhood where I had grown up. I had known my neighbors all my life, and, except for an occasional outburst, the neighbors were pretty set in their ways and were generally quiet and considerate. You could always count on peaceful afternoons and quiet evenings. Since I had never been faced with the problem of constant noise, it was not something I consciously thought about. It didn't occur to me that this place could turn into a zoo of wild kids and party animals.

"Also, I moved into my townhouse in October, when the children were in school, most of the neighborhood was working, the weather was cold, and not many people were outside. The few times I visited the unit before I purchased it, I didn't stay long and didn't hear any of the neighbors, or maybe I just came on relatively quiet days. Anyway, I didn't pay much attention.

"But something else aggravated the problem. It seemed like we had a Gresham's law of neighborhoods. Bad residents were driving out good ones. Since I came from a neighborhood where people rarely moved, I had naively assumed that the neighbors I had when I moved in would be my neighbors for many years. At least in the beginning I did have relatively quiet neighbors beside me and in back. Within a year they were both gone. In their place came a divorced man who partied constantly, and a young single woman behind me who played her stereo from 8:00 A.M. to 10:00 P.M.—I think to accompany her barking dogs.

"On top of this, parking was another problem. Each unit had an assigned parking space. When I visited the units before buying, many of the spaces were empty so it looked like parking was plentiful. But, of course, then most people had been at work. Weekends and evenings it was a different story. Since most units had more than one car, parking was clearly inadequate. I also learned that residents totally disregarded the parking rules. Sometimes cars were even abandoned. Repeated calls to the police were all in vain."

Apathy Prevails

"Later, when some of us tried to reform our homeowners' association to develop and enforce stricter rules, we ran into a brick wall. Too many of the units were owned by absentee investors. They didn't live here and didn't care about unruly residents. And they certainly didn't want to put money into maintenance and upkeep of the property."

Ann's mistake is common. She didn't think to verify her subconscious assumptions. She assumed her new neighbors would behave in a considerate and friendly manner. As she learned to her regret, the facts contradicted her assumptions. Before buying, she should have determined the compatibility, stability, and cooperativeness of her future neighbors.

MISTAKE #

Those people were a bunch of snobs.

LESSON: *Want to socialize with neighbors? First find out whether you'll fit in.*

In today's world of hectic schedules, easy travel, and instant communication, our chief socializing may take place on a catch-as-catch-can basis with friends and relatives located across town or across the country. Unlike the past, many of us today seldom get together with neighbors—we may not even know their names. The old notion of sipping morning coffee at the neighbors' kitchen table seems as outdated as TV reruns of *Leave It to Beaver.*

To Abe and Lucille Hoskins, though, the idea of neighborhood meant neighborliness. That's the type of neighborhood they each had grown up in and had become accustomed to while raising their own children. Abe and Lucille were also a living example of the American dream. Starting life poor and lacking a college education, by their mid-forties Abe and Lucille had achieved an income of $230,000 a year and a net worth (primarily equities in rental houses) of $1,800,000. Their income and wealth placed them near the top in their Midwestern town. They were definitely among the town's well-to-do.

But Abe still worked at the steel plant, and whenever their tenants moved, Lucille still cleaned their rental houses. Following the model of Sam Walton, Abe drove an old pickup truck. Lucille bought her clothes at Kmart. The one extravagance they both wanted (and could certainly afford) was a home in Woodshire, the "best" neighborhood in their city.

After much searching, the Hoskinses found a Woodshire home they fell in love with. They put an offer in the first time they saw it. The house was exactly what they wanted.

Sadly, though, as Abe and Lucille discovered, the neighborhood didn't want them. Although in appearance and convenience it left nothing to be desired, in neighborliness it failed on every count. Not only did the neighbors seldom socialize with each other, they overtly snubbed the Hoskinses with an unspoken attitude: "Since you're not credentialed professionals and lack a college degree, you're not as good as us. We choose not to acknowledge your existence."

Neighbors Make the Neighborhood

Many homebuyers could ignore this nasty attitude and go on with their lives. Not Abe and Lucille. They didn't want to merely own a house, they wanted to feel like they were part of a community. That didn't happen. Within two years the Hoskinses sold their dream house in Woodshire and moved back to their old home on South 14th Street (which they had kept as a rental). "Those people in Woodshire were a bunch of snobs," Lucille told her friends. "We didn't fit in."

Houses and lawns, trees and shrubs, streets and sidewalks, parks and playgrounds, schools and libraries, shops and restaurants: these are the parts of a neighborhood you can see. But look beyond these physical characteristics. Find out who lives in the neighborhood. Is there a feeling of community? Where do the people work? What are their educational backgrounds? What are their ages? Are they primarily married or single? Do they have children? What are their lifestyles and attitudes? Are they neighborly? Do you think you will fit in? Does it matter? Had the Hoskinses investigated these questions, they would have prevented their homebuying mistake.

MISTAKE # **45**

You're saying we can't build a fence around our yard? Isn't that unconstitutional?

LESSON: State and local governments can regulate the use of your property down to the smallest detail.

The Fifth Amendment to the U.S. Constitution declares that no person shall be "deprived of life, liberty, or property, without due process of law; nor shall private property be taken for public use without just compensation." In addition, nearly all state constitutions include clauses similarly written to stop governments from encroaching on an individual's property rights.

In interpreting these protective clauses, though, courts have defined "taking" quite narrowly. In effect, courts have said governments may squeeze an owner's rights as tightly as they want—so long as an owner still enjoys some minimal use of the property. As Nicole and Brett Gates learned to their dismay, a neighborhood prohibition against backyard fences by the Village of Inverness was perfectly legal.

Government Restrictions: For and Against

Government regulations can work for you or against you. If your neighbor is planning to build a second story onto his home that will block your view of the bay, you'll be more than eager to remind him that the added height of his remodeled home will violate the building height regulations. Conversely, when you learn you aren't allowed to rent out the room above your garage to a local college student, you may feel government has gone too far. After all, isn't a "man's home his castle"?

e, there's nothing objective about government restrictions. 're for or against them usually depends on what you intend to do with your property—and what you want to prevent your neighbors from doing. Nor are property restrictions uniform among neighborhoods and communities. One neighborhood might encourage accessory apartments; another might prevent them. Jackson Heights might allow in-home businesses; Fairview may outlaw them. All this means that before you buy a home or a building lot, investigate the government restrictions that will apply to you and your neighbors.

Allan Funt's Surprise

Consider what happened to Allen Funt, best known for his *Candid Camera* movies and television shows. Mr. Funt bought 1,200 acres of land near Monterey, California. He intended to build four buildings on the site: a house, a guesthouse, a barn, and a stable. The California Coastal Commission (the zoning authority over the 1,200 acres) refused permission. Instead, the commission allowed Mr. Funt to build two structures and ordered him to grant the public a 300-acre scenic easement through the site. To top that, the commission further specified that Mr. Funt situate his home and landscaping such that, after dark, no passersby would be able to see the home's lights.

The government probably won't regulate you to the same degree that the California Coastal Commission has regulated millions of Californians. But here are the types of restrictions you might face:

- *Height restrictions.* Most homes are limited in height. You may not be able to add a second or third story.
- *Side yard, front yard, and backyard restrictions.* Land-use laws typically require a home to be set back a certain distance from each of the site's boundaries. You may not be able to build onto the house or garage.
- *Floor area ratios.* These regulations limit the maximum square footage of your home relative to the size of your lot.
- *Use restrictions.* These laws may prevent you from operating an office or business from your home.
- *Occupancy laws.* These regulations may limit the number of people who can live in your home. On occasion, they also

may prevent more than three or four singles from sharing a home.

- *Rental unit prohibitions.* You may not be permitted to rent out a basement suite or add on an accessory apartment.
- *Energy conservation.* These laws may apply to anything from window size and placement to retrofitting your toilets with water-saving devices.
- *Nuisance ordinances.* These include virtually anything you do that annoys your neighbors or vice versa. Fence heights, barking dogs, overhanging trees, car parking, practicing musical instruments, public nudity (sunbathing au naturel in your backyard)—the list goes on.
- *Remodeling and renovation.* Nearly any serious remodeling or renovation will require a permit and government approval.
- *Historic preservation.* Should you buy a historically significant home or a home located in a designated historical district, any changes you make to the home will have to conform to prescribed aesthetic and architectural standards.

Your Realtor Will Not, and Should Not, Advise You about Regulations

Jason Shields, an Ohio Realtor, says that homebuyers pay too little attention to zoning and building regulations. "They buy a home with big plans. Then they find out they can't do what they want to do. Because I can't give legal advice," Jason points out, "I tell them to talk over their intentions with a lawyer, a reputable contractor, or the city planner. But they forget or let it slide and end up disappointed.

"Sometimes it also works the opposite way," Jason adds. "By failing to check neighborhood zoning, they get all upset when an apartment building starts to go up two blocks over. Or maybe they don't like their neighbor operating a repair shop out of his garage and parking four or five cars along the street. Either way, I try to emphasize that the laws will help determine the character of the neighborhood. So they ought to make sure they get the protection they want—yet not so restrictive as to interfere with their own plans. It really is a matter of finding the neighborhood with the right balance."

MISTAKE # **46**

No need to worry; those laws are never enforced.

LESSON: Beware of nonconforming and illegal property uses.

Some of the homes you look at will not conform to the neighborhood's existing zoning laws or building regulations. It's not uncommon to walk into a home and find a built-on den that sits too close to the property line, an illegal basement rental suite, or maybe outdated wiring. If you ask the real estate agent or sellers about the violation, they might say something like, "Don't be concerned, those laws are never enforced." Cy Torre, though, found out differently.

Cy bought a four-unit flat in Waukegan, Illinois. It was his way of getting over the affordability hurdle to home ownership. Cy lived in one of the units and collected rents from the other three apartments to cover a big part of his mortgage payments. At the time Cy bought the fourplex, the neighborhood was zoned single family and duplex. Cy knew his fourplex violated the law, but so did a number of triplexes and fourplexes in the area. The seller told Cy, "There's nothing to worry about. It's been this way for years and no one's ever said anything." So Cy bought the flats without investigating further.

Beware of Neighbor Complaints

Cy had chosen this neighborhood because it was being revitalized. Recent buyers had begun to spruce up their homes, clean up the nearby park, and establish a neighborhood crime watch program. They also began to complain about parking.

Since this was an older neighborhood, many homes lacked garages, and few enjoyed enough on-site space to park two cars. As a result, these younger recent homebuyers (who owned more cars than the previous older homeowners) often found themselves driving around the block several times before they could find a parking space. Joining with other neighbors, they put pressure on the mayor to solve the problem.

Whenever some neighborhood group complains about inadequate parking, the first casualties are owners of homes with illegal suites or flats. "Get rid of those illegal tenants and there would be enough parking spaces for us homeowners."

And that's how the mayor solved the problem. He sent investigators out to count mailboxes at all properties in the neighborhood. Owners with more than two boxes were cited for violating the zoning ordinance and ordered to bring their properties into compliance within 60 days. Cy not only had to spend $2,200 to remove kitchens and take out several walls, his rental revenues went down. In the long run, Cy will benefit from these changes through increased property values in the neighborhood. In the short run, he suffered a severe cash crunch.

In Cy's case, his building violations were illegal. Whenever you own a property that *illegally* fails to conform to existing zoning or building regulations, you run the risk that an enforcement campaign will require you to make costly repairs or renovations. (A more costly example is that of Lawrence Ginsburg, a New York City developer who was forced to remove the illegal top 12 stories of a 31-story apartment building he had constructed five years earlier. In addition to losing the rental income of 12 stories, Mr. Ginsburg had to pay $1 million for their demolition.)

Nonconforming Uses

Sometimes zoning or building regulations are changed and existing uses are grandfathered. Once grandfathered, they become nonconforming uses, but not illegal. Still, nonconforming uses pose two risks.

First, the governing powers may change their minds. If they choose, they usually can take away or phase out a grandfathered use. Political winds blowing from a different direction, or offended neighbors who raise a fuss, can lead a nonconforming use to a premature death. (In Palo Alto, California, complaining homeowners forced the political powers to get rid of a nearby office building. In a compromise, the owners of the office building were permitted a 15-year phaseout.)

As a second risk, you might lose permission for a nonconforming use if you suspend or discontinue it. Say you operate a home business that doesn't conform to existing laws but has been grandfathered. If you shut down your business for several months, you may not be allowed to reopen it.

Small Fire, Big Repairs

I once owned a rental house that had a sub-par 60-amp electrical system that was grandfathered. Current building codes specified a minimum of 100-amp service. Unfortunately, the house experienced a small fire and the wiring was damaged. But the building inspector wouldn't permit a small repair. Instead, he pointed out that the law required me to rewire the entire house to comply with present standards. A $200 fire cost $2,000 to repair.

Throughout the United States, as many as 50 percent of houses and small apartment buildings may fail to comply with a current zoning ordinance, building regulation, or environmental restriction. Especially if you're buying an older home, you may not be able to avoid noncomplying properties. Just don't buy blind. Discover violations. Learn whether they're illegal or merely nonconforming. And think through what risks they might present.

As the risks grow bigger, your offering price should drop. If you're expected to bear the risk of noncompliance, the sellers should discount their price to make up for it.

MISTAKE # **47**

We live in Naperville, but our kids can't go to Naperville schools.

LESSON: *Your address doesn't necessarily tell you where you live or the services you are entitled to.*

The city address for my previous home is Berkeley, California, and I received mail service through the Berkeley post office. But for purposes of zoning, building codes, school district, and property tax rates, the house falls within the jurisdiction of Oakland, California. Within the city of Dallas, Texas, the self-contained high-income community of Highland Park is known for the high quality of its schools. But if you live on the west side of the freeway that slices through Highland Park, your kids must attend Dallas public schools.

Will You Live Where You Think You Will Live?

Throughout the country, city addresses, school districts, and governing jurisdictions do not necessarily coincide. Your address does not give all the information you need. What is true for school districts also stands true for services such as fire and police protection, trash pickup, water, sewage and utility hookups, and cable television. Before you buy, verify the school district, property tax rates, and municipal services that will apply to your home-to-be.

Also, when you're talking to the secretary or clerk at the school district headquarters, the planning agency, or the tax assessor's office, describe specifically where the house is located. In Urbana, Illinois, Marlene Watts asked school personnel whether her home-to-be on Florida Avenue would put her kids in Wilson Junior High, which was the school she wanted. The secretary Marlene talked to replied yes. The correct answer was no. True, residents on the south side of Florida Avenue were within the Wilson Junior High School district. But homes on the north side of the street, where Marlene had moved, were not. Florida Avenue was the dividing line. It wasn't enough to live on Florida. You had to live on the south side of the road.

Avoid Marlene's mistake: Verify municipal boundaries, school districts, tax rates, and services. As odd as it sounds, your house might not be located where you think it is located.

MISTAKE # **48**

We didn't know there were stables nearby. The wind was blowing from a different direction the day we looked.

LESSON: *Find out if any foul odors periodically intrude into the neighborhood.*

In the town where I was raised, relatively few homebuyers wanted to live in the southwest part of town. Six or eight days a month a local chemical plant released huge amounts of what smelled like hydrogen sulfide (which smells worse than rotten eggs). This foul odor just hung in the air. Today, due to tougher environmental laws, industrial emissions don't cause the problem they once did. Still, not all noxious odors have been eliminated. So if you are relocating to an area you don't know well, do some sniffing around.

Industrial emissions aren't all you need to think about. Kevin Conroy remembers the day he and his wife looked at the suburban development where they bought a lot to build their new home. "It was a crisp, cool afternoon in early November," says Kevin. "We were looking forward to getting out of the city into the clean, fresh country air. And that's what we found."

"Then, one day during the following spring when we were pretty well along with our construction, we were almost knocked over by the strong odor of horse manure. We hadn't known it, but we soon learned that riding stables and a large horse farm were located less than a half-mile in back of our development. Overall, we were lucky. The wind doesn't come from that direction very often. But when it does...."

MISTAKE # **49**

No one told us we had bought in a flood plain.

LESSON: Ask your real estate agent or mortgage lender if your home is located in a flood plain. Then buy flood insurance.

Every year throughout the United States, thousands of homeowners suffer financial losses due to floods. All too often these losses could have been prevented. A case in point is Emily and Dennis Bruner. The Bruners bought their home in a flood plain. In and of itself, there's nothing unusual about that. Millions of homes are located in flood plains. But (according to the Bruners), no one—not the previous homeowners (the sellers), the real estate agent, or their mortgage lender—explained to them the area's flood potential.

Consequently, the Bruners didn't buy flood insurance. Sure enough, several years after they had moved into their home, the Des Plaines River overran its banks. A torrent of water rushed through their home at a depth of five feet. Their home's foundation was destroyed, as was its interior, all of their furniture, and their personal belongings. Not counting the drowning of their Yorkshire terrier and the emotional trauma of losing their life's possessions, the Bruners' direct dollar losses totaled $60,000.

As if this weren't bad enough, their mortgage lender pushed the Bruners for full payment of their outstanding mortgage balance. The Bruners were without a home, without personal belongings, and saddled with a mortgage debt of $91,381. Bankruptcy looked like their only solution.

Eventually, when threatened with a lawsuit for failing to advise the Bruners to buy flood insurance, the mortgage lender backed off and forgave their debt. Yet, even with debt forgiveness, the Bruners were out their direct losses and their accumulated home equity. They avoided bankruptcy, but their failure to buy flood insurance cost them their life's savings. Flooding is a real risk that many homeowners face. But you can't judge the flood potential of a neighborhood by driving through it. You need historical data. That's why the federal government has drawn up flood maps and designated certain areas as flood zones.

Of course, just because a home is located in a flood zone doesn't mean a flood is imminent, or even likely. But do you prefer safe or sorry? To be safe, buy flood insurance. (In fact, your lender may require it.) Your homeowners' insurance policy will not pay for flood losses. Also, look at the site's drainage patterns. In some cases, homes tend to flood because they are poorly situated—even when they are clear of a government-designated flood zone.

MISTAKE # **50**

After a downpour, we can't drive down these roads.

LESSON: *Think bad weather. Will you be able to get to and from your home?*

More than likely, you won't shop for homes when it's raining so hard you have to hunch over the steering wheel to see where you're driving. Likewise, on days when ice and snow cover the ground, you'd probably rather stretch out on the sofa, read a book, or watch a football game. For the great majority of homebuyers, bad weather is not the best time to go out looking at houses. The best time to look at houses is when the sun is shining and you feel like getting out and driving around.

But on nice days, you won't see whether snow or rain makes the roads leading to and from a home inaccessible. "We wanted to move out to the country," says Steve Rankin, "but we didn't think what we would encounter driving into town during heavy winter snows or rains. Unfortunately, with bad weather, you can't drive down these roads. Sometimes it takes a couple of days for the snowplows to clear the roads. Then, if we're dumped on again, we're stuck for another couple of days.

"When it rains hard, our dirt road leading to the county highway becomes so muddy, you can hardly use it. We had to buy a four-wheel drive."

Of course, dirt roads aren't the only potential source of trouble. More than a few cities and suburban developments have improperly graded streets and inadequate sewers for water runoff. I've seen neighborhoods where, after a heavy rain, the kids get out and go "swimming" in the streets.

Also, it's not uncommon for houses situated below grade to receive a flood of water flowing from the streets into their driveway, garage, or basement in heavy rains. If you live where it sleets and snows, look at the grade of your driveway. Is it so steep you will have trouble pulling in or out?

Shop for your home on those nice days. But think bad weather. When it rains or snows, can you easily travel to and from your home?

MISTAKE # **51**

We seldom see the sun here.

LESSON: *Discover your metro area's microclimates.*

Does your metro area have microclimates? In and around some cities, within commuting distance of a central business district, a July day might bring fog and 60-degree temperatures in one neighborhood, 70 degrees and rain in another, and 90 degrees and sunshine elsewhere.

Oceans, lakes, rivers, hills, mountains, bays, and even tall buildings can affect weather patterns.

Within a 15-mile radius of downtown Vancouver, British Columbia, rainfall varies from 15 inches to more than 100 inches per year. In San Francisco, the Cow Hollow and Marina District neighborhoods enjoy noticeably less fog and more sunshine than other neighborhoods located near the zoo and the Pacific Ocean. If you live in Walnut Creek (20 minutes from the San Francisco Bay Bridge), you'll find many summer days over 80 degrees. To city residents, though, 80 degrees feels like a heat wave. In the Los Angeles metro area, Ventura residents breathe relatively clean air, while in Palmdale residents have suffered through up to 150 smog-day warnings a year. Skyscraper buildings not only block sunlight, they can create strong gusts of wind. Don't try walking near the Sears Tower in Chicago on windy days.

If you live in a metro area with microclimates, you may know how weather differs among local neighborhoods and communities. If you are moving to a new area, talk to Realtors or call a government weather station. To avoid unwelcome surprises, it pays to know the weather patterns before you choose a neighborhood.

MISTAKE # **52**

We bought outside the city limits to avoid its high property tax rates.

LESSON: *Property taxes are only one part of the equation. Also compare government services.*

Many homebuyers flee the cities to locate in rural or suburban areas where they can find lower property taxes. That's what motivated Jack Byers and his family. "We wanted to buy a home out in the county," says Jack. "We knew that once we moved beyond the city limits, tax rates would drop 30 percent. But I forgot about services. Out here in the country, we pay for our own trash collection, we are assessed separately by the fire district, and the city's water and sewage lines don't run out this far. That means we have to maintain a well and a septic tank.

"We don't have gas lines either," Jack continued. "So our energy costs for drying clothes, home heating, water heating, and cooking are higher. Nor are we connected to cable television. And because the fire station is a volunteer outfit three miles away, we pay more for homeowners' insurance than people in the city.

"I don't want to complain," Jack added. "I'm just saying we didn't look at homes in the city because we wanted lower taxes. Now it looks like after we consider everything, living in the country's actually costing us more."

Sometimes it's easy to get so concerned about cutting taxes, you forget that cities do provide services. So, when shopping locations, compare tax rates. But also compare what services your taxes buy.

MISTAKE # **53**

The city cut our services and raised our taxes.

LESSON: *Determine whether the community is solvent.*

Everybody would like more services, better schools, and lower taxes. But many Americans are getting the opposite. Some cities, counties, and states throughout the United States are incurring revenue shortfall. But aside from political semantics, the results are usually the same: higher taxes and cutbacks in schools, libraries, street repairs, fire and police, and social services. "The month after we moved in," says Shannon Brown, "they jacked up tax rates, canceled the bus service, and raised the tolls for the bridge."

If you're buying a home in a community that's running a deficit, beware. Since state and local governments can't borrow with the same reckless abandon as the federal government, at some point—sooner rather than later—someone's got to pay. And as likely as not, that someone will be you. Property tax rates will head up. You will pay more for less.

Look to the Future

As you look to the future, find out the financial condition of the community. Does it balance its books? Or is it headed toward a financial crunch? As an added precaution, ask your Realtor or the city treasurer's office about the level of the community's bonded indebtedness. Sometimes communities that expect rapid growth float bonds (borrow money) to pay for new streets, roads, sewage facilities, parks, libraries, schools, and fire stations to support development and an increasing population. (In California, these are called Mello Roos bonds.) Over time the bonds will be paid off by taxing all the residents in the new developments. As long as growth continues as expected, financing improvements with bonds doesn't create a problem.

However, if growth stalls or the local economy falters, early residents may end up with a serious problem. After the Colorado oil bust stalled growth in that state, new developments and communities went bankrupt. Some owners of $100,000 houses were getting property tax bills for as much as $12,000 a year. Most owners didn't pay. They just walked away from their houses. Lawyers for the tax authorities, mortgage lenders, and bond holders were left to litigate over the remains.

The Colorado experience was extreme. But it illustrates a basic rule: Understand the risks of owning a home in a community that extravagantly spends more than it takes in.

MISTAKE # **54**

Everyone around here seems apathetic. They've accepted decline.

LESSON: Look for communities and neighborhoods with an entrepreneurial let-us-make-things-better spirit.

Communities improve when they look at their strengths, search for ways to overcome problems, and develop a can-do attitude. Communities decline when people fail to fix "broken windows." Ask Paul Dillon. As he pounded the for-sale sign into his front yard, Paul says, "We didn't want to move, but everyone around here is so apathetic. They've accepted decline. We just don't want to be here as it happens."

More than 100 years ago, Henry Grady, editor of the *Atlanta Constitution,* used the funeral of a man to describe the dying of nearby Pickens County, Georgia:

> The grave was dug through solid marble, but the marble headstone came from Vermont. It was in a pine wilderness but the pine coffin came from Cincinnati. An iron mountain overshadowed it, but the coffin nails and the screws and the shovel came from Pittsburgh. With hard wood and metal abounding, the corpse was hauled on a wagon from South Bend, Indiana. A hickory grove grew near by, but the pick and shovel handles came from New York. The cotton shirt on the dead man came from Cincinnati, the coat and breeches from Chicago, the shoes from Boston; the folded hands were encased in white gloves from New York, and round the poor neck, which had worn all its living days the bondage of lost opportunity, was twisted a cheap cravat from Philadelphia. Pickens County, so rich in undeveloped resources, furnished nothing for the funeral except the corpse and the hole in the ground and would probably have imported both of those if it could have done so. And as the poor dead fellow was lowered to his rest, on coffin bands from Lowell, he carried nothing into the next world as a reminder of his home in this, save the halted blood in his veins, the chilled marrow in his bones, and the echo of the dull clods that fell on his coffin lid.

The residents of Pickens County could not see their own opportunities and potential. Is this the type of community or neighborhood you're considering? Or is there an active entrepreneurial spirit that declares, "We can make things better. We can and will determine our own future." It was this spirit that lifted Pittsburgh, Denver, Austin, and Houston from their economic fall. It's this spirit that has invigorated neighborhoods like South Central Los Angeles, Candler Park (Atlanta), Mt.

Rainier (Washington), South of Market (San Francisco), and North End (Boston). For an excellent guide to revitalizing neighborhoods, see *Fixing Broken Windows* by George Kelling and Catherine Coles, 1996 (Free Press).

MISTAKE # **55**

The sellers said it was only 25 minutes to downtown.

LESSON: Commuting to work? Test-travel the route before you buy.

"True, it was only 25 minutes to downtown by train," recalls Andrew Ho. "But that was if you arrived at the platform on Saturday afternoon just as the train was about to pull out.

"If you're leaving our house to get to work by 9:00 A.M., you'd better be out the door by 7:30. With the morning traffic backup at 95th, it can take 20 to 30 minutes just to get to the Sommerville station. Then parking (when you can find it) and walking to the platform takes another 5 to 10 minutes. And at commuter hours, the train takes 40 minutes, not 25. Next comes an eight-minute walk to the office. So that's about an hour and a half if everything goes without a hitch—which you can't always count on.

"We liked the house so much," Andrew adds, "I wanted to believe I could get to work in 30 to 40 minutes. I don't really blame the sellers for misleading me as much as I blame myself. Rather than discover the facts, I preferred to be blinded by illusion."

When buying a home, it's easy to accept illusion. You tell yourself what you want to believe. To help avoid this mistake, test-travel your commute *during the hours you will be commuting.* You might find that a so-called 30-minute trip actually puts you en route for an hour or more.

MISTAKE # **56**

We didn't walk the neighborhood.

LESSON: *Walk and talk the streets where you plan to locate.*

Carol and Wendy Tabor bought their first home in a San Francisco neighborhood that looked pleasant enough when they discovered it on one of their weekend excursions. But the Tabors learned after they moved in that the neighborhood was infested with drug dealers. A crack house was located just two doors down from their home. Shocked and hurt by what they now know, the Tabors are suing their real estate agent and the sellers of the property. Carol and Wendy complain that the agent and the former homeowners should have told them about the neighborhood drug problem.

Carol and Wendy are probably right. Yet, to some degree they share responsibility for this mistake. Before offering to buy the home, they should have walked the neighborhood and talked to the people who lived there—not just to get the facts on crime, but to discover other vital information that could help them decide whether the neighborhood would meet their expectations. For example, here are some questions you might want to ask:

- Are the neighbors friendly? Do they welcome newcomers, or are they standoffish?
- Where are most people in the neighborhood employed? What are their occupations? Are their jobs and employers solid or unstable?
- Are there any recent or planned zoning changes? Street widenings? Commercial or apartment construction?
- Do the streets flood when it rains hard? Are the streets cleared promptly after a snowfall?
- Is the neighborhood plagued with noisy neighbors or other disturbances?

- What types of people are moving in and out of the neighborhood? Is it heading upscale, downscale, or holding its own?
- Is there an action-oriented homeowners' association that works to improve the neighborhood?
- If residents could improve three things in the neighborhood, what would they be?
- Do residents think they receive good public services for the taxes they pay?
- What schools do neighborhood children attend? What are their strengths and weaknesses? Who's doing what to improve them?

In addition to talking with residents, walking the neighborhood can help you sharpen your observations:

- Look closely at the houses. Do they show signs of neglect? Or do nearly all residents show pride of ownership?
- Are the yards well landscaped? Have residents accented their homes with flowers, shrubs, and attractive plantings?
- Do you hear any disturbances or detect unpleasant odors?
- Are the parks and public spaces well kept? Or are they littered with sacks from Burger King or McDonald's, marred by graffiti, and populated by derelicts?
- Do houses show multiple mailboxes or cars lined up in driveways?
- Do you see signs of remodeling, improvements, or renovation?

Your real estate agent and the sellers *should* tell you about the neighborhood. But you learn even more when you experience it for yourself.

CHAPTER 6

Is This Home for You?

Based on your carefully thought-out list of possibilities and priorities, does this home feel right? Think where you are now in life—and where you plan to be in the future—will this house meet your most important goals? Does it fit within the amount you want to spend (invest)? Does the home offer good value?

To answer these questions, examine the house closely. Envision its livability. Estimate maintenance and repair costs. Imagine how it might meet your everyday patterns of living. By reading through the experiences and mistakes in this chapter, you'll see how to carefully inspect a house and make a good homebuying decision.

MISTAKE # **57**

Our agent said it was a lot of house for the money.

LESSON: *"A lot of house for the money" can sometimes mean "a lot of money for the house."*

"We had been looking for a two-or three-bedroom, two-bath house," recalled Tyrone Jones. "That size was all we needed or wanted. But our agent alerted us to a great bargain that had just come on the market.

The house had four bedrooms, three baths, and 2,400 square feet. At a price of $289,500, our agent told us it was really a lot of house for the money. "Since I can't pass up a bargain," Tyrone continued, "we decided to take a look. Based on the price information our agent gave us, I figured we could buy this house for less than $120 per square foot [p.s.f.]. Other houses we had considered were priced at $250,000 for around 1,600 square feet. That works out to more than $156 p.s.f. Compared to these houses, the bigger one seemed cheap.

"And even though other houses were more in line with what we were looking for, we didn't want to pass up this deal. So we bought it. In hindsight, I think we decided wrongly. To buy the house, we pushed ourselves financially. And, the house didn't give us the warmth we wanted. Besides, it costs too much for upkeep. Instead of getting a lot of house for the money, we're paying a lot of money for the house."

Tyrone and his wife fell into the bargain trap. They sacrificed their basic goals for a good deal. When someone needs a good buy just to afford a house, shopping for a bargain makes sense. Or if you find a home that fills your most important needs and you buy it at a bargain price, that's even better. But think twice before you commit yourself. Don't grab a great deal unless you have placed "great deal" as your top priority.

Sometimes a Bargain Is Not a Bargain

To Tyrone, getting a price of $120 p.s.f. as compared to $156 p.s.f. seemed like a moneywise decision. But Tyrone later realized that the larger home required higher property taxes, insurance, utilities, mortgage payments, and maintenance expenses. As his experience shows, don't merely think "a lot of house for the money." Figure the extra costs of owning the house over time. Do you want to spend money for rarely used unnecessary space? (Before you answer this question, consider whether creativity can help you turn the extra space into productive uses.)

Just as important, think carefully when you compare the per-square-foot costs of homes of different sizes, quality, and design.

- Smaller homes nearly always cost more per square foot than larger homes of the same quality. The expensive components of a house (baths, kitchen, heat and air, plumbing) don't increase proportionately as a home increases in size. When comparing large to small, ask whether the difference in price and operating costs makes the larger home a better buy than a smaller home.

- Dollars-per-square-foot works best when you compare homes of the same size, features, and quality. Tyrone should have compared the p.s.f. price of the large home he bought to more similar homes. If he found that other comparable large homes typically sold for, say, $135 p.s.f., only then could he have concluded that his home (at $120 p.s.f.) might present a bargain.

- Before finally deciding, Tyrone should have compared the homes according to their livability, energy efficiency, architectural style, and condition. Price per square foot serves as only one standard of value.

MISTAKE # **58**

Our agent was part order-taker, part chauffeur, and part narrator—but she didn't give us the help we needed.

LESSON: *Know what services to expect from your agent.*

Peter Chen reflects, "We didn't really know what to expect from a real estate agent. Ours was friendly enough. But she hardly did anything that we couldn't have done for ourselves. She seemed like she just wanted to take our order, chauffeur us around, and then act as an announcer."

"She'd say things like 'What kind of home are you looking for? What neighborhood do you want? What price range fits your budget?'

"The problem," says Peter, "is that we weren't sure what, where, or how much. That seemed to frustrate her. When she did drive us around to look at houses, she didn't seem to know very much. Once inside a house, she would simply announce, 'This is the living room. This is the kitchen. This is the master bedroom.' Even as first-timers, we do know a kitchen when we see one.

"But," Peter continued, "she was nice, so we didn't want to hurt her feelings and switch agents. In the end, we realized we made a mistake by sticking with her. With a better agent we could have explored more options and made a better choice. In fact, after it was over, we laughed because we realized how silly it was for us to stick with an agent we would not recommend to our friends."

A Good Agent Does More Than Show Houses

Peter Chen and his wife fell into a trap that catches many first-time homebuyers. They call a real estate office about a listing, get hooked up with an agent who wants to show them houses, and then stay with the agent by default. You prevent this mistake when you know what services to expect from an agent and then work only with an agent who delivers.

Here are the ways a real estate professional should help you make a better homebuying decision:

- Talk through your housing possibilities and priorities. Guide you to clarify and rank your potential choices.
- Review your finances, help you improve your borrower profile, and suggest finance plans and lenders that can maximize your affordability. (Alternatively, your realty agent may put you in touch with a loan agent who will help you improve your borrower profile.)
- Suggest trade-offs and compromises that will match your priorities.
- Inform you about neighborhoods, communities, and developments that seem right for you.
- Provide market facts, such as recent comp sales prices and time-on-the-market data for homes similar to the ones you're interested in.
- Alert you to good buys as soon as (sometimes even before) they come on the market.
- Require the sellers of homes you're interested in to prepare a Seller Disclosure Statement. A disclosure statement warns you about defects that can mar the desirability of a home or its neighborhood.

- List ways that you might improve a home (redecorate, remodel, renovate) to enhance its market value or better meet the needs of your family (preferably both).
- Stay in touch with your homebuying efforts from beginning to end. Verify that the loan representative, real estate agent, and underwriter are actually completing their assigned tasks according to schedule.
- Anticipate, prevent, or overcome roadblocks or problems that may arise. Keep you fully informed. Pave the way for a smooth and successful homebuying experience.

You may not want all of the services mentioned above. But certainly insist on more service than order-taker, chauffeur, and announcer. Successful real estate agents have worked with hundreds of homebuyers. They've run into all types of homebuyer problems, obstacles, and goals. By requiring agents to deliver a variety of services, you gain the benefit of their expertise and experience. The best realty agents don't *sell* real estate. They help people become homeowners. A good agent works with you until you're sure you've found the right home.

MISTAKE # **59**

Our agent never mentioned ...

LESSON: *Always ask sales agents (or sellers) for specific factual disclosures that list the defects of a home and its neighborhood.*

One of the most misunderstood topics in real estate is the legal concept of "disclosure." Because the laws and practices of disclosure are constantly changing, many home sellers, buyers, and even sales agents have become confused.

From the early 1900s up to the 1960s, real estate agents represented sellers. Legally, agents worked for the interests of property owners. With respect to homebuyers, the rule was *caveat emptor,* "let the buyer beware." In most home purchases, the law required neither sellers nor their agents to reveal a home's defects. If you didn't discover a home's crumbling foundation or inadequate wiring, that was your tough luck. You had little recourse against the sellers or the agent. Unless the sellers or their agent gave explicitly false warranties or representations—"That roof never leaks"—you were assumed to have bought the home in as-is condition.

Today, the doctrine of caveat emptor is dead. From the late 1960s and still evolving up through the present, innumerable court decisions, federal and state laws and regulations, and real estate licensing standards have sealed the coffin on "let the buyer beware." The general rule has become "let the sellers and their agents beware."

Today the law gives little comfort to sellers or realty agents who fail to disclose a property's serious defects. Whether you're working with a seller's agent, a buyer's agent, or a dual agent, anyone who fails to reveal a property's serious defects can be held liable for that omission. Yet, even with the death of caveat emptor, plenty of room still exists for confusion, misunderstanding, and deception.

Serious Defects

First, consider the term serious. What kinds of defects qualify as serious? At one extreme is a Massachusetts case. A house had a dangerously defective gas heater. On several occasions the heater had malfunctioned. The home's owner and soon-to-be seller was told by a repairman that the heater could easily start a fire. Even with this warning, the seller did not replace or correctly repair the heater. Nor did he inform the eventual buyers of the home.

Shortly after buyers took possession, the heater exploded. The results were fatal: Two members of the family died. The court held the seller criminally liable. He was convicted of involuntary manslaughter and sentenced to 15 years in prison.

Defects in a home that could likely lead to extensive property damage, injury, or death are serious. Both sellers and agents must disclose them or suffer the consequences. But what about substandard wiring that is in good condition and has never created a problem? That's a gray area. What about several light switches and electrical outlets that don't work? Those are probably not serious.

Due to these gray areas of liability and uncertainties—not to mention potential injury or loss of life—insist that sellers tell you *all* of a home's problems. Many sellers, and some agents, have not adjusted to the death of caveat emptor.

To illustrate: Consider this question from a would-be seller. In a letter to Q&A newspaper columnist Nina Groskind, a homeowner writes that he knows his home has "several flaws, some minor, some more significant." He then asks (fully prepared to hide as much as possible), "What obligation do I have to 'tell all' to people interested in purchasing my home?"

Ms. Groskind answers that the homeowner might be able to get away with "nondisclosure." But (1) he'd better not tell his real estate agent, because the agent would have to pass the information along to the buyer; and (2) the owner should not make any explicit false statement that could mislead any prospective new owners of the home. It's sellers like these that you must guard against.

Known or Suspected Defects

As you try to get as much information as you can about a prospective home and neighborhood, another type of problem arises. What if the seller or the agent doesn't know about the termites in the foundation or the wood rot under the roof? What if they don't know, but only suspect, a defect might exist? In the case of no knowledge, courts generally rule that sellers or agents can't be expected to disclose what they don't know. However, ignorance doesn't offer an airtight defense.

Laws in many states require owners or agents to make certain kinds of property investigations. In Massachusetts sellers must test their homes for urea formaldehyde foam insulation. In California real estate agents must visually inspect most homes they list for sale. Even further, some judges and juries have held sellers or agents liable for not disclosing defects they should have known about or reasonably suspected might exist—even though they claimed no direct knowledge.

In a far-reaching California case, a realty firm was held liable for not disclosing that a home's hillside location made it susceptible to damage from mudslides. The agent claimed no knowledge or expertise on the topic of mudslides. The court said "too bad." Even if the agent didn't know, he should have reasonably suspected there might be a problem.

As you can see, inspections and disclosures can confuse everyone involved in a homebuying transaction. In so many ways the law is ambiguous or simply not well understood. That's why the false assumptions about disclosure and nondisclosure contribute to so many homebuying mistakes. The traditional tendency of sellers to hide or understate defects adds to the potential for error.

But there's also another long-standing practice in homebuying that can divert you from getting the information you need to make a good decision. It's called "puffery."

Beware of Puffery

"This is a great neighborhood. You're really getting a bargain. This home's in first-class condition. You'll just love the people here. Oh yes, it's very quiet." Often homebuyers who don't get the information they need fail because they unconsciously accept puffery in lieu of facts (see Mistake #39). None of these statements actually includes any factual content.

Some unethical agents (or sellers) purposely use puffery to mask their lack of knowledge—or as an explicit attempt to avoid disclosure. These agents have learned to couch their comments in terms of puffery or opinions because opinions permit them to escape liability for misleading you.

"You said this was a great neighborhood," complain the angry homebuyers to the agent who sold them their home.

"Well, it is a great neighborhood," responds the agent. "Sure there's a crack house several doors down and I know the drive-by shootings can be annoying. But the neighborhood association is working hard to turn things around. All this community spirit really does make this a great neighborhood. You just can't find that spirit and feeling of togetherness in many neighborhoods these days."

By the agent's definition, the neighborhood is great. Can you prove that your definition of "great" outweighs the agent's? Did the agent misrepresent the neighborhood? Were his comments merely sales puffery and a matter of opinion? If you took a case like this to court, you would probably stand a better chance of winning today than in years past. But in most states you'd just as well spend your money on lottery tickets as on lawyers.

Exceptions to the Laws of Disclosure

Although society is moving away from the doctrine of caveat emptor, the evolving laws still omit some types of sellers, properties, and transactions. Government agencies, financial institutions, auctioneers, and court-appointed trustees may be excluded from some disclosure laws. Buyers of commercial and investment real estate receive less protection than homebuyers. And if you're buying at a foreclosure sale or through probate, you will probably be buying as is. In some states, FSBOs (owners who sell their homes without an agent) need not meet the same high standards of disclosure required of real estate agents.

Rules to Follow

Today's laws of disclosure make homebuying less risky than in the past. Yet, disclosure laws don't complete the difficult task of information gathering. They scatter into many gray areas, they may be circumvented by puffery, they may not be understood adequately by agents or sellers, and such laws frequently carve out exceptions for certain types of people, properties, or transactions.

So buy proactively. Don't expect others to reveal all they know or should know about a property and its neighborhood. Exercise initiative. Follow these guidelines:

- Ask your real estate agent (or lawyer) to explain fully the laws of disclosure that apply to homebuying in your area. Learn how disclosure laws may not apply; learn the types of nondisclosure problems that are prone to arise in the homes or neighborhoods you're looking at.
- Ask your agent questions that require factual answers. Don't accept opinions. Probe for details.

- Ask the sellers to prepare a written list of every defect, problem, or shortcoming of their home and neighborhood. If anything is not 100 percent perfect, tell them you want to know about it.
- Stay alert for agent or seller evasions such as, "I believe," "I think," or "As far as we know." If the sellers or their agent don't know, then follow up with further inquiry or investigation. Many homebuyers mistakenly accept these kinds of seller or agent hedges.
- Hire professional inspectors to examine the condition of the house, its component systems (heating, air conditioning, electrical, ventilation), and built-in appliances.
- Closely inspect the home and neighborhood yourself. In the end, it's going to be your house. Successful homebuyers take charge of the inspection process.
- Assume everyone you're working with is acting in good faith. But take precautions as if they weren't. Trust, but verify.

MISTAKE # **60**

We didn't hire a professional inspector. My dad knows all about houses.

LESSON: *Ask your dad, brother-in-law, or Uncle Harry to inspect your home as an additional safeguard. But don't substitute family members or friends for a professional inspection.*

If a friend or family member "knows all about houses," you may be tempted to skip a professional inspection and save yourself $200 to $400. Don't do it. Marci Alvarez tells why.

"When we bought, we were short of cash. So I asked my dad to inspect our house for us. He has worked as a painter, a carpenter, and even built a den and an extra bath for my parents' house. With all that experience, I figured he would be able to discover any trouble spots. Unfortunately for all of us, he missed some type of problem with the fuse box and the wiring. After we moved in, we must have blown a dozen fuses, and several wall outlets kept getting really hot every time we plugged something in and turned it on.

"When I told my dad about the problem, he tried to fix it, but I think he just made it worse. Eventually, we did get an electrician out to the house. By the time he finished rewiring, the bill went past $1,900."

"If that wasn't bad enough, my husband first blamed me and next blamed my dad. They argued over it for several weeks. It was not fun. Spending $1,900 for circuit breakers or whatever it was the electrician charged us for was bad enough. But the family turmoil was even worse."

"Then, after I thought the whole episode was behind us, my dad insisted on giving us a check for $1,900. We didn't want it. But there was no way we could refuse without more arguing. Now we have the $1,900, but I feel guilty about accepting the money and regret ever getting my dad involved in the first place."

Don't Burden Parents or Friends

When it comes time to get your home inspected, hire a professional house inspector. Professional inspectors evaluate dozens of houses a month. They know what to look for. They own the necessary tools of their trade. They learn to recognize signs of problems in their early stages so they can caution you about what to expect in the future. Moreover, professional home inspectors take on financial liability for any mistakes they do make. (For more on inspections, see www.ashi. com.)

Ask your family and friends to join with you to celebrate your new home. Don't ask them to shoulder the responsibility of inspecting a home. If tempted, remember Marci's shocking experience.

MISTAKE # **61**

We didn't think a new home needed to be professionally inspected.

LESSON: *Even when you're 100 percent sure of your builder's reputation, buy some peace of mind. Secure a professional inspection.*

"Christine Estep is weary—weary of paying for a home she can't live in," opened a front-page article in the *Miami Herald*. Christine Estep is one of the tens of thousands of homeowners whose homes were damaged by Hurricane Andrew. But instead of having her home repaired, Christine and the other 343 homeowners in her Village Homes condominium complex are about to see their homes demolished. The relatively new complex was "so riddled with construction defects" that engineers have recommended tearing down all the units and rebuilding from scratch.

To make matters worse, the developer of the complex was the well-known Florida development company, Arvida. At the time of the first phase of construction, Arvida was a subsidiary of the Walt Disney Company. After Disney, another company of high standing, JMB Realty, became Arvida's parent. In a multimillion-dollar case like this, accusations fly among homeowners, architects, lawyers, engineers, and contractors. Yet, no one disputes the engineers' basic conclusion that the construction quality of the units in the Village Homes complex failed to meet even minimum standards of safety.

Engineers, as well as government investigators, say the homes had undersized foundations, inadequately designed roof trusses, masonry walls without necessary steel reinforcement, unanchored support posts, and missing hurricane straps. Now you might wonder, aren't newly constructed homes inspected and approved by government building inspectors? How could major defects slip by? A lot of other people are asking the same questions. But it's not the first time.

Government Inspectors Sometimes Fail to Do Their Jobs

Over the years many cities throughout the United States have been rocked by permits-for-sale bribery and payoff scandals. In fact, Janet Reno, former attorney general of the United States, once worked as Florida's prosecuting attorney for Dade County (Miami). In that job she led a drive to investigate the government building inspection process. Ms. Reno never prosecuted anyone for a crime, but her office did file charges for lax enforcement of building codes.

A county investigator discovered that one building inspector inspected and approved seven newly built houses in *five minutes*. A former building inspector in Dade was quoted by the *Miami Herald* as saying, "It was a farce. The building and zoning department for years pushed quantity, not quality."

Although it will be years (if ever) before a complete accounting of errors and responsibilities are tallied up and assigned to the various parties involved in Christine Estep's case, the construction defects and lax inspection practices that brought about Christine's losses are all too common. Just because a home is new (or nearly new) does not mean it's defect-free. A few builders and developers are crooks, others are careless, some need to cut corners temporarily to stay solvent, and others just plain make mistakes. Any way you look at it, new does not necessarily mean perfect.

Avoid unpleasant surprises. Employ a professional inspector even when you're buying a new or recently built house or condominium.

MISTAKE # **62**

I thought lead paint had been outlawed years ago.

LESSON: *Environmental concerns have come home.*

When your concerns turn to the environment, you may think of disappearing habitat for spotted owls, illegal killings of elephants for their tusks, or perhaps clear-cutting the Amazonian rain forests. But some of the most dangerous environmental problems may lie right where you live.

Jackie Shattuck and her husband, Mike, recently bought a home. Their inspection report showed the house to be nearly defect-free. The wiring, plumbing, roof, foundation, and appliances were in good condition. Unfortunately, the Shattucks thought only of the physical condition of their home. They forgot to check its environmental quality. That mistake cost them nearly $5,000.

"Lead paint," Jackie recalls saying when she heard the bad news. "I thought it had been outlawed years ago."

As a matter of law, Jackie was right. Once it was learned that lead-based paints could cause serious illnesses, including brain damage (especially to children), this toxic metal was phased out of use in household paints. Prior to 1977, though, lead was a common ingredient. Although no one knows exactly how many older homes still have layers of lead-based paint lurking under less toxic (and more recent) paint layers, estimates place the number somewhere between 20 and 40 million. "If you're buying a home built before the late 1970s," advises lead specialist Stephanie Pollack, "assume there's lead until proven otherwise."

Removing the danger of lead-based paint (which is called *deleading*) requires trained specialists with special equipment and protective gear. Depending on the size of the house and the number of rooms affected, deleading a home can easily cost $3,500 and may run up to $6,000 or more. Without deleading, paint chipping and flaking through natural wear can create a health hazard. Should you begin sanding, tearing out walls, or other particle-disturbing remodeling efforts, lead-based paint becomes a clear and present danger. Inhaling lead paint dust can cause permanent respiratory or neurological damage.

Other Environmental Concerns

Lead-based paint isn't the only contaminant you need to check before you buy. San Francisco Board of Supervisors member Angela Alioto, an outspoken environmentalist, discovered an old, long-out-of-use buried oil tank in her home's yard. To remove the tank and clean up the soil cost her $9,000. When journalists questioned the councilwoman, she admitted she had not had her home inspected for environmental dangers before she bought it.

Environmental dangers can threaten health and sometimes cost thousands of dollars to remedy. This is one instance where "better safe than sorry" really applies. The exact type of environmental dangers you confront will vary depending on where you live, the age of the home you're planning to buy, and the type of building materials used in your area.

Talk with local or state environmental agencies. Many of these agencies have published environmental booklets that are written especially for homeowners. You might also pick up an environmental booklet from your local Realtor. When risks are slight, you may decide against a full environmental inspection, but at least stay alert for these types of problems:

- Lead-based paint (federal law mandates disclosure)
- Lead pipes or lead solder
- Asbestos (commonly found in many types of building supplies, materials, and floor tiles)
- Formaldehyde, especially urea formaldehyde foam insulation
- Contaminated ground water
- Volatile organic compounds (VOCs are found in most household chemicals, adhesives used with wall-to-wall carpeting, and pesticides)
- Radon (a gas released by radioactive decay that rises up from the ground especially into the lower levels of a home)
- Underground heating oil tanks
- High-power electrical lines and transformers (whether these actually produce any hazards is subject to debate)
- Mold (If mold is listed as a possibility from your general inspector, then call a mold specialist to inspect the property. Even new homes can have mold issues, and older homes that have gone through renovation or new roofing may not have had the proper ventilation put back into place, therefore creating a mold issue that was not preexisting before the renovation or new roof.)

In our industrial world, no one can escape all contaminants. Still, at least identify risks, assess their relative dangers, and estimate costs of cleanup. Many state, federal, and local laws now apply to environmental hazards. Some of these laws mandate seller disclosures. Others require that you be given various forms or booklets. Whatever the case in your area, actively investigate. The environmental quality of a home ranks just as important as the condition of its roof or furnace.

MISTAKE # 63

We now know why the sellers put up paneling in the downstairs den.

LESSON: *Be cautious of recent redecorating, repairs, or remodeling by sellers. They may be hiding a problem.*

"If you want to get top dollar for your house when you sell, put it in tip-top condition." Over the years, this advice from books and real estate agents has encouraged millions of homeowners to clean up, paint, wallpaper, panel, or otherwise redecorate and repair their homes before they place them on the market. "Package your home for profit," writes Peter Percelay in his book by the same title. "By effectively packaging your home, rather than just putting it on the market, you can reap thousands of additional dollars on your sale."

Percelay then goes on to tell his readers, "Your goal is to give buyers confidence in your product…. But you should never use packaging techniques as a way of hiding serious problems or defects in your home." Yes, and you should never inflate your resume, pad your expense account, or bring pens and pencils home from the office. But some people do.

Within our society, there are dishonest practices that, if perhaps not widely accepted, are at least widely practiced. Hiding a home's defects through redecorating or remodeling seems to be one of them.

When you're shopping for a home, stay alert to this possibility. Many people who consider themselves honest have nevertheless imbibed too much of the spirit of caveat emptor. More than 200 years of this attitude hasn't been eradicated by two decades of consumerism. Sally Roth knows from experience.

Sally bought a home that was built into a hillside and had a lower level den. Not long before the sellers had put their home up for sale, they had "packaged it for profit" by installing wood paneling on the walls of the den. Not only did the paneling add a nice aesthetic touch, it perfectly hid the water stain marks where water had poured through during the rainy season. Because Sally moved into the home in July, she didn't learn of the problem until the wet months of December and January.

Most people who prepare a home for sale want to enhance its appeal. They're not trying to hide anything. But some people are. If you find a home that has been freshly painted, plastered, paneled, wallpapered, repaired, or redecorated, closely inspect the improvements. As diplomatically as you can, secure written disclosures and warranties that pertain specifically to the condition of the property before the improvements were made. Assume the sellers are honest, but inspect the home as if they weren't. Again, I remind you: Trust, but verify.

MISTAKE # **64**

After we moved in, the sellers' remodeling contractor put a lien against our home. And we had to pay it!

LESSON: Ask to see the sellers' receipts. Verify that all recent work on the home has been paid in full.

Every state allows contractors to place liens against a home for unpaid work or materials. The exact nature of these laws differs, but they generally give firms and tradesmen 60, 90, and sometimes up to 180 days after they have completed their work to file a lien.

In Rob Shoo's case, his sellers had remodeled a back porch into a sunroom at a cost of $2,700. The work was completed in late February. In March the sellers placed their house up for sale. In early April Rob put in his contract and the owners accepted. The transaction closed in mid-May. On May 27 the Dependable Construction Company filed a mechanic's lien for unpaid wages and materials.

As a matter of law, the sellers were financially liable for the charges. But the mechanic's lien establishes a valid claim by Dependable Construction against the house—regardless who owns it. The lien sits in the public records as a cloud on the home's title. Unless Rob can get the sellers to write a check for the amount they owe, he will have to write a check himself. As long as the mechanic's lien remains valid, Rob cannot sell or refinance his home.

To avoid this potential mistake, check the sellers' receipts for any work that has been performed recently on the house. As further precaution, ask the sellers to sign an affidavit stating that either all work performed has been paid in full, or no work to the home has been completed within the past 90 days (or whatever other statute of limitation for filing liens applies). If you buy a home with recent improvements, verify whether the contractors have been paid. If you don't verify, you risk paying for them twice—first when you buy the home, and once again when you pay off the lien to clear the home's title.

MISTAKE # **65**

We should have looked at the utility bills.

LESSON: *Energy audit a home before you buy it.*

"We were renting a house just about the same size as the one we bought," says Patty Snyder, "so we thought we knew how much our utility bills would run in our new home. Boy, were we wrong! Our heat and air-conditioning bills nearly doubled. Utilities now average $430 a month. We should have gotten copies of the sellers' utility bills."

The recent run-up of oil and natural gas prices has brought this homeowner expense back into view. Total utility costs can amount to $3,000 to $5,000 a year or more. With utility bills at these levels, an energy-efficient house can save you $750 to $2,000 a year. I've talked with some homeowners in Maine and Vermont who, after installing super-energy-efficient improvements, have reduced their total winter heating bill to as low as $900 a year.

Check the Home's Energy Usage

One simple way to check a home's energy usage is to go over the sellers' utility bills. That won't tell you everything because you'll have to adjust for their family size, lifestyle, and comfort zones. But if you find their winter heating or summer cooling bills top, say, $300 or $400 a month, you may want to find out why.

Besides looking at utility bills, closely check windows, doors, appliances, water heater, furnace, and air conditioner. Do these promote energy conservation? What about the site placement and exterior design of the house? Is the home situated to protect against north winter winds as it brings in sunlight from the south? What about water usage? Fresh water for households is becoming a more expensive resource. Does the yard require heavy watering? Are the showers and toilets equipped with water-saving devices? Is it likely your local or state government will require an energy retrofit for the home at some time in the future?

In many parts of the country, utility costs rank right after mortgage payments as the largest household cost—higher than property insurance, maintenance, or property taxes. Because an energy-efficient house can save you thousands of dollars, explicitly include this cost when you compare houses.

MISTAKE # **66**

Those little repairs and renovations sure can add up.

LESSON: Little things can mean a lot.

If you buy an existing home, you may want to paint and wallpaper, lay new carpeting, repair wood rot around the eaves, enclose a porch, put in a skylight or two, restore the hardwood floors, strip the paint and refinish those oak doors, patch the roof, and maybe remodel a bath and kitchen.

How much money, time, and effort will these repairs and renovations add up to? If you make a reasonable estimate, double it, and add a 25 percent contingency factor, you may come close to an accurate answer. Some unwritten law of the universe states that everything costs more and takes longer than you originally thought. This law certainly applies to putting a house into shape.

Compare it to paying bills. You sit down to write a few checks for $50, $100, maybe $200, and all of a sudden the checking account balance drops $1,650. How do all those little checks add up to such a large amount?

When you evaluate a home, realize that little things do add up. As you think about the repairs, redecorating, and renovation you'd like, make a comprehensive list. Check figures with qualified contractors or suppliers. Most important, don't keep a bunch of little numbers running around in your head. Put all the figures down on paper and add them up.

Redecorating and renovation can boost your home's value by thousands of dollars. But the amount of your *profit* depends on how accurately you anticipate your costs.

MISTAKE # **67**

Before we could add central heat and air, we had to spend $1,800 for new wiring and ductwork.

LESSON: *Often, repairs and renovations can't be made without incurring other necessary costs.*

To replace a roof may cost $3,500. But if the plywood under the shingles has suffered wood rot (water + wood = rotten wood), your costs could climb to $4,500 or more. If interior ceilings and supports have been water-damaged, the costs could go higher.

When Jagdish and Carrie Sheth bought their Galveston, Texas, home, they planned to spend $2,800 to put in central heat and air-conditioning. Their actual bill totaled $4,600. Although Jag and Carrie figured right about the cost of the heat and air unit, they forgot to add the cost of upgrading the 100-amp electrical system to 200 amps. The upgrade was necessary to power the heat and air-conditioning system safely. Also, because the previous heating in the house had been gas floor heaters, the home lacked ductwork. Together, the electrical upgrades and new ductwork pushed their costs above the Sheths' original estimates.

One Thing Leads to Another

Often, planned repairs and renovations cost more than you originally figure because the work you want can't be performed by itself. To do this, you must first do that. In home repair and renovation, one thing leads to another.

Unfortunately, many contractors calculate cost estimates for only their basic work. Some purposely lowball bids to get you committed. Then they "discover" other work that they must (or should) perform. In other instances, it really is impossible to know the full extent of necessary repairs until well into the work. For example, all competent heating and air-conditioning contractors know the necessary electrical upgrade their heat and air units will require. However, roofing contractors may not know how much wood damage a house has suffered until they rip off the old shingles.

There is no perfect way to handle this problem. But you can try to get a no-surprises estimate. As a matter of good communication, make sure your contractor (or other cost estimator) understands that you want to know the costs (or at least the nature) of all labor and materials necessary for a total repair or renovation. Also ask for a worst-case/best-case range of estimates. Then you have a lower and an upper limit. None of these solutions is perfect, because even the best no-surprises estimate can miss the mark. (The construction budget for Australia's world-famous Sydney opera house began at $6 million. Costs at completion exceeded $100 million. Now, that's a real cost overrun.)

Home repairs and renovations may require unanticipated expenses. If you buy a home that needs work, recognize that you risk cost overruns. Use this fact to help negotiate a lower price. You can reduce risk through good planning and thorough inspection. But it's tough to eliminate it entirely.

MISTAKE # **68**

The house *looked* great. I just didn't like cold showers, listening to my son's favorite radio station, or lugging groceries up the stairs.

LESSON: Looks aren't everything. Evaluate a home's livability.

The feeling's great when you see a house you fall in love with. High ceilings, hardwood floors, lots of natural light, a large country kitchen, a big stone fireplace, beautifully finished woodwork: The house could be featured in *Architectural Digest*. Before you jump to make an offer, though, evaluate whether the house will work for you. Don't mistake great looks for livability.

Walk the Floor Plan

As a start, walk the floor plan—not for the purpose of viewing the rooms, but to judge internal accessibility and convenience. In your daily living patterns, what rooms will require frequent travel between them? How many steps is it from the master bedroom to the kitchen, the laundry facilities, or the main living area? How convenient is the parking (garage, carport, street)? Can you easily carry groceries from your car to the kitchen?

Enter the kitchen. Can you work efficiently between the stove, sink, and refrigerator? This area is called the work triangle. A poorly designed work triangle can add hundreds of steps a day to food preparation and cleanup. Measure the kitchen counter, cabinet space, and placement. Are cabinets and counters situated to provide enough room to prepare and store food conveniently?

Before leaving the kitchen, turn on the dishwasher. How loud is it? Can you hear it as you walk to other rooms of the house? What about televisions, radios, and stereos? Where will you place them? Take a radio from room to room. Can you play it without hearing the sound elsewhere in the house? Problems with noise rankle many homeowners and family members. Do you really want to hear rap music blasting from your son's bedroom at 10:00 at night?

What about privacy? Does the floor plan of the home provide enough private space? Can family members retreat from each other when they want to?

Check the bathrooms. How conveniently located are they? How long must the water run before you get hot water? How strong is the water pressure in the showers? Does the pressure ebb when someone flushes a toilet or turns on a faucet or another shower? Does the water temperature hold constant? Can you hear a running shower or flushing toilet throughout the house? Are the bathrooms well illuminated with natural or artificial light?

From the Outside In

Once you've completed a livability inspection of a home's interior, go outside. Admire the azaleas, the hedges, the flowers, the expansive yard. Now, think: How much care and expense will this greenery require? Do you want to spend weekends pulling weeds, trimming bushes, and cutting grass? Can you afford to pay someone else to do it for you? Cast your eyes around the exterior of the home. Will it require frequent painting or staining? How much time and money will you spend to maintain the appearance and condition of the home?

Go to the front entrance. Will visitors stand in the rain until you let them in? Or is there an area that protects against the weather? Step inside the house. Is there a coat closet nearby? What would incoming visitors see? Piled-up dirty dishes in the kitchen? Children's toys scattered about? A pristine formal reception area and living room? Do you even care what visitors will see?

Sum Up Your Thoughts

Consider the house as a whole. Does the home reflect a sense of scale and proportion? Are some rooms too large, others too small? Does it include enough closet and storage space? Will the home heat and cool evenly? Or will it develop hot spots and cold spots? Is differential zone heating and cooling possible?

Now evaluate. Bring your thoughts together. Are the good looks superficial? Or are they integral to your needs and to the design, function, and livability of the home?

Realty agents love to show homes with curb appeal. They like homes they can advertise as a "decorator's dream." Agents know most homebuyers prefer a home that looks good, a home they can show off to friends and relatives, a home they can be proud of. All perfectly reasonable. Few buyers want to own the ugly duckling of the neighborhood. But when comparing houses, stay detached. Don't fall in love with appearance. First, figure out whether the home could live well for you and your family.

MISTAKE # **69**

We *had* such great views.

LESSON: *Before buying a house with a view, determine whether the view is protected.*

Heather Caldwell loved the townhouse she bought. It was close to the city center, yet the development was surrounded by trees. "We felt like we were living in a forest," Heather remembered. "At least for a while."

One year after Heather bought her new townhouse, the developer began phase two of the project. The bulldozers arrived, down went the trees, and that was the end of Heather's view of the woods. But her disappointment didn't end there. Once the second phase of the project was sold out, trees along the road leading into the complex were cut down. In their place, the developer built a strip shopping center topped with an orange roof. "Within less than four years," Heather said, "we lost our wooded views and tranquil setting."

In Chicago, Fred Paine bought his one-bedroom condominium at Lake Point Towers because it offered spectacular panoramic views of the city from his living room and bedroom. Three years later, Fred's view had changed. Instead of city lights, Fred looked straight into another high-rise. Not only had Fred lost his view, he had lost his privacy.

On the outskirts of Orlando, Florida, Mindy and Ron Lange bought their home because its lot bordered a grove of orange trees. Then central Florida was hit with back-to-back winter freezes. The orange trees were killed. Instead of replanting, the grower sold his land and moved his business to Homestead. The Langes' property now backs up to another subdivision. Gone forever are the views and privacy the orange groves provided.

Only Pay for Protected Views

Before you buy a home with a view, check to see how well that view is legally protected. Will zoning laws, building regulations, or environmental restrictions keep someone from blocking or destroying your view? Many homebuyers pay a premium price for a home with a view, only to lose not only the view but also thousands of dollars in property value. Although you can't get 100 percent protection because the government might change the laws, at least know what chance you're taking.

Both Heather Caldwell and Fred Paine mistakenly believed their views were permanent. Had they checked the zoning laws or developer's plans, they would have discovered the views were temporary. Naturally, the Langes couldn't have forecasted back-to-back record-setting winter freezes. But, had they investigated the area, they would have discovered that even before the killer freezes, many orange growers were selling their groves to subdivision developers. With this knowledge, the Langes may have decided to look elsewhere, or they may have chosen to offer a lower price for the home.

Never assume your view will last. Before you buy, look into the future. Then adjust your price accordingly. Or, look for another property.

MISTAKE # **70**

I didn't notice that the house was situated on two lots.

LESSON: *An extra lot can mean extra value.*

Ralph Wozniak tells how he missed out on several hundred thousand dollars. "Some years back," says Ralph, "I was looking at houses in the well-established Point Grey neighborhood. My choice came down to two houses. One was sitting on a normal 33-foot lot. The other was built on a 50-foot site that included two 25-foot buildable lots. To my way of thinking, the houses were about equal in pros and cons. Both were priced at a little over $100,000. In the end, I bought the house with the 33-foot lot because I preferred its kitchen. The fact the other house was sitting on two buildable lots didn't affect my decision one way or the other. That was my mistake."

Lots Appreciate More Than Houses

Here's why Ralph should have noticed the profit potential offered by two lots. Four or five years after Ralph bought, home prices in Point Grey started spiraling upward. They went from an entry level of around $90,000 up to around $200,000. Ralph recalls that at the time he was feeling pretty happy with himself. His home had grown in value to around $225,000. Then he heard the two-lot house he had passed up had just sold. The price was $395,000.

It wasn't the homes in Point Grey that were appreciating, it was the lots. This time around, the two-lot house was not sold to a homeowner. It was sold to a builder, who promptly tore down the house. In its place she built two houses—one on each lot. These two new homes sold for $475,000 each.

When Ralph judged his home to be worth around $225,000, he was wrong. His house was worth $25,000 to $35,000. His lot was worth $190,000 to $200,000. Remember: Houses seldom appreciate much. Only in times of rapid inflation in construction costs will a *house* increase in (nominal) value. In most instances, it's the *land* value that's going up. When you own two *buildable* lots, you double your chance for gain.

Find Bargains in Slow Markets

In hot markets, smart homebuyers quickly learn that a home with two lots means extra profit potential. They bid up its price. In slow markets, though, buyers don't give it much value. Since they don't expect appreciation, they're not willing to pay a premium for a two-lot house. To them, an extra-large site just means a bigger yard. So if you're buying in a slow (or uninformed) market, there's a good chance you can buy a second lot for a relatively small amount of money. Generally, the best places to look are older neighborhoods (especially neighborhoods that show strong potential for turnaround or even well-kept neighborhoods that are moving upscale).

Depending on how a home is situated on a two-lot site, you might put the extra lot to immediate use. If the size is big enough, you might subdivide the site. This would permit you to sell the extra lot by itself. Or you might build another unit (house, cottage, carriage house) that you could rent out and hold as an investment. Given these possibilities, think carefully before you reject a house with two or more buildable lots. You might pass up big hidden value.

MISTAKE # **71**

We focused on problems, not possibilities.

LESSON: *Before you reject a home, think through its possibilities.*

To some homebuyers, shopping for a home amounts to one frustration after another. If a house isn't too large, it's too small; or maybe it's a long commute to work, is located in a less desirable school district, needs too much work, lacks enough light, is too expensive, or has the wrong floor plan or architectural style. Whatever the home's features, these home-buyers can easily point out problems. They reject everything they look at because no house feels right.

Tom and Joan Search in Vain for the Perfect House

Past friends of mine went through this stage. Tom and Joan wanted to own their own home for more than two years. They earned good incomes and had saved down payment money. They worked with good real estate agents. They diligently pored over the real estate classified ads. And during two years of looking, they must have inspected 80 to 100 houses, maybe more. Yet, they never bought.

Why? Because to them every home they inspected had some problem, defect, or flaw. Tom and Joan said they knew exactly what they wanted and wouldn't settle for anything less.

Although at the time my friends didn't realize it, the difficulty of their home search was not what they thought it was. They described their problem as "We just can't find what we're looking for." But their real difficulty was attitude. When they walked into a house, they immediately began to find fault. In their mind's eye, they thought they could imagine exactly what they wanted, and if the house they were inspecting in some way violated their wish list, they rejected it—no ifs, ands, or buts.

No Perfect Spouse, No Perfect House

Then one day when Tom was talking with me about the couple's inability to find a home, I changed the subject and asked, "Tom, why did you marry Joan? You've complained that she's overweight, and she hates football. And you know she's always trying to get you to stop fishing and hunting."

When I finished, Tom immediately began to defend Joan, list her good points, and emphasize how well they got along together (which of course I knew). Then the light bulb went on in his mind. He stopped his praise of Joan and said, "All right, I see what you're getting at. I may not be perfect, and Joan may not be perfect, but we still have a good marriage. So why not stop insisting on the perfect house and find one that will work for us?"

"You got it," I answered.

Several months later, Tom and Joan bought a triplex, renovated it, lived in it for several years, sold it at a profit, and then built a custom-designed house. After they moved in, I asked Tom, "Well, now that you've custom built your own house, do you have everything you wanted?"

Tom smiled and said, "Do we have the perfect marriage? No. Do we have the perfect house? No. We love each other and we love the house, but nothing's perfect."

Are you frustrated shopping and comparing homes? Then think of Tom and Joan. Shift your sights from what's wrong with a house to what's right—or what could be made right. Much of this chapter describes mistakes in homebuying that commonly result from failing to spot a home's defects, flaws, or features that don't suit your priorities. But you also can become too critical and reject houses too quickly. Strike a profitable balance. List problems. But also look for ways to make a less-than-perfect house work for you. You can trade up later.

CHAPTER 7

Negotiate Win-Win

Negotiators typically fit into one of three types of nego-tiating styles: (1) adversarial, (2) accommodating, and (3) win-win. Lawyers typically practice the adversarial style. Adversarial negotiators make outrageous demands. They push, pull, or threaten to move you as close as possible to their position. Adversarial negotiators don't care whether their opponents end up pleased. All they care about is winning for themselves.

In contrast to the adversarial approach, the accommodating nego-tiator tends to give in to every request or demand. Accommodators feel powerless to effect the outcome they want. They feel helpless due to lack of money, time, information, knowledge, or experience. Accommo-dators detest conflict. They would rather lose than stand their ground. When negotiating through a real estate agent or other third party, ac-commodators typically delegate too much responsibility. Accommoda-tors often say things like, "Oh, just do what you think is best" or "Let's just sign and get the whole thing over."

Negotiate Win-Win

When you negotiate win-win, you may adopt a little of the adversarial style and maybe a little of the accommodating style. Overall, though, you adopt a cooperative perspective. Win-win negotiators recognize that every negotiation brings forth multiple issues, priorities, and possibili-ties. They also recognize and respect the other party's (not opponent's) concerns, feelings, and needs. Win-win negotiators do not operate along a single line of contention (e.g., price).

Win-win negotiators work to create a strong, mutually beneficial agreement that all parties want to see completed. By reading through the homebuyer experiences and mistakes in this chapter, you will learn to shape a win-win agreement. Moreover, you'll stand up to those adversarial hardballers and avoid becoming a passive-accommodator.

MISTAKE # **72**

We thought our agent represented us.

LESSON: *Before you begin to work with a realty agent, set ground rules for your relationship.*

You will probably negotiate your purchase contract through a real estate agent. So, understand how agents can work for you—or against you. During the past several years, "who represents whom" has ranked as one of the most controversial issues in homebuying. Until recent years, nearly all realty agents were employed by sellers to find buyers for their homes. Under this traditional system, you may have worked with an agent who advised, counseled, and helped you negotiate your home purchase. But as a matter of law, that agent was most likely a subagent of the sellers—not "your" agent. Here's how the traditional system worked and why it has sparked so much confusion.

Under the traditional system, a home seller might sign a listing contract with Fox Realty. In turn, Fox Realty would place this listing in a multiple listing service (MLS). The MLS probably included dozens of other real estate agencies that employed hundreds, maybe thousands, of real estate agents. Let's say one of these other cooperating realty firms is Hoosier Realty, and Joe Salesman works for Hoosier Realty as a sales agent. You meet Joe through your local church.

You call Joe. He sets up a meeting where you discuss your housing needs, how much you're willing and able to invest in a home, and the neighborhoods you prefer. With this information, Joe suggests some homes to show you. If all goes well, you find a home you like and tell Joe to make an offer. Joe advises you about the price, terms, conditions, and contingencies and then helps you negotiate a purchase agreement with the sellers through their listing agent, Sally Saleswoman, who's employed by Fox Realty. After some give and take, you and the sellers strike a deal. Everyone seems satisfied.

What's Wrong with This Picture?

What's wrong with the way this transaction was handled? Your agent, Joe, was representing you and looking out for your interests. Sally Saleswoman was representing the sellers and advising them about their interests. Or at least that's the way it may seem.

But, in fact, under the traditional sales system, Joe didn't represent you. As a salesman with Hoosier Realty, a firm that had joined with Fox Realty as a cooperating broker, Joe owed his allegiance to the sellers—not to you.

As a matter of law, Joe was required to relay to the sellers your statements like, "We have to have this house. It's the best one we've looked at." Or, "Let's try an offer of $375,000, but we'll go to $395,000 if we have to." Or perhaps the sellers learned you had told Joe, "We're really pressed for time. Our apartment lease is ending and this is the only house we've looked at where the sellers are willing to give early possession." Or maybe you believed Joe when he ran a bluff and told you, "The sellers won't budge. Their absolute low dollar is $395,000." So, thinking you had no choice, you offered $395,000.

The Traditional System Upsets Many Homebuyers

How would you feel if you later learned the sellers were really experiencing a cash crunch and were so eager to sell they would have accepted a price of $370,000 for their home? Yet, your agent, Joe, the man you trusted enough to share your confidences, never mentioned this fact to you. In effect, Joe's silence hid this juicy bit of information that would have strengthened your negotiating power. Wouldn't you feel angry and cheated? After all, Joe led you to believe he was representing you, but in reality he was working as an agent of the "enemy." You might even think about suing Joe for deception.

That's exactly what Sheila and Jeff Buck did. The Bucks sued their agent because, "We thought our agent represented us, when she really was working for the sellers. Had Diane told us she was duty bound to the sellers, we never would have told her our top dollar. We're sure she used the information against us."

States Create *Agency* Disclosure Laws

To help you and other homebuyers prevent the mistake of the Bucks (and their agent), nearly all states have enacted some type of agency disclosure laws. In addition to agency disclosure, state laws and the National Association of Realtors are making it easier for you to use a buyer's broker or buyer's agent when you shop for a home and negotiate a purchase agreement.

Under these laws, real estate agents disclose to you the types of agency relationships that are legal in your state, explain their meaning, and then give you a choice. Although state laws differ, you usually can select from three or four choices:

1. You can choose the traditional system where you work with an agent or subagent of the sellers.
2. You can choose dual agency. Here the agent helps both sellers and buyers but agrees not to divulge confidential information that could give one party an unfair advantage over the other.
3. You may employ a facilitator. A facilitator owes no fiduciary responsibility to either potential buyers or the sellers. He or she acts as a mediator. The idea is to find agreement, not to play the role of advocate.
4. As a fourth option, you might use a buyer's agent, who should represent your interests exclusively. Buyer's agents can't legally pass along your confidential information to the sellers. But they can pass along to you any information about the sellers they know that could strengthen your hand in negotiations.

Space doesn't permit a full look at the pros and cons of each of these types of agency relationships. Here, I mainly want to warn you that "your" agent may be working for the sellers. Also, many state laws don't require agents to disclose their allegiances until you're ready to make an offer on a property. By that time you already may have revealed your finances, how well you like the house, or that your landlord has ended your lease and you have to find someplace to live within the next 60 days.

Follow This Advice

Set ground rules for your relationship *before* you begin to work with a realty agent. Each type of agency has its advantages and disadvantages. As long as you know the ground rules for what you can disclose and what you should keep to yourself, you can work with any type of agent. Mistakes occur when you don't set the ground rules up front.

In addition, evaluate your agent's character, competence, and knowledge. The type of person you choose to work with is just as important as the type of agency relationship. Most real estate professionals—people who are committed to a career in real estate—don't view homebuying and home selling as an adversarial contest. Buying (or selling) a home is not like filing a lawsuit. In contrast to lawyers whose ethics permit them to mislead and deceive, consumer laws (as well as Realtor ethics and personal reputation) oblige realty agents to treat all buyers and sellers fairly.

Nevertheless, many homebuyers now choose buyer's agents. It is the wave of the future. But in many areas, dual agency and traditional (seller) agency still account for a large number of buyer relationships. No matter what type of agency you choose, remember: It's tough to negotiate your best deal when the agent passes along your confidential information to the sellers.

MISTAKE # **73**

I tried to buy directly from an owner to save the commission, but instead lost $10,000.

LESSON: *Buying without an agent can cost you more than you save. Be careful.*

When Dan Boatman decided to stop renting and buy his own home, he called several real estate agents whose names he had seen on for-sale signs. "They didn't impress me much," says Dan. "One just wanted to talk all the time and never listened. Another one kept showing houses and neighborhoods he didn't know anything about. I'd ask him questions and he would answer, 'I dunno, but I can find out for you if you want.' This was a hassle I didn't need.

"So I decided to concentrate on for sale by owners [FSBOs]. That way I wouldn't have to deal with agents. And I could get the sellers to lower their price since they would save the commission. It seemed like a smart move. Unfortunately, I got suckered. My smart move cost me $10,000. That's a mistake I won't make again."

Dan actually made not one but three mistakes.

Don't Choose Agents Randomly

First, Dan selected agents randomly. He might as well have flipped open the yellow pages to the real estate section, pressed his finger to the page, and started telephoning. The chances are that if Dan or anyone else merely pulls an agent's name out of the telephone book or off a for-sale sign, he or she is not going to find a first-class professional. Real estate sales follows the same 80–20 rule found in most fields. The top 20 percent of the agents do 80 percent of the business.

To locate a real estate professional, ask relatives or friends for recommendations. Read the newspapers for the names of top producers. Call the sales manager of the most highly regarded real estate firms and find out who among their agents has provided the highest quality services to the most buyers. In other words, work with an agent who has a proven track record. Helping people buy and sell homes requires knowledge, competence, and possibility analysis. Don't settle for a chauffeur. Only work with a pro. Dan Boatman failed to understand this critical difference.

FSBOs Don't Always Sell at Lower Prices

Second, Dan mistakenly believed that if he bought directly from an owner he would get a lower price. Because the owners wouldn't have to pay a commission, they could pass along their savings to him. But why would they want to? Most sellers don't take on the burden and expense of selling their own home so they can give buyers a better price. They do it to pocket more money for themselves.

In fact, as often as not, people who try to sell their own homes over-price them. They hope to find some bargain-hunting buyers who will be hoodwinked into believing they are saving money because no agent gets involved. In addition, even if the home is priced right, it may suffer from hidden defects. In today's lawsuit-happy world, professional agents will insist that sellers disclose their home's shortcomings. In contrast, own-ers who sell on their own are noted for "forgetting" about the erratic furnace or the fuses that blow every time the toaster and microwave are turned on at the same time.

Always Place Deposits in Escrow

Third, here's how Dan lost his $10,000. After negotiating the price and terms of their purchase agreement, the sellers asked Dan for a deposit of $10,000. This amount would be credited against his down payment at closing. Dan knew deposits were customary, and since he planned to put a total of $25,000 down, a $10,000 good-faith deposit didn't seem unreasonable. So he wrote the sellers a check. That was his biggest mistake.

As it turned out, Dan could not get his financing approved within the 30 days allowed by his purchase agreement. To make matters more diffi-cult, other buyers wanted the house and (unlike Dan) they had secured preapproval from their lender. The sellers gave Dan an extra week to close, but to no avail. He couldn't close. The sellers went ahead and sold to the other buyers.

When Dan asked for his deposit back, the sellers told him they would send him a check after the other buyers completed their purchase. Should that deal fall through, they promised to give Dan another chance to come up with his financing. Dan reluctantly agreed because he really wanted the house. But the new sale did close. The sellers moved to Ta-coma. And Dan never again saw his $10,000.

Dan hired a lawyer who wrote to the sellers and demanded they re-turn his deposit. The sellers' lawyer responded that Dan had forfeited the deposit when the sellers had given him extra time and yet he still couldn't get his financing put together.

Dan disagreed. "We didn't discuss anything about forfeiture," Dan told his lawyer. "Well," the lawyer said, "we can sue them. But that will cost more than $10,000, and I can't guarantee you'll win, or that if you win, you can collect. There's not really anything I can do. You might as well kiss your $10,000 goodbye."[1]

Guidelines to Follow

No one denies that, on occasion, you can negotiate directly with sellers and save money. I've gone this route many times. But if that's the route you choose, proceed with caution.

1. If you buy direct, you'll give up not only the services agents provide to help you find a home, but also the services that ease you through negotiation, financing, and closing.
2. Get the home professionally inspected for condition and appraised for value.
3. Beware of easy seller financing. Although OWC is great at times, on occasion some sellers will use it as bait to lure in unsuspecting buyers and sell them a problem property, a property that's overpriced, or possibly both.
4. Open an escrow closing account for your deposit with a title insurer, escrow firm, or realty firm. (In fact, even when buying from an FSBO, you can still employ a buyer's agent to help negotiate a win-win agreement and provide other services that will keep your transaction progressing smoothly. In these cases, many by-owner sellers are willing to pay a two or three percent sales commission to your agent.)

---

[1] Dan may have been able to use his state's long-arm statute and sue the sellers (without heavy legal costs) in his local small claims court (up to the applicable small claims limit). However, that possibility goes beyond the scope of this discussion.

MISTAKE # **74**

We didn't know we could withdraw our offer.

LESSON: *You may withdraw your offer at any time before the sellers accept it.*

As you prepare an offer to purchase a home, decide how long you want to give the sellers to accept it. Real estate sales contracts often include a clause that reads something like this:

> This offer prepared and delivered to the Sellers by the Buyers on __
> _____, 20___, at _____ and shall remain open
> for ___ days, *or until revoked by the Buyers.*

In regard to this clause, some homebuyers overlook or misunderstand the meaning of the last six words. In effect, these words give you the right to withdraw your offer any time before the sellers have accepted it. If you tell the sellers you'll leave your offer open for three days, but then change your mind, notify your agent (preferably in writing, but that's not always essential). Even if your contract doesn't include these words or something similar, you still may withdraw your offer.

Many agents forget to fully explain a buyer's right to withdraw. Agents don't like to emphasize the point because homebuyers (especially first-time buyers) often have second thoughts about their decision to buy. To squelch these worries, the agent might gloss over your right to pull back. He or she might lead you to believe you're obliged to keep the offer on the table for the specified number of days.

Of course, you shouldn't withdraw just because you get cold feet. Get rid of negative emotions by replacing them with thoughts of how much you're going to enjoy the home and home ownership. But if you discover new information (you're getting transferred or you've noticed a shortfall in your bank balance), or if you run across another home that better fits your needs, then feel free to exercise your right of withdrawal.

Counteroffers Kill Offers

Keep in mind, too, that if the sellers change any part of your offer, you're released from obligation. Any counteroffer kills a previous offer. Should you offer $489,500 and the seller counter with a price of $489,501, your bid of $489,500 is dead. You could bring it back to life if you wanted. But if you reject the sellers' $489,501, they can't unilaterally declare (without your agreement), "Okay, then, we'll accept $489,500."

From a negotiating standpoint, keep the sellers guessing about what you plan to do. Let them know you're considering other options. The sellers should realize that if they wait too long to accept your offer, or if they counteroffer too high, they could lose you as a prospective buyer. Maintain a cooperative, win-win demeanor. But don't tip your hand.

MISTAKE # **75**

We never met the sellers. We didn't know anything about them.

LESSON: *Get to know as much as you can about the sellers.*

Some sales agents do everything they can to keep buyers and sellers away from each other. For good reason. Agents have seen sales fall through because of personality clashes. Or they fear that sellers (because agents of yesteryear nearly always represented sellers) might give away a choice bit of information that will help the buyers.

"Why are you selling?" the buyers ask.

"Oh, Mack's been transferred," the sellers respond. "We have to be in Omaha by the end of next month."

Although the keep-the-buyers-and-sellers-apart sales strategy sometimes is best, as a rule I reject it. Before you make an offer, learn all you can about the sellers. What kind of people are they? Do they seem generous and open? Are they rigid and argumentative? Do they show pride in their home? Are they reluctantly moving? Are they eager to leave? Why are they selling? Have they bought another home? What are their important needs: emotional, personal, and financial? What are their worries and concerns?

What Do the Sellers Really Want?

The sellers aren't really trying to sell a house. They're reaching for more distant goals. Selling their home is a means to those ends. The sellers won't judge the price and terms of your offer by absolute standards. They will judge it according to how well it helps them move toward what they want to achieve. That's why you must get to know the sellers. Without understanding their needs, you miss a great opportunity to find high value/low value win-win trade-offs that can benefit both of you.

Say the sellers previously accepted two offers that fell through because the buyers couldn't arrange financing. With these experiences in their background, the sellers may be quite anxious. They don't want to be strung out again. If you can assure them that you have the resources to buy (bank statements, credit report, preapproval letter, job security), they likely will give you a lower price or other concessions.

Broaden Discussions beyond Price

Too frequently, homebuyers and sellers aim their negotiating toward price. The sellers want a higher price. The buyers want a lower price. Stalemate. Steer around this trap. Meet the sellers, talk with them, learn all you can about their perceptions, past home-selling experiences, feelings, and needs. But keep in mind that agent concerns about personality clashes are valid. When meeting and talking with the sellers, follow these guidelines:

- Meet the sellers as soon as possible. The sooner you get a fix on who they are and what they're like, the better you can begin to map your negotiation strategy. Sellers respond more openly with information when you first look at their home. At that point they're eager to please. They want to excite your interest. If you wait to meet them until after you've made an offer, they'll guard their disclosures more closely.
- Get concessions before you begin negotiations. "You're asking $165,000, is that right? Just so we can fairly compare your home to others we're looking at, have you thought about how much less you

would accept?" Or: "You're asking $165,000, right? What personal property—appliances, drapes, rugs, patio furniture, gazebo, etc.—are you planning to include?" Or maybe: "How much financing will you carry back?" When you innocently suggest concessions, you're not negotiating with the sellers. You're not even asking for concessions. You're merely gathering information to rank the sellers' home against other houses that are up for sale. Sensing you are exploring other options, many sellers will sweeten the deal before you write your offer.

- Inquire, don't interrogate. The way you ask your questions stands more important than the questions themselves. Phrase them as innocuously as you can. Don't intimidate, accuse, threaten, or debate. Remember Peter Falk as Columbo, the perpetually "disoriented" detective. Columbo didn't interrogate suspects. He gently probed. Use similar tactics. Encourage the easy flow of information. Don't try to extract it.

- Establish rapport. Find common ground. Talk about the last Cubs game, the weather, or perhaps a shared hobby. Negotiations are about people, not money. Treat the sellers as people, not merely owners of a house you might want to buy.

- Compliment, don't criticize. As you walk through the sellers' home, sincerely note their beautiful grandfather clock. "Does it have an interesting history? How long have you owned it?" Comment on other belongings they seem to take pride in. Have the owners decorated or remodeled their home with taste, flair, or creativity? If so, tell them. What about the yard? Do the sellers have a green thumb? Can you genuinely admire their tomatoes or roses?

  At this first meeting, put forth a cordial attitude. Establish a *relationship* bank account so you will have something to draw on later if you need it. To sharply criticize the sellers' home won't loosen them up to accept a lower price. But it may very well turn them against you and make later negotiations more difficult. (Of course, also corral your enthusiastic exclamations: "Wow! This is exactly what we want. It's so much nicer than the other houses we've seen.")

- Share information about yourself with the sellers. Let them get to know you. Skip the bravado. But accent personal characteristics that tell the sellers you're decent, credible people who like (not love) their home. Trust and relationship-building can't travel a one-way street.

MISTAKE # **76**

The worst they can do is say no.

LESSON: *The worst they can do is say get lost.*

Lowball offers destroy trust. When you lowball the sellers, you signal that you're a win-lose negotiator—with the sellers as the losers.

Joan McGill recalls her lowball experience. "We really wanted this house," says Joan. "But my husband considered himself a hotshot negotiator. Even though the house was priced just a little over market at $325,000, he convinced me we should start with an offer of $260,000. 'All they can say is no,' he assured me. 'At the worst, they'll probably compromise. We can still get the house at a bargain price of around $290,000 to $300,000.' Well, he clearly missed that one. We got the house all right—at a price of $325,000. After our lowball offer, the sellers simply refused to negotiate with us. They just said, 'The price is $325,000. Take it or leave it.' So we ate crow and took it."

Most sellers are emotionally attached to their homes. A lowball offer insults them. Besides, if the sellers have listed their home with a realty agent, they have a good idea of how much it is worth. And if they doubt the agent's price, 9 times out of 10 the sellers figure higher, not lower. What chance does a lowball offer have of getting accepted? Slim or none.

Put yourself in the shoes of a seller. Your home is worth $310,000. Out of the blue, someone offers you $250,000. How would you respond? You'd probably think: (1) the buyers don't know what they're doing, so there's no point in even talking with them; (2) they think we're so ignorant we don't know the value of our own home, and they're trying to take advantage of us; (3) the buyers believe we're desperate and they want to prey on our misfortune; or (4) the buyers aren't serious buyers—they are just shotgunning lowball offers to see what might turn up. (In fact, this tactic is taught in some of the get-rich-in-real-estate seminars.)

When you lowball, you'll probably wipe out the possibility of a win-win purchase agreement. Most sellers respond to a lowball offer by flat-out rejecting it, counteroffering at the full asking price, or telling the buyers to get lost. This is not to say you'll never find ignorant or desperate sellers who will accept a lowball offer. And, if your priority is to buy at a bargain price—without regard to a specific house—then lowballing can work. But, as the McGills learned, lowballing generally creates ill will and provokes seller retaliation.

MISTAKE # **77**

We thought the sellers had accepted our offer.

LESSON: *Get the sellers' signatures on the contract.*

"We had been going back and forth with offers and counteroffers," says Keith O'Hara. "We kept trying to find that magic combination of price and terms that would click for both of us. Finally, it seemed like we found it. We were working with our agent in her office late Friday afternoon and she came up with a solution that would work for us. Next she called the sellers' agent to ask him to run it by the sellers before we wrote it up in a revised contract. About 20 minutes later the sellers' agent called back. He said we had a deal. The sellers could live with our solution.

"Our agent printed out a new copy of the agreement. We signed it, and she said she would visit the sellers later that evening to get their signatures. 'Congratulations,' she told us. 'You've just bought a great house. I know you're going to be happy with it.' We were elated.

"But our spirits came crashing down less than 24 hours later. That's when we learned the sellers had accepted a better offer that another agent brought them on Saturday morning. Our agent had dropped the ball. She hadn't kept her 7:00 P.M. appointment with the sellers. Because of a personal conflict, she had rescheduled the appointment for 1:00 Saturday afternoon. By that time, the sellers had already accepted the other offer with the provision that we would be allowed to match it. We couldn't. So we lost the house."

Never assume you have a deal until the sellers have signed the contract. Their oral acceptance isn't binding. Once upon a time you could count on people to honor their word—regardless of whether it had been committed to writing. But for many people, those days are gone. To be safe, if you receive an oral commitment to an agreement you want to see fulfilled, get the signatures as fast as possible. Don't give the sellers time to change their minds, change the terms, or find a better offer.

MISTAKE # **78**

The listing handout said "wet bar/sink" included.

LESSON: *Itemize in writing all personal property and fixtures included in the sale.*

Exactly what are you buying when you buy a home? Does the sale price include that $2,500 Tiffany light fixture hanging over the dining room table? Does it include the gazebo in the backyard? Does it include blinds, rugs, carpeting, appliances, or the window air conditioner? Does it include the mailbox? What about the lightbulbs in the ceiling lights and outdoor flood lamps?

"We couldn't believe it," recalls Jay Martin. "We got into town after dark around 9:00 P.M. We went right to our newly bought house, eager to spend our first night there, even though the moving van wasn't scheduled to arrive until the next day. We opened the front door, reached for the light switch, and flipped it on. Nothing happened. At first we thought the electric company had turned off the power. But when we felt our way to the kitchen, we could hear the refrigerator running. We opened the door to the fridge expecting to get some light; nothing happened.

Like lost souls in the dark, we wandered from room to room, flipping on every light switch we could find. Still no light. Finally, we borrowed a flashlight from a neighbor, and we quickly discovered the problem. The sellers had taken every lightbulb in the house—including the bulbs from inside the refrigerator and oven."

What Is a Wet Bar/Sink?

When Forrest and Dyan Alberts bought their home, the Realtor hand-out that described the features of the house listed a "wet bar/sink." In looking at the home before they bought, the Alberts admired the bar, its fine quality wood, anD ITS UNIQUE DEsign. In fact, they had compli-mented the owners on the bar.

But when the Albertses moved into their new home, the bar was gone. Remaining were the marks on the floor where the bar had stood. "Where's the bar?" Forrest inquired of the real estate agent.

"Oh," she said, "that was the sellers' personal property. The bar wasn't included in the sale."

"What do you mean, 'not included'?" Forrest shot back. "The house listing handout you gave us said the wet bar/sink was included."

"That didn't refer to the bar," the agent said. "That referred to the wet bar sink. You get the sink, not the bar. That bar was worth over $2,500."

I once bought a house that had a large antique mirror bolted to the bricks above the mantel on the fireplace. When I took possession of the house, the mirror and the bolts were gone. I got the holes where the bolts had been.

Assume Nothing, List Everything

Each of these stories teaches the same lesson: Never assume the sell-ers plan to leave any personal property with the house. Sellers have re-moved items as trivial as lightbulbs and mailboxes. At times they remove items of high value, such as chandeliers, gazebos, and wet bars. They may even take things that are bolted to floors, walls, or ceilings. There have been court cases where after contracting with buyers, sellers have removed toilets and furnaces. No matter how obvious it is to you that the item belongs with the house, the sellers may entertain different ideas.

In some instances, the sellers merely show their pettiness. In others, the sellers interpret ambiguity in their own favor. And sometimes sellers take things that they know rightfully belong to the buyers. But they may justify their actions: "Those buyers stole the house from us, so it's only right we even the score." Or, with larceny in their hearts and a keen sense of the impractical, the sellers may say to themselves, "What are the buyers gonna do, come to North Dakota to get us?"

There is a body of law (real property, fixtures, personal property) that defines what stays and what goes in a homebuying transaction. Like all law, though, it's riddled with contradictions, conflicting court opinions, and gray areas—not to mention the difficult and expensive burden of using lawyers to enforce a claim, even when you're sure the law favors your view. (I've heard of a Yiddish curse that says, "May you have a lawsuit you believe you can win." You might also recall Dickens's *Bleak House*.)

The law may offer recourse but rarely satisfaction. To prevent mistakes about what goes and what stays, assume nothing. List everything included in the home's sale price. Go through the house room by room with the sellers and your real estate agent. Identify, itemize, and write out. Leave no chance for doubt, confusion, or ambiguity. Then attach the signed list to both your copy and the sellers' copy of the purchase agreement.

Don't Rely on Oral Promises

Never depend on an oral promise of the sellers. "You're such a nice couple," the sellers say. "Since we have no use for them in our new house, we'll leave you the washer and dryer. They're old, but they'll serve you until you can buy your own."

When making their promise to you, the sellers may not know their daughter also needs a washer and dryer. Where will these appliances end up when the daughter says, "Mom, you know I hate going to the laundromat. If you're giving your washer and dryer away, you should give them to me." At that point, if you haven't written the washer and dryer into your purchase agreement, even the most well-intentioned sellers may be tempted to help their daughter at your expense.

MISTAKE # **79**

We fell in love with the house and had to have it.

LESSON: Keep your love to yourself. Put your options on the table.

In his best-selling book *You Can Get Anything You Want,* Roger Dawson, the world-renowned negotiating expert, tells how a negotiation slipup cost him $30,000 when he was buying his family's home. Roger writes that one day while teaching his daughter to drive in the secluded hills of Southern California, he spied the house of his dreams. "Everything about the house was perfect," he says, "and it was for sale."

Posing as a reluctant, if not altogether indifferent, buyer, Roger relates how he plotted his negotiation strategy—only to see it evaporate when his wife and daughter returned to look at the house without him. "They oohed and aahed over every feature, and by the time they were through with their tour, they had demolished my reluctant buyer plan," says Roger.

It also didn't help matters when his wife told the sellers Roger really thought their house was wonderful. At that point the sellers knew the Dawsons were hooked. Roger says with a ticket price of $15, many people think a tour of Hearst Castle is expensive. But he calculated that one house tour by his wife and daughter cost him $30,000.

Express Like, Not Love

When talking with sellers, walk a fine line. Show interest, develop a co-operative, problem-solving attitude, and hold your tongue if tempted to criticize. Yet, do not lavish praise. Nor should you tell yourself, "This is the perfect house, we've simply got to have it."

Keep your options open—both in your own mind and in the minds of the sellers. When the sellers believe you've scratched other houses off your list, they'll naturally use that information to bolster their own position. When you tell yourself that nothing else will do, you abandon the strongest negotiating power any buyer has—the willpower to walk away. Once you relinquish your walk-away willpower, you might as well hand the sellers a blank contract and tell them to fill in the numbers.

MISTAKE # *80*

Our negotiations centered on price.

LESSON: To most sellers, price is the main event. It's up to you to win agreement by emphasizing other important points.

"The mistake many home sellers make," says Realtor Bill Sloane, "is that they stop listening if the purchase price offer is too low." Sloane is pointing out a well-known fact. To most sellers, price is the main event. Everything else is warm-up. That's why lowball offers knock negotiations off the track before they even get going.

When you realize this fact, however, you can use it to your advantage. By not pushing the sellers too hard on price, you may get nearly anything else you want. Here's an illustration from one of my early homebuying experiences.

A Truly Win-Win Agreement

The sellers and I were sitting at their dining room table drafting a contract point by point. The first point was price. Although the sellers had their house priced fairly, I offered $10,000 less. The sellers rejected. I said, "Well, let's put that issue on hold and see if we can agree on some of the other points." In abbreviated form, here's how those other points went:

- The sellers agreed to a lease-purchase plan with closing 15 months after I took possession of the property.
- The sellers agreed to a cash deposit of just $5,000.

- They agreed to give possession within six weeks.
- They agreed to let me store all my household furniture in their den for the month prior to my taking possession of the property. (I had sold my previous home and was giving quick possession to the buyers, so I was going "homeless" for a month.)
- The sellers agreed to include in the sale about $4,000 worth of furniture and appliances.

These people were the easiest sellers I had ever dealt with. But when we eventually returned to price, they still didn't want to budge. After we talked some more, the husband said, "Look, here's what we paid for the property. At what you're offering us, we would take a $6,000 loss. We want to at least get what we paid."

Here's where negotiation experts differ. Some would say at this point you've got the sellers committed to everything but price. Hang tough and you can still get the price concession you want. The sellers are so close to a deal, they won't let you walk away. If they did, they would just have to start over again with someone else—if and when that someone else appears. If they're smart, the sellers won't take that risk.

For reasons explained earlier (and later, see Mistake #83), I don't endorse this view. If the sellers have been willing to yield on every point that's important to me, why not let them score a point, too? Besides, once you've gotten nearly all you want, why push so hard you might upset the entire applecart? So, adopting a win-win approach, I increased my offer by $7,000 on the promise the sellers would take responsibility for cutting down and removing a dead tree from the backyard. They quickly agreed. We had a deal that pleased us both.

How to Bargain for a Low Price

Let's return to the beginning of these negotiations. What would have happened early on if we had heavily debated price? Even if I had been able to pull the sellers down to my offer, that "success" probably would have destroyed my chances of getting all the other things I needed to make the deal work. A hollow victory indeed.

However, on other occasions, I have reversed this approach. When through early inquiries I've learned the sellers have needs stronger than price, I emphasize how I am willing to help them meet those needs (e.g., their preferred possession date, their need to know the transaction is actually going to close). Then, once the sellers understand they are receiving nearly all the terms and conditions they want, I feel I can justify my request for their concession on price.

Remember, sellers do not demand their price for purely economic reasons. For many, price is laden with emotional content. A low offer doesn't just hurt their pocketbook. It hurts their feelings.

When you singlemindedly negotiate price, as likely as not, one party "loses" and the other party "wins." In contrast, when you negotiate (search for) an *agreement,* you and the sellers can both gain.

MISTAKE # **81**
___

"Split the difference" sounds like a good compromise to me.

LESSON: *Don't compromise, conciliate.*

In negotiation lore, the story is told of a mother who hears her two children bickering at the dinner table. Each child wants the only remaining slice of pie. Tiring of this debate, the mother takes the slice, cuts it in two, and gives half to Craig and half to Shawn. "There," she says, "as you get older you must realize you can't have everything you want. You must learn to compromise. Remember this as an important lesson."

This well-intentioned mother thought she was teaching her kids a valuable lesson, whereas, in fact, she had imprinted them with one of the greatest obstacles to win-win negotiating. By splitting the difference before fully exploring her children's wants and a range of options, this mother mistakenly framed her kids' debate along a single continuum. Compromise simply meant deciding how to split the piece of pie.

Look for Ways to Enlarge the Pie
Had the mother framed the problem multidimensionally, more than likely she could have figured out a better solution. What if one child re-

ally preferred the crust? What if the children shared a television set and each preferred different programs? What if the children shared after-dinner cleanup responsibilities? What if the children had money from an allowance? What if Shawn didn't really want the pie, but simply liked to torment Craig?

Had the mother recognized a range of wants, trade-offs, and outcomes, she may have produced results more satisfying (or just) for both children. The true art of negotiating doesn't depend on one's readiness to strike a compromise. It depends on seeing beyond a single either/or issue.

Conciliation Sparks Creativity

In Mistake #80, I told how the sellers I was buying a home from agreed to let me use one of their rooms to store household furniture. Alternatively, I wanted an earlier date of possession, but they wanted a later date. What would have happened had we focused our negotiations exclusively on possession date? I would have said, "I have to be out of my present home on February 1. I need possession on that date."

The sellers may have responded, "We can't get into our new home until March 1. A February 1 possession date is out of the question. We can't possibly give you possession before February 28."

"Okay," I might say if I'm thinking compromise, "let's split the difference. I'll agree to February 15. I'm willing to meet you halfway."

Although meeting the sellers halfway sounds like fair play, many times it doesn't make sense, or it overlooks another more satisfying outcome. In this case, February 15 wouldn't work for either of us. So that position never found its way onto the table. By looking at my real problem—what to do with my furniture for a month without incurring the cost and inconvenience of multiple moves into and out of storage—we solved the issue by temporarily storing my household goods in a large room they used but didn't really need. We both liked this outcome.

Nine times out of 10, thoughtful conciliation beats win-lose compromise.

Compromise Provokes Extremes

Too often, people who negotiate to compromise open with offers at the extreme. If you believe the sellers will split the difference, it's to your advantage to offer $95,000 for a $120,000 house. Should the sellers agree to meet you halfway, they will sell you the house for $107,500.

But few sellers are that obliging. The tactic of bid low and compromise is too familiar to work effectively. As negotiating expert Herb Cohen likes to emphasize, "A tactic perceived is no tactic at all." You're more likely to negotiate successfully if you bake a bigger pie. Expand your knowledge of wants, needs, trade-offs, and possibilities. To loosely paraphrase Emerson, "foolish compromises are the hobgoblins of little minds."

MISTAKE # **82**

We let our agent negotiate for us.

LESSON: *Use an agent as an intermediary, but negotiate for yourself.*

Writing in *Real Estate Today,* a national trade magazine for Realtors, sales agent Sal Gebbia tells of an offer he received on one of his listings. Sal says that after receiving the purchase offer from a buyer's agent, this *buyer's* agent told Sal, "This is their [first] offer, but I know this couple will go up to $250,000. They really want the house."

"Of course," Sal adds, "I told my sellers that information, and we were pleased with the outcome of the transaction."

The lesson here is plain. Never let your agent negotiate for you. Don't give your agent information you do not want the other side to learn. Don't let on to your agent that you're willing to pay a higher price than your first offer. Use your agent as fact finder and intermediary. But guard your emotions, confidences, and intentions.

Many buyers (especially first-time buyers) mistakenly rely too heavily on their agents to actually come up with the terms of their offer and carry out their negotiations. These buyers will ask their agents, "What price do you think I should offer? What's the most you think I should pay? Will the sellers concede points or agree to carry-back financing?" Then the buyers follow whatever the agent recommends.

Such buyers abandon their own negotiating responsibilities. If you follow their example and shift decision making to your agent, you should keep the following in mind.

You May Be Working with a Subagent

Remember, you may be working with the sellers' subagent. As a subagent, your Realtor's legal duty is to the seller. In favoring the sellers' interests, the agent may persuade you to boost the price or terms of your offer. Or the agent may disclose your confidences to the sellers.

As a practical matter, many subagents do not strictly follow the letter of the law. Even though technically they represent the sellers, in their heart and efforts they may feel more loyalty to you. I know many subagents who work hard for their buyers—even at a loss to their sellers.

Nevertheless, since you don't know for sure how your agent will use the information you share, carefully limit your disclosures. Likewise, when offering price and terms, rely on your agent for facts about the sellers, selling prices of comp houses, neighborhood statistics, and general market conditions. Listen to the agent's price recommendations and accept the benefits of his or her experience. But don't delegate your decision making. You may be led into giving up more than you need to.

Be Cautious of Buyers' Agents

Increasingly, brokerage firms and sales agents promote buyers' agency. Because sellers are represented by their own agents, buyers also need someone to look out for their interests. Marilyn Williams, a Vancouver, Washington, real estate broker, says, "Buyers should think of their agents as attorneys. Would you want to have one attorney representing both parties in a divorce settlement?"

At first glance, this idea sounds reasonable. Yet, even if you choose to employ a buyers' agent, you still need to guard your disclosures and negotiating strategy. First of all, like the agent Sal Gebbia referred to earlier, even buyers' agents may disclose your confidences—either intentionally or unintentionally.

Second, we're all subject to subtle influences. A buyers' agent may talk you into offering a higher price or better terms because it will make his or her job easier. In which case do you think your agent will work hardest for you: when the agent knows you offered $685,000 but said you're willing to go up to $750,000, or when you offer $685,000 and say "If they don't accept this offer, there's four or five other houses I'd like to look at"?

Watch What You Say

Regardless of whether you're working with a sellers' subagent, a buyers' agent, a dual agent, or a facilitator, watch what you say. Don't tell your agent everything and then turn the negotiations over to her with the simple instructions, "Do the best job you can," or "Why don't you try $135,000 and if that doesn't fly, we can go to $145,000."

In fact, it doesn't matter whether we're talking about lawyers, insurance agents, financial planners, real estate agents, or any other type of professional relationship; conflict of interest always lurks in the background. Again, tread a fine line. Release enough information to achieve the results you want, but not so much that you invite your agent to sacrifice your interests to the interests of someone else (including your agent).

MISTAKE # **83**

We pushed to get the absolute best deal we could.

LESSON: *The deal's not over 'til it's over.*

"We chose to work with a buyers' agent," recalls Barry Tausch. "We felt a buyers' agent would push harder to get us the best deal possible. As it turned out, we pushed too hard.

"We knew the sellers were getting a divorce. The wife had moved out of the house and in with her boss. Without income from the wife's paycheck, the husband was facing tough times. He couldn't handle the family expenses on his own. Although they had a lot of equity in the house, the husband was hurting for cash. He needed a fast sale. By using this information to our advantage, we got the sellers to come down at least $20,000 to 25,000 below market. Bad deal for them. Good deal for us.

"The only thing we had to agree to was a 30-day close. We didn't think this would be a problem because we already had been preapproved. But it was. There was one foul-up after another.

"In the meantime, the sellers got a backup offer for $7,500 more than our price. To make a long story short, the husband held such resentment against us for 'stealing' his house, he wouldn't cut us any slack. As soon as we missed the loan commitment date, he demanded payment. When we couldn't deliver, he pulled out of our contract and sold to the backup buyers."

Leave Something on the Table

Negotiating expert Bob Woolf says, "There isn't any contract I have negotiated where I didn't feel I could have gone for more money or an additional benefit." Why "leave money on the table?" Because skilled negotiators know, "The deal's not over 'til it's over." If you push too hard, you create resentment and hostility in the other party. Even if they've signed a contract, they'll start thinking of all the ways they can get out of it. Even worse, if you stumble on the way to closing, they won't help you up. They'll just kick dirt in your face.

Especially in the purchase of a home—where emotions run strong—you're better off leaving something on the table. The purchase agreement only forms stage one of your negotiations. Later, you might encounter problems with respect to property inspections, appraisal, financing, possession date, closing date, surveys, or any number of other things. Without goodwill, trust, and cooperation, unpleasant setbacks on the way to closing can throw your agreement into contentious dispute.

CHAPTER 8

The Best Loan at the Lowest Cost

"It's easier than ever for young people to buy a home,"
writes Bill Rumbler of the *Chicago Sun-Times*. Lend-
ers and builders are bending over backward to help first-time buyers.
They're lowering interest rates, reducing (or eliminating) down payments, and cutting closing costs. "On top of that," reports Rumbler,
"many lenders, builders, and credit counselors provide homebuyer
counseling."

The *San Diego Union-Tribune* agrees. "Now's the time to go from
renter to homeowner. The government *wants* to put people into their
own homes and is encouraging lenders to woo first-time buyers."

With new loan programs, easier qualification, and expanded homebuyer counseling services, you're nearly certain to find a loan that can
move you into home ownership. Educate yourself, plan your finances,
and avoid costly mistakes. As you learn from the homebuyer experiences
in this chapter, you will discover how to (1) save money on your mortgage, (2) buy with little or nothing down, and (3) shape up your credit
profile. (For more on qualifying and affordability, see Chapter 11.)

MISTAKE # **84**

We never heard of special financing for people like us.

LESSON: If you have the will, you can find a way.

"We always heard that to buy a house you needed 20 percent down and excellent credit," says Rene Wolpe. "Otherwise we would have bought years ago. Until we heard of the government's home ownership initiatives, we never knew we could qualify for special financing."

The Wolpes made the most common and most costly mistake in real estate. They excluded themselves from home ownership because they mistakenly believed they couldn't qualify for financing. But as Kathy Ortiz of the San Diego Home Loan Counseling Center points out, "There are a lot of loan programs, and there is a program for almost everyone."

Ortiz goes on to say that most of the people she helps are like the Wolpes. They don't realize how many different ways there are to finance a home. "A large majority of our clients come in here really hesitant and lack the confidence that they can qualify. But when they leave, they leave with confidence because they have developed an understanding of the homebuying process and they know their options."

Javier and Maricela Samaniego are living proof of what Kathy Ortiz is referring to. This young couple with a 16-month-old son never believed they could own their own home. They were paying $950 a month for rent and had meager savings. But thanks to Union Bank's Economic Opportunity Mortgage, they were able to buy. "I thought that without this," says Maricela, "we would have had to come up with more money, and since we didn't have much money to work with, it really helped us a lot…. We now have so many plans for the house. It really changed everything for us. The money we were paying in rent is now going somewhere."

With the help of Realtors, homebuilders, mortgage lenders, government agencies, and home counseling centers, hundreds of thousands of Americans like the Wolpes and the Samaniegos are discovering that traditional rules of mortgage financing no longer block most renters from home ownership. In today's push to expand home ownership (especially among minorities and low- to moderate-income individuals and families), lenders are reaching out to all creditworthy (not credit perfect) people who want to become homeowners. Although you must check to see what's available in your area, here's a brief sampling of the types of home finance programs you might use.

Community Reinvestment Programs

For years civil rights activists and various consumer groups have accused banks and other mortgage lenders of "redlining." According to critics, bank officers take a red marking pen and draw a circle around minority or low- to middle-income neighborhoods. "These areas are too risky," say the bankers. "We can't finance homes there. Property values may go down."

When bankers cut off mortgages to a neighborhood, they set in motion a self-fulfilling prophecy. If people can't get money to buy and fix up homes, the neighborhood will decline. Fortunately, lenders now recognize a more positive truth. If they make loans, people will invest in their own homes. Neighborhoods will turn around. Values will increase.

In response to neighborhood activists, federal antidiscrimination laws, the National Home Ownership Strategy, and the profit motive, mortgage lenders are rolling out the red carpet for borrowers who in past years may have been turned away. "We are in a heavy campaign to spread the word to the community that home ownership is not out of reach for low-income families," says mortgage specialist Fred Thomas III. "This is truly a window of opportunity for folks who previously were shut out of the homebuying system."

Loan Details Differ

The specific details of these community reinvestment home-finance plans differ among lenders. Some offer low- or no-down-payment plans. Others eliminate or reduce closing costs and fees. Most relax qualifying standards and offer counseling to help individuals and families shape up their finances, improve their credit, and become familiar with the process of buying a home. A large number of lenders combine all these benefits into one program.

Ray Sims of GE Capital Mortgage Services says, "We expect to create business where we haven't seen it before.... We see this as a potentially large underserved market."

Even though community reinvestment loan programs are geared toward lower- to middle-income borrowers, the income limits may go up to $40,000, $50,000, or even $90,000 a year. Sometimes no limits apply. American Savings Bank has advertised, "If you pay $1,000 a month or more for rent, you should consider buying a $200,000 home." Don't rule yourself out because you think you earn too much money. Most community reinvestment home finance programs reach well into the middle class.

State and Local Governments

"It's a great program," says Rebecca Hoffreiter. "Anybody that needs it should go for it." Rebecca's talking about a home finance plan sponsored in part by the Pennsylvania Housing Finance Agency. Under this innovative lease-purchase plan, renters can move into home ownership with as little as $1,000 in up-front cash. Then for a period of one to three years, a part of the homebuyers' monthly payments go into a forced savings account. Once they build up enough money for a five percent down payment, the buyers obtain a mortgage and close on their purchase.

"This is certainly a great program, and we're really excited about it," says Craig Cunningham. Craig is director of marketing for K. Hovnanian, one of the new homebuilders who agreed to participate in this lease-purchase program. On the other side of the country, Harry Jensen of Jensen Mortgage says, "We're putting people in $180,000 homes who could have only qualified for a $120,000 home. At the beginning, the Realtors I know were incredulous." Harry's praise is aimed at a shared equity mortgage plan sponsored by the San Diego Housing Commission.

Under this plan, the Housing Commission contributes up to $25,000 in down-payment funds. Homebuyers need only come up with three percent of the home's purchase price from their own pocket. As an added advantage, the city Housing Commission's down-payment money doesn't require any monthly repayments. If the homeowners sell within 15 years, they must then repay the down-payment money along with some profit to the Commission. On the other hand, after 15 years the loan is completely forgiven.

Throughout the United States, both state and local governments are creating dozens of programs that offer special assistance financing. There are low-interest mortgage bond programs, mortgage credit certificates, low-cost home repair or renovation loans, down-payment assistance plans, and even sweat equity and urban homesteading. Some states have created their own version of the VA (U.S. Department of Veterans Affairs) mortgages. Also, if you're a government employee (teacher, firefighter, police officer, etc.), your town or city may have developed an easy-purchase home finance plan for you.

Fannie and Freddie Get Creative

The largest suppliers of mortgage money in the country are two congressionally chartered corporations called Fannie Mae and Freddie Mac. Since the kickoff of the National Homeownership Strategy several years ago, these lenders have relaxed their underwriting standards and lowered down payments for first-time buyers.

Through loan programs sponsored by Fannie and Freddie, you can borrow as much as 95, 97, and even 100 percent of your home's purchase price—up to $359,650 (2005). Fannie and Freddie also permit you to buy 2–4 unit properties with a low down payment. Even better, they will agree to approve much higher loan limits:

- 2 units @ $460,400
- 3 units @ $556,500
- 4 units @ $691,600

If you are buying a property that's located in Alaska, Hawaii, Guam, Puerto Rico, or the U.S. Virgin Islands, Fannie and Freddie increase each of their respective property limits by 50 percent.

I strongly encourage you to weigh the advantages of buying a 2–4 unit property. Not only will your tenants pay most (if not all) of your monthly mortgage payments, but you can gain more dollars each year from appreciation because you will own a higher-priced property. At, say, 4.0 percent appreciation, a $300,000 property gives you a $12,000 yearly gain, whereas a 4.0 percent value increase on a $650,000 property equals $26,000. Over 5 years, that totals more than $70,000. With the larger property, you will also gain more equity through amortization (mortgage payoff).

Fannie Mae permits homebuyers with excellent credit to borrow their down payment from family; obtain a gift, grant, or loan from an employer; or even take a cash advance against a credit card.

Fannie and Freddie are both committed to creating new and easier ways for people to own homes. As long as borrower default rates (foreclosures) remain low, these giant mortgage lenders will "keep their doors open" to almost any homebuyer who can demonstrate financial responsibility. For more on new homebuying programs from Fannie and Freddie, go to their respective websites at www.fanniemae.com and www.homesteps.com.

Where Else to Look

To locate community reinvestment mortgages, first-time buyer loan programs, or other special assistance finance plans, talk to Realtors, loan officers, mortgage brokers, government agencies, and homebuying counselors. Read the business and real estate sections of major newspapers in your city or state. You're sure to find an easy qualifying, low- (or no-) down-payment home finance plan with your name on it.

MISTAKE # **85**

We thought the FHA loaned only to low-income people and involved too much red tape.

LESSON: *Don't overlook loans insured by the Federal Housing Administration (FHA).*

"We earn $88,000 a year," says Sam Wright. "We didn't know we could get an FHA loan, since we stand above the low-income category. Anyway, whenever you get involved with the government, you've got too much red tape to wade through."

Sam has made a common mistake. Many Americans wrongly believe that FHA mortgage loan programs are intended only for low- to middle-income individuals and families. In truth, the FHA places no limits on income. It doesn't matter whether you earn $12,000 a year or $120,000. As long as you have acceptable (not perfect) credit and earn enough to make your mortgage payments, you can qualify. As for red tape, the FHA does apply rules and regulations. But these shouldn't present a problem for borrowers who are working with a DE (direct endorsement) lender. These lenders can complete the loan paperwork directly, without submitting it to FHA for prior approval.

Two Drawbacks of FHA Loans

Compared to other home mortgages, FHA loans have two drawbacks. First, if you plan to buy a higher-priced home, FHA loan limits may be too low. For 2005, maximum FHA loan limits range between $172,632 and $312,895. The top limits apply to high-cost areas such as Boston, San Francisco, San Diego, and New York. The lower loan limits apply to the more moderate housing cost areas such as many of those found in north central Florida, Arkansas, Alabama, and West Virginia. (However, no matter where you live, you can find some homes suitable for FHA financing. For example, even high-cost San Diego has neighborhoods where some homes sell for less than $312,895.

Just like Fannie Mae and Freddie Mac, FHA permits larger loans (with small down payments) for 2–4 unit properties:

	Low Cost Area	High Cost Area
2-Unit	$220,992	$400,548
3-Unit	$267,120	$484,155
4-Unit	$331,968	$601,692

Again, I encourage you to recognize the financial gains that you can achieve when you own a multiunit property. After a few years, you can buy the single-family house that you might prefer and hold on to your 2–4 unit as an investment. After a few more years, you can trade up this smaller rental to a larger investment property (tax free, I might add).

A second drawback of FHA loans is cost. Compared to many mortgages, FHA insurance and fees can add several thousand dollars to your closing expenses. To offset these higher expenses, though, the FHA does let you roll most of the costs into your loan. You don't have to pay much at closing. Also, due to a record level of financial reserves, FHA has sliced 40 percent off its fees, making it more competitive with private mortgage insurance.

Benefits of FHA Home Financing

Overall, in deciding whether to use an FHA loan, weigh its somewhat higher costs against these seven benefits:

1. *Low down payment:* Usually five percent or less.
2. *No savings required:* Even the relatively small FHA down payment need not come from your own cash savings. Your parents or other close family members may loan (or give) this money to you.
3. *Easier qualifying:* FHA lenders often will not be as picky as Freddy or Fannie (i.e., conventional) lenders. FHA exists to expand home ownership.
4. *Higher qualifying ratios:* This means FHA loans expand your buying power (see Mistake #86).
5. *Counseling:* HUD/FHA offers counseling through hundreds of not-for-profit organizations located throughout the country. These counselors help plan your finances to achieve home ownership. Should you suffer a layoff, health problem, or other financial setback after you've bought your home, FHA counselors can reduce your mortgage payments and help you solve your budget problems. FHA discourages "quick trigger" foreclosures.
6. *Streamlined refinance.* If you finance your home with an FHA loan and mortgage interest rates drop, you can streamline an FHA refinance to take advantage of the lower rates. Streamlining means you don't have to jump over any qualifying hurdles again. A streamlined refinance requires no credit check, no income verification, no appraisal, and no points. No conventional lender offers this super deal.

7. *Assumability.* When you sell your home, your buyers can, with easy qualifying, assume your FHA fixed-rate mortgage at the same rate you're paying. If interest rates fall, they too will be able to streamline a refinance at the new lower rates.

These last two FHA benefits, streamlining and assumability, provide especially good value. Several years back, when hard times hit some homeowners, they weren't able to refinance their conventional loans because their income, their home's value, or both had fallen. They were stuck with old mortgages of 9 to 13 percent even as current market rates then fluctuated between 6.5 and 8 percent. In contrast, through streamlining, FHA borrowers were able to cut their mortgage payments by hundreds of dollars a month—even when they could not have otherwise qualified for refinancing.

As a further benefit, FHA assumability gives you a competitive edge over other sellers when you put your home up for sale. If interest rates are high, you can pass along your lower rate to buyers. If market interest rates have fallen, you or your buyers can streamline a refinance. Your buyers avoid the hassle and cost of taking out a new loan. In addition, it's usually easier to qualify for an FHA assumption than for a new mortgage.

For many homebuyers, I strongly believe that the benefits of FHA loans outweigh their drawbacks. Although you must decide what's best in your circumstances, don't casually ignore FHA. During the past five years the FHA has helped more than 3.5 million Americans become homeowners. This is one government agency that is working hard to move Americans and immigrants into home ownership.

HUD Homes

HUD (the U.S. Department of Housing and Urban Development) is the parent of FHA. In those situations when FHA borrowers hit hard times and default on their loans, HUD takes back the property and offers it for sale. The exact deals HUD offers depend on the number of homes it has to sell relative to the number of potential homebuyers.

When HUD sales are slow and foreclosures high, HUD creates buyer incentives. In robust markets, incentives become less generous and HUD prices its homes closer to their market values. Nevertheless, even in hot markets, patience, perseverance, and maybe a little luck can get you a good buy on a HUD home. At present, HUD homes are piling up in states such as Indiana, Ohio, and Georgia. Yet, in California, most HUD homes sell quickly at or above HUD's asking price. To learn what's happening in your area, go to hud.gov. Click on HUD homes. You can then follow the links to your state and county. Check regularly because local markets can change quickly.

HUD does not sell directly to buyers. To bid on a HUD home, you must go through a real estate agent who is authorized by HUD. To find these agents, look through the realty firm ads in your local newspaper or consult the yellow pages of your telephone directory. You might also call the HUD office nearest to where you live and request a list of their registered agents.

If you want to stop renting now, a HUD home might prove to be your best opportunity. Put a HUD agent to work for you. There are no guarantees, but passing up this possibility could be a mistake. Nearly anyone (with tolerably good credit) can afford to buy a HUD home. (For a thorough discussion of buying HUD homes, VA homes, and other types of foreclosures, see my forthcoming book *Investing In Real Estate, 5th Edition*, 2006 [Wiley].)

VA Mortgages

If you have served in the armed forces (including the National Guard), contact the VA (Department of Veterans Affairs). Your years of service may qualify you for a VA certificate of eligibility. With VA eligibility, you can buy a home priced up to around $359,650—with virtually *no cash* required for a down payment or closing costs. Some new homebuilders even advertise, "Veterans—$1 Moves You Into Your Own Home." If you are an eligible veteran with tolerably good credit, don't overlook this possibility. (See www.va.gov.)

Nonveterans Can Also Benefit from VA

Nonveterans can use VA programs in two ways. First, you can assume a VA mortgage that has been originated by an eligible veteran. Say a veteran bought and financed a $200,000 home two years ago. Now she finds she has been transferred to another area and wants to sell. Her current loan balance equals $203,000 (at the time of purchase, some of the closing costs were added to the mortgage). Today's market value of the home is $207,000. Pay the veteran $4,000 (or whatever amount you both agree to) and, with a small assumption fee, you can simply take over the veteran's mortgage. A quick, low-cost, low-down-payment way to buy a home!

Another VA possibility: nonveterans can buy a VA foreclosure (REO). Similar to FHA, VA "takes back" some of the properties it finances when veterans default. It then offers these houses and condominiums on easy terms to anyone (veteran or nonveteran) who meets VA's (relaxed) qualifying standards.

To locate VA-owned properties, go to va.gov. Click on home loan, which will take you to the home loan guaranty page. Look to the left sidebar and click on property management. From that link click on ocwen.com, which is the bank that manages VA foreclosures. You will then see a map of the United States, which you can follow to locate properties within the states and cities where you might buy. Also, because VA lists all of its homes for sale with local Realtors, you can call an agent who specializes in these types of listings (ocwen.com shows the listing agents for its VA properties along with property descriptions; you can also link to VA foreclosures at hud.gov).

Currently, nonveteran homebuyers can buy VA-owned properties with nothing down (but some closing costs). Investors may place as little as 5.0 percent down, but with 20 percent down they receive streamlined loan processing. In 2005, VA offered 30-year loans at an APR of 5.783 percent.

My recent search of California turned up just two VA properties. But Ohio shows 156 properties; Georgia listed 292; and Texas leads with 462 VA houses for sale. So, keep in mind that the numbers of HUD/VA homes for sale varies greatly by city and local market conditions.

MISTAKE # **86**

We wanted a fixed-rate mortgage. ARMs were too risky.

LESSON: *Before you pass up an ARM (adjustable-rate mortgage), understand and explore your options.*

"When we started shopping for a home," recalls Ari Kyle, "I read that you should avoid an ARM whenever you can get a 30-year fixed-rate mortgage for less than 10 percent. Since at the time, 30-year mortgages were around 8 percent, we didn't even consider an adjustable rate. With fixed rates that low, why take the risk of an ARM?"

Although Ari asked this question rhetorically, the answer is not as obvious as he thinks. In fact, like Ari, many homebuyers pass up ARMs without considering why an adjustable-rate mortgage might prove their best choice. To help you decide, answer these six questions:

1. Is there a strong probability you will sell your home within seven years?
2. Do you expect your income to increase during the coming years?
3. Would you like to increase your home purchase price range by $10,000 to $40,000 or even more?
4. Would you like to cut your closing costs by $1,000 to $3,000?
5. Do you expect to keep your home for more than seven years?
6. Do you enjoy a financial cushion in your budget and savings accounts?

If you can answer yes to at least three of the above questions, you might profit with an ARM.

Save Money with ARMs

The shorter the length of time you plan to own your home, the more you should consider an ARM. You can nearly always find an adjustable that will cost you less than a 30-year fixed-rate loan if you plan to sell within seven years. Take a look at 5/25 or 7/23 (sometimes described as 30/5 or 30/7) adjustables.

These types of ARMs fix your interest rate and monthly payments for the beginning five or seven years of the loan. Then they periodically adjust to keep your rate in line with the market. Even this limited type of ARM may save you between .5 and 1.5 percent in interest rates as compared to a fixed-rate mortgage. For instance, at a time when 30-year fixed-rates were at 7.25 percent, I saw several 5/25 ARM plans with interest rates as low as 5.75 percent.

On a $100,000 loan, your payments for a 7.25 percent 30-year fixed-rate loan would cost $682 a month. If you selected the 5/25, your payments would drop to $583 a month. Although the rate differences between 30-year fixed-rate loans and various types of ARMs change daily, it pays to at least take a look. When you plan to sell within seven years, the chances are good you can find an ARM that limits your risk at the same time it reduces your monthly payments.

Moreover, if your income is going up, you should be able to handle any increases in your ARM's monthly payments.

Qualify for a Larger Mortgage

ARMs help you qualify for a larger mortgage. They do this in two ways. First, because ARMs typically start with lower interest rates, for the same amount of monthly payment, you can borrow more. A payment of, say, $1,250 a month will pay off a loan of $187,885 at 7.0 percent over 30 years. With an ARM's qualifying interest rate of, say, 5.5 percent, you could borrow $220,152. Second, if you can afford it, some ARM lenders will qualify you with more liberal qualifying ratios. For example, with a fixed-rate loan, the lender might limit your payments to $1,250 a month. But with an ARM, the lender might qualify you for a monthly payment of, say, $1,350. Instead of borrowing $202,915 (with a 7.0 percent fixed-rate loan), the 5.5 percent ARM with liberal qualifying would permit you to borrow $237,764.

Lower Points and Fees

To further encourage you to use an ARM, sometimes ARM lenders cut their loan origination fees and closing costs. This benefit, however, may not be the advantage it once was. To meet competitive pressures, many lenders also have been offering low cash-to-close deals on fixed-rate loans. Nevertheless, at least compare adjustable- and fixed-rate mortgages on the basis of cash you need to close.

Longer-Term Cost Savings

An ARM will probably save you money if you plan to sell within seven years. But you also might save money over the longer term. Here's why.

Say you're faced with a choice between a 30-year fixed-rate loan at 7.25 percent and a 7/23 that starts at 6.0 percent. You want to borrow $300,000. With the fixed-rate plan, your payments will cost $2,046 a month. With the 7/23, you'll pay $1,798. For at least the first seven years, you'll save $248 a month, for a total of $20,832.

Instead of pocketing this monthly savings of $248, though, add it to your monthly mortgage payments. Even though you're only required to pay $1,798, you go ahead and pay $2,046 ($1,798 + 248 = 2,046). This tactic causes you to pay down your outstanding mortgage balance much faster. By making these extra payments, your mortgage balance after seven years would have fallen to approximately $248,086. On the other hand, your mortgage balance with the fixed-rate plan at 7.25 percent would have dropped to just $274,488. Obviously, if you sell at this point, you're way ahead of the game with the ARM.

But what if you don't sell? As long as your new adjustable rate stays below 9.5 percent, your monthly mortgage payments won't amount to any more than $2,522—about the same as you've been paying. At 10.5 percent, your payments would increase only to $2,744 a month. Now, what if interest rates are lower when your loan adjusts after seven years? Not only will you have accumulated an additional $35,159 in home equity, but your monthly payments won't increase and may actually go down.

These figures are illustrative only. Because the *relative* costs of ARMs versus fixed-rate loans change frequently, you must work numbers with your mortgage loan advisor that are current at the time you buy your home. Still, this basic fact holds true: The right ARM can put some homebuyers thousands of dollars ahead of where they would have been with a 30-year fixed-rate mortgage.

The Fixed-Rate Solution

Some mortgage loan officers agree with everything I have just stated, but they still argue that for most homebuyers the fixed-rate mortgage (FRM) can give comparable benefits with less risk. Here's their reasoning:

1. Some fixed-rate loans can be obtained without heavy front-end costs and fees. Therefore, the total first-year costs of ARMs versus FRMs may not differ as much as is commonly supposed.
2. Should interest rates fall, you can inexpensively refinance your no-cost FRM at the lower interest rates. (Of course, this refinance option presumes that both you and your home continue to meet the current qualifying and *loan-to-value* [LTV] requirements.)
3. Instead of using an ARM to qualify for a larger mortgage, locate a special first-time buyer fixed-rate mortgage that offers easier qualifying, a lower-than-market interest rate, or perhaps both. Or get your seller to *buy down* the FRM interest rate for the first two or three years of the loan.
4. With an FRM you need not worry about payment shock. (Payment shock results when a quick jump in an ARM's interest rate boosts your mortgage payment by hundreds of dollars a month.)
5. Even if you plan to sell within three to seven years, take the security of a fixed-rate mortgage. Why? Because your plans may change. Or, if interest rates dramatically increase (say, from 5.0 percent to 7.5 percent), you may not be able to qualify for a loan on another house. In other words, higher interest rates may put your move-up possibilities on hold until interest rates fall. Then you would be stuck with your high rate ARM.

The Debate Continues

Which is best? An ARM or a fixed-rate mortgage? No one can answer that question. It depends on how FRM points, fees, and interest rates compare to those of ARMs at the time you buy. Plus, the answer depends on your personal financial situation as well as your "sound sleep" quotient. And remember, those zero-cost FRMs generally come with higher interest rates. They're not zero cost. You just pay the costs over time.

Will an ARM save you money? Can you afford the risks of an ARM? Can you sleep soundly with the knowledge that your mortgage payments could increase? Don't prejudge the answers to these questions. Get together with a savvy loan rep who will explain a variety of loan products and potential outcomes. Compare dollar amounts. Don't focus on small percent changes in rates. A two percent change in your mortgage rate can affect your payments by hundreds of dollars a month.

Review the numbers relative to your circumstances. Then choose the best loan for your needs. To locate the best loan at the lowest cost, don't rely on uninformed beliefs. Contrast savings and risks.

MISTAKE # **87**

We didn't negotiate for seller financing.

LESSON: *Even when you qualify for financing from a mortgage lender, consider seller financing.*

Julio and Tara Scott had only enough cash for a 10 percent down payment. So when they bought their home, their bank charged them a higher interest rate and required them to buy private mortgage insurance (PMI). In addition, because the mortgage insurer applied tight qualifying standards, the Scotts weren't able to buy as much house as they wanted. In other words, they ended up paying more and getting less.

What the Scotts overlooked was a financing method referred to as an 80–10–10 sale. Here's how this technique works: You put 10 percent down; you borrow 80 percent of your home's purchase price from a mortgage lender; and the sellers carry back the other 10 percent as a seller-financed second mortgage.

Save on PMI

Because under this plan the bank has made an 80 percent loan instead of a 90 percent loan, it faces less risk. In exchange for this lower risk, the bank will drop its requirements for PMI, perhaps give you a better interest rate, and possibly relax its qualifying income ratios or other credit standards. You can buy more house for less.

Benefits to Sellers

What's in it for the sellers? Why would they accept this kind of deal?

First and most important, the sellers get their house sold. For most sellers, that's their number-one priority. When you write your offer, you make an 80–10–10 plan a condition of the contract. Second, because it's easier to qualify at the bank for an 80 percent loan, the sellers can feel secure that your purchase will actually close. Many sellers fear they will pull their house off the market for four to eight weeks, then their sale will fall through, and they'll be back at square one. Anything you do to reduce this fear stands out as a plus in the sellers' eyes. (A preapproval letter also helps achieve this goal.)

Third, the interest rate you agree to pay the sellers will exceed the amount they could earn on their money in a certificate of deposit or savings account. With CDs paying four to six percent, a return of seven to nine percent to the sellers on a second mortgage can look pretty good. Fourth, an 80–10–10 sale will probably take less time to close than a 90–10 sale with private mortgage insurance.

Other Variations

Of course, an 80–10–10 sale represents just one variation of combined seller–bank financing. If you're really short of cash, you could try for an 80–15–5 plan, or even an 80–20–0. In fact, any combination is possible. If your credit score is too low, you could decrease the bank's percentage to 60 to 75 percent—say 70–20–10. Just remember: The lower the bank's loan-to-value ratio, the greater your chance for loan approval, the less likely you'll have to buy PMI, and the lower your interest rate.

Eliminate the Bank Altogether

Homebuyers who can't qualify for bank financing know they must turn to some type of seller financing or an (increasingly rare) nonqualifying mortgage assumption. But even when you can qualify for bank financing, you might still go for a completely seller-financed purchase. Here are four reasons why seller financing works to benefit you:

1. You can often get the sellers to accept a lower interest rate than typical mortgage lenders.
2. Sellers don't charge application fees, "garbage" fees, or loan origination fees. You need less cash to close.
3. Seller financing involves less paperwork and a quicker closing.
4. You can tailor the exact terms, amounts, and payment schedule to the needs of you and the sellers.

More than 40 percent of homeowners in the United States and Canada own their homes free and clear. These homeowners are prime candidates to carry back all or part of your financing. But sometimes you have to do more than ask. You have to make seller financing an essential condition of your purchase offer. Then itemize and explain the benefits. If you make your offer reasonable and responsive to the sellers' needs (remember win-win), you'll find that many can be persuaded to accept.

MISTAKE # **88**

Those were the fastest two years of our lives.

LESSON: *Beware of financing that falls due in less time than it takes to wear out a pair of shoes.*

"We never worried about it at the time," says Ruth Mehta. "We were sure interest rates would come down and our home would appreciate. We couldn't imagine any trouble refinancing. But interest rates didn't come down. Our home didn't appreciate. And those were the fastest two years of our lives."

When Ruth and her boyfriend, Sid, bought their home, they used a 70–20–10 financing plan. They borrowed 70 percent of their home's price from the bank, the sellers financed 20 percent, and Ruth and Sid put 10 percent down. This technique made it easier for the couple to qualify for bank financing, and it saved them money. Not only did the bank give them a lower interest rate, the sellers even agreed to accept an interest rate less than the bank was charging. But here's the catch: Ruth and Sid agreed to pay off the sellers' balloon loan within two years. And they couldn't do it.

Ruth and Sid had fallen into a common trap. Sometimes sellers who carry back financing will grant their buyers favorable terms for a year or two. After this short term, the seller financing falls due. The buyers then have to either come up with the money themselves or arrange new financing.

Risks of Short-Term Financing

Although in and of itself, there's nothing wrong with short-term financing, it does present risks that many homebuyers ignore. Ruth says, "We were so eager to stop throwing rent money down a rat hole, we were willing to accept almost any terms the seller wanted. Back then, two years seemed like a long time. With the prospects of home ownership so close, we shut our mind to the risks. As far as we were concerned, there weren't any. We told each other interest rates had to come down. We told each other our home would probably go up in value by at least 10 percent. Talking between ourselves was like talking in an echo chamber. Neither of us listened critically. We just repeated what the other one said."

Sid and Ruth's sleepless nights and anxious days demonstrate the risks of short-term financing. Over a period of one to three years, no one can accurately predict interest rates or home appreciation rates. Although it's often easy to tell yourself you'll be able to refinance, often experience has proven otherwise.

Minimize Those Risks

In fact, as many Southern Californians and New Englanders learned in the early 1990s, home prices can fall (in the short term) even when interest rates are heading downwards. Many of these homeowners couldn't refinance their short-term seller carrybacks. Although a new loan would have meant lower payments, their home values would no longer support the amount of mortgage they needed.

To prevent getting caught in refinance limbo, do the following:

1. Insist on a second mortgage loan term of at least five to seven years. Don't risk short-term future shock for the immediate joy of home ownership.

2. If you do agree to a shorter-term loan, include an escape clause that extends your due date if home values are depressed or if interest rates have risen.
3. As another safeguard, develop a plan to create value. Shorter-term finance plans work best when you buy a home at a bargain price. Then redecorate, remodel, or renovate to boost its loan value (or future selling price).

Special Note on Lease-Options

One of the most popular short-term seller finance plans is the lease-option. Most lease-option agreements call for buyers to execute their option to buy within one or two years. Usually, buyers use this time to save money for a down payment, strengthen their credit record, or pay off some of their other bills. For tens of thousands of former renters, the lease-option has been their ticket to home ownership.

If you choose a lease-option, you face the risk that interest rates will go up before you are able to buy. Just as with short-term mortgages, protect your position. Write a clause into your lease-option agreement that gives you more time to close if interest rates head north. Especially follow this advice if you're paying substantially more for your option and lease payments than you would be paying in straight rent for another similar home. Don't leave yourself wide open to the danger that you won't qualify for the financing you need to pay off the sellers as scheduled.

MISTAKE # **89**

I paid $2,500 down to lease-option a townhouse, then found out that no bank would give me a mortgage.

LESSON: *Not all properties or down payments meet lender rules and regulations.*

Like many tenants, Eric Coffey was tired of wasting money on rent. But financially, he wasn't quite ready to buy. Eric wanted time to pay off his car loan, cut down his credit card debt, and build up more savings for a down payment and cash reserves. So he decided to look for a seller who would give him a lease-option.

"After just three weeks of searching," recalls Eric, "I felt lucky because I found just what I wanted. It was a large end-unit townhouse with two bedrooms, two-and-a-half baths, fireplace, and a lower-level study. At $129,500 it was priced right, and the seller agreed to an 18-month lease-option. Our terms looked like this: I paid $2,500 to move in; my monthly rent payment was $1,500; and out of that $1,500, I received a *rent credit* of $500 a month toward the purchase price.

"I was quite pleased with this arrangement," Eric continues. "Everything went well for the first 16 months. Altogether, I had accumulated a total of $18,000 toward my down payment. I had the option payment of $2,500, rent credits of $9,000, and additional savings of $6,500. That was more than enough for a 10 percent down payment and closing costs. I had even paid down my bills like I planned."

Be Wary of Complexes or Buildings Populated by a High Percentage of Renters

"But my bank still turned down my loan," says Eric. "The loan representative said too many unit owners in the complex were renting out their townhouses instead of living there themselves. To further complicate matters, the bank would not count my rent credits as part of my down payment. I'd been doing business with this bank for eight years. I had never made a late payment on my car loan or bounced a check. Yet the lender wouldn't make the mortgage. I began to panic that I was going to lose the townhouse and all the money I'd put into it.

"In the end, we did get things worked out. The bank made a 70 percent loan, the seller carried back 20 percent, and I contributed my 10 percent. But it was really touch-and-go for a while."

When Eric entered into his lease-option agreement, he ignored the fact that many lenders won't give mortgages for condo, townhouse, or co-op complexes with high numbers of renters. Once a building or complex drops to less than 60 or 70 percent owner occupancy, lenders believe values in the complex may start to decline. When a property tips toward rentals, upkeep and maintenance often deteriorate.

"Funny Money" Down Payments

Eric also faced a second problem. Some lenders are suspect of "funny money" down payments. They prefer cash down from your bank account. If you want to use your car, a stamp collection, or rent credits as part of your down payment, the lender may feel you and the sellers are manipulating the numbers. In the past, many lease-option sellers have simply overpriced the homes they were selling. In exchange, they give buyers a large rent credit so it appears that they're building equity—at least on paper. But in fact the rent credit is just whittling down the price to where it should have been to begin with.

Say you agree to pay $330,000 for a condo (or house) that's actually valued at $300,000 (see Chapter 4). Over two years you build up $11,000 in rent credits that you want to count toward a down payment. From the lender's viewpoint, those rent credits are funny money. Even after counting them against your purchase price, you'll still owe more than the home's worth. So the lender says no deal. You've got to come up with a lot more real cash for your down payment.

To solve both these problems, first avoid condo, co-op, or townhouse developments that are close to tipping toward renters. (This is good advice regardless of whether you're using a lease-option.) Second, make sure your option terms can pass a lender's sniff test. If your agreement doesn't smell right, the lender probably won't go for it. The lender will try to make sure your rent levels, rent credits, and purchase price make sense in terms of the market. A lender doesn't want to make an 80 or 90 percent loan-to-value ratio loan that actually turns out to be a 95 or 100 percent loan.

MISTAKE # **90**

We paid too much for our mortgage.

LESSON: *Learn the tricks of the trade.*

Until several years back, some real estate agents routinely received kickbacks from mortgage lenders. Although RESPA (the Real Estate Settlement and Procedures Act) supposedly outlawed this practice, it was common in many cities throughout the United States for lenders to pay agents under-the-table referral fees. In fact, unethical agents even *demanded* lenders pay them kickbacks for bringing in loan customers.

Beth and Ted Cippolla were one couple who fell victim to such a deception. "We trusted him," says Beth. "He told us we didn't need to waste time calling a dozen lenders because he had a special arrangement with a mortgage company who would give his buyers the best mortgage terms possible. He had a special arrangement, all right. But the arrangement wasn't to get us the best deal. It was to get Harold [their agent] a free trip to Hawaii. He cost us an extra $900 in closing costs and one-quarter percent on our mortgage interest rate."

In an effort to stamp out abuses like those the Cippollas suffered, HUD has cracked down on illegal kickbacks and referral fees. In several well-publicized court cases, HUD has gone after offenders with civil fines and criminal prosecutions. In addition, HUD has strengthened its rules and regulations. "Under current law," says HUD division director David Williamson, "if agents aren't providing a bona fide financial service, they aren't entitled to referral fees, extra compensation, or anything else of value."

So, become a savvy borrower. Don't accept your real estate agent's referrals without first checking the rates, terms, and qualifying standards of other lenders. HUD's rules can work well only if you think for yourself. Count on your real estate agent to advise and suggest. But, it's up to you to choose. (To easily compare loan rates and terms, go to www.hsh.com, www.interest.com, www.mortgagequotes.com, or www.iown.com.)

Loan Originators Can Increase Your Costs

In today's competitive mortgage market, most mortgage originators (loan representatives) work on commission. They want to find you a loan. Otherwise, they don't get paid.

The bad news is that loan originators earn higher commissions when they place you into higher-cost loan products. If your loan officer says, "The best I can do is a rate of 6.75 percent and two points," don't take that as a final quote. Just like a car salesperson (or any other type of salesperson), the loan officer may be testing your reaction.

If you accept, great. If you balk, the loan officer can say, "Oh, wait a minute, I've just thought of something else. Maybe I can get the lender to shave a point off those origination fees. They owe me a favor."

Protect Yourself

To protect yourself against paying too much, ask to see the loan officer's rate sheet. The rate sheet shows the wholesale cost of the loans. The bigger the spread between the wholesale rate and the interest rate and fees you pay, the larger the loan officer's commission. In fact, ask the loan officer straight out, "What's the amount of your commission on this loan?" If it's $4,000, you know that more than likely you've been placed into a high-cost loan. If the commission is $400, there is far less chance you're being taken for a ride. (Typical commissions run about 1 to 1.5 percent of the amount you borrow.)

Of course, neither the wholesale-retail spread nor the amount of the loan officer's commission—taken together or separately—provides the entire picture as to whether you are getting the best possible loan for your needs and financial qualifications. But it is one important piece of the puzzle. Don't passively accept a loan originator's quotes. Investigate and negotiate.

Credit Blemishes

Traditionally, mortgage lenders have classified borrowers into the credit categories of A, B, C, and D. (Today, though, most lenders rely on credit scores. Yet, the principles remain the same.) The lower your grade (score), the more you must pay for a mortgage. But just like in school, the grade (score) you receive depends on who's doing the grading. Even with credit blemishes, one mortgage lender might give you an "A–", another might downgrade you to a B or even C status—and, correspondingly, persuade you to pay a higher interest rate and fees. (At the same time, of course, the loan rep earns a higher sales commission.)

If you get downgraded because of credit blemishes, don't meekly accept that verdict. Ask why. Is the loan rep bamboozling you so he or she can make more money? Or do you really deserve the downgrade? Also, learn how long it will take—or what you can do—to reach "A" status. Maybe you should defer buying until you can qualify at lower rates and costs.

To give you an idea of how credit scores affect loan pricing, go to my-fico.com. At the time of this writing, the figures were:

- 720–850 / 6.0%
- 700–719 / 6.13%
- 675–699 / 6.66%
- 620–674 / 7.81%
- 560–619 / 8.53%
- 500–559 / 9.29%

Remember, though, these figures represented averages. When you show high cash reserves, low qualifying ratios, higher down payment, or persuasive compensating factors, you can negotiate a rate lower than the averages (at the time you're mortgage shopping).

Subprime (Predatory) Lenders

Beware of those lenders who prey on people whose credit reports show credit stains such as foreclosures, repossessions, writeoffs, multiple lates, and bankruptcy. Such lenders frequently advertise "Bad credit, no problem." More often than not, these lenders charge high fees, high interest, and high prepayment penalties. When their borrowers miss a payment or two, they prefer to foreclose quickly rather than attempt a loan workout (as is the case with reputable lenders).

If you thoroughly shop the market of reputable lenders and can't obtain approval, do not turn to a predatory lender. Instead, try to arrange seller financing or delay buying for a year or so until you shape up your financial fitness. In recent years, a number of high profile predatory lenders have suffered fines running into the tens (or even hundreds) of millions of dollars for their unethical and illegal lending practices. Do not become prey for these predators.

Also, talk with several mortgage companies. If your blemishes consist of nothing more than a few late payments, you can probably find an A-grade mortgage. Even when you've suffered more serious setbacks, it's sometimes possible to provide an excuse that will move you into an A category (see Mistake #93).

Loan originators earn higher commissions if they persuade you to accept higher fees and interest rates. If your credit is severely blemished (low credit score), you may face little choice. You may have to pay more for your loan than A borrowers (but still subject to negotiation). Nevertheless, don't naively accept the higher rates. Learn the specific reasons and then seek second, third, fourth, or even fifth opinions. One mortgage broker told me that as many as 40 percent of "B" and "C" borrowers could have been qualified with an "A" or an "A–" grade.

Discriminatory Pricing versus Negotiating Skills

Back in Chapter 2 (Mistake #16), we talked about two types of mortgage discrimination: (1) stereotypical ("We don't make loans to _____. They're bad risks."), and (2) discrimination through "neutral" rules or practices that adversely impact some identifiable groups of borrowers (e.g., African Americans, Hispanics, immigrants, women, singles, and single-parent families).

As company policy, lenders have nearly eliminated stereotypical turndowns. However, studies do indicate that some borrowers pay more for their mortgages than other borrowers—even when their credit records and incomes are fairly similar. As it turns out, the borrowers who pay more are the borrowers most likely to fall into some legally protected category. Does this suggest that lenders are engaged in illegal discriminatory pricing? Not necessarily.

It does suggest, though, that these borrowers fail to negotiate their interest rates and loan fees. When the loan rep says, "Gee, this is the best I can do," these borrowers are more likely to accept the loan on the terms offered. They don't realize that they should respond with their own negotiating gambit, "Really, that's the best you can do? Well, Providence Mortgage quoted us a better deal. Sorry, we're just wasting our time here." Or, "We found rates less than that on the Internet. You're not trying to put one over on us, are you?"

No matter who you are, many loan originators will charge you higher interest and fees—if you let them. If you fear the lending process, fail to negotiate aggressively, or are uneducated about mortgage loan practices, you are prime game—regardless of your race, sex, ethnicity, nationality, or family status.

To protect yourself, assert yourself (politely, of course). For when some loan reps sense a vulnerable and powerless prey, they go for the kill.

30-Year Loans versus 15-Year Loans

Mortgage lenders joke among themselves about the many telephone calls they receive where the caller asks, "What's your best rate?" Nine times out of 10, the caller really means, "What's your best rate on a 30-year, fixed-rate mortgage?" Yet, the 30-year, fixed-rate mortgage is nearly always the most expensive loan over the short run—and it's more expensive than the 15-year, fixed-rate loan over both the short run and the long run. Consider the comparisons on a $200,000 loan shown in Table 8.1. The original monthly payments on a 30-year loan cost less than the payments on a 15-year loan. But that's where the advantage ends. After five years you will still owe $187,751 for the 30-year loan (compared to a $152,729 balance on the 15-year loan). And after your first 10 years of ownership, you'll owe $82,432 more on your 30-year loan as compared to the 15-year loan ($170,602 − $88,170 = $82,432). And after 15 years, your 15-year mortgage will be paid off, but you'll still owe $146,591 on your 30-year loan. In total, the 30-year loan will cost you not only a much slower payoff, but also $158,318 in additional interest expense.

Why do borrowers choose the higher-cost 30-year loan? The answer is the lower monthly payments for the first 15 years. The original lower payment helps borrowers qualify for a larger mortgage. Borrowers also

Table 8.1	**Comparison of 30-Year and 15-Year Fixed-Rate Outstanding Loan Balances***		
	30 Year Fixed-Rate @ 6.75%	_15-Year Fixed-Rate @ 6.25%_	_Difference_
Monthly Payment	$1,297	$1,715	$ −418
Balance @ 5 yrs	187,751	152,729	35,022
Balance @ 10 yrs	170,602	88,170	82,432
Balance @ 15 yrs	146,591	00	146,591
Balance @ 20 yrs	112,972	00	112,972
Balance @ 30 yrs	00	00	00
Total Interest Paid	266,990	108,672	158,318

*Original loan at $200,000

say they don't want to pay down their loan quickly. They would rather invest their extra money. Or they say, just for safety, we want the 30-year loan's lower payments, but we plan to go ahead and make larger payments so we can get rid of this debt faster.

Only you can judge whether any or all of the above reasons may influence your choice of loans. But before you decide, compare the 15-year versus 30-year numbers. Experience proves that for many homebuyers, the 30-year loan proves more costly.

Prepayment Penalties

Some borrowers choose the higher-cost 30-year mortgage with the idea of refinancing into a 15-year loan later when rates drop or when their income goes up. If you adopt this strategy, be careful. Some lenders (especially, but not exclusively, in the subprime market) now insert prepayment penalties into their mortgage contracts. If you pay off your loan early (say, within the first three to five years), the lender may stick you with a $2,000 to $4,000 penalty (or more).

Loans with prepayment penalties aren't necessarily bad because these loans are originated at slightly lower interest rates. For instance, you might be offered a 30-year, fixed-rate loan (no penalty) at 6.5 percent, but with a prepayment penalty, the rate drops to 6.25 percent.

Unfortunately, some loan reps don't fully explain these choices, nor do they automatically give you the interest rate break that loans with prepayment penalties warrant. Once again, a word to the wise: Ask your loan rep to advise you fully concerning the features and costs of the mortgages that you are evaluating. If your loan includes a prepayment penalty, make sure you get a discounted interest rate.

Points versus Interest Rates

Nearly all lenders trade off points (fees paid at the time the mortgage money is loaned) and interest rates. Say you're looking at the choices shown in Table 8.2.

The question is, "Which of these choices is the lowest cost?" The answer: It all depends on how long you keep your mortgage. If you keep your loan for more than three years (36 months), the 6.75 percent/ 3 point loan will save you the most money. Although you must pay an ad-

Table 8.2 **Illustration of Different Payback Calculations***

$100,000 Mortgage at 30 years

Interest Rate	Points/Amount	Monthly Payment	Months to Break Even
1. 8.0	0/0	$733	00
2. 7.75	1/$1,000	$716	58 months
3. 7.5	1.5/$1,500	$699	44 months
4. 7.25	2.0/$2,000	$682	39 months
5. 6.75	3.0/$3,000	$648	35 months

*These figures represent hypothetical comparisons. In practice, they vary among lenders, loan products, and mortgage market conditions.

ditional $3,000 at closing to get this lower rate, this loan will save you $85 a month over the 8.0 percent/0 points loan. In comparison to the 8.0 percent mortgage, you'll earn your $3,000 in points in just over 35 months ($3,000 ÷ $85 = 35.29). After that, it's all gain.

The above figures are for purposes of illustration only; the actual trade-offs you see will differ from these. Yet, this type of calculation is a good method (though not precisely accurate) to select the lowest loan *based upon your expected circumstances.*

A trustworthy and competent loan rep will go over interest rate/points trade-offs with you to figure out which look best for you. A greedy loan rep will steer you into the interest rate/point combination that yields the largest sales commission. Don't ask your loan rep, "Which one is best?" Instead, ask him or her to work through the numbers with you. Then, after the explanation, you decide.

Closing Costs and Fees

At the time you apply for a loan, your lender will provide a "good faith" estimate of the closing costs and fees that will be charged at settlement. In addition to points (discussed above), closing costs may include charges for an appraisal, credit report, prorated taxes, mortgage application, flood insurance, title insurance, mortgage insurance, homeowners' insurance, garbage fees, and numerous other expenses that can total in the thousands of dollars.

The question is, how can you reduce the amount of these costs that you have to pay? First, before you apply for a loan, get some idea of the closing costs that buyers typically pay. Then, in your home purchase negotiations, shift some of these costs to the sellers (or at least keep this tactic in mind). Second, in some markets and for some loan products, lenders differ greatly in the costs they levy against buyers. When shopping lenders, compare costs and fees as well as points and interest rates. Third, if the closing costs seem high (or even if they don't), ask the lender to reduce or eliminate them. It is perfectly reasonable to question and negotiate a lender's costs and fees.

Watch Out for Bait and Switch

Above, I placed "good faith" in quotation marks. That's because some lenders will quote you one amount for costs, fees, points, and interest rate. Then, after they get you deep into the loan process, they will "discover" a credit blemish or some other "defect" in your application. "Sorry," such a lender might say, "you'll have to pay more because ..." At that point, don't give in without a fight. You may be targeted for the old bait and switch sales tactic. If you do suspect this type of unethical (and perhaps illegal) behavior by the lender, tell them to honor their commitment or you will file a complaint with the state licensing board or the Federal Trade Commission (FTC). Also, you could switch lenders and demand that the offending lender forward your file to the new lender. That way, your new approval process won't start over from square one.

Bad Faith Lock-Ins

Some unethical lenders also play tricks with lock-ins. At the time you apply for a loan, the lender may (for a fee) lock you in to an interest rate of 6.25 percent for say, 45 days. Then, if market interest rates head up, the lender may "discover" problems in your application that delay settlement beyond the 45 days. "Sorry," the lender says, "rates have increased, and we have to bump you up to 6.75 percent."

If you believe that the lender has purposely dragged its feet to push you into a higher rate, don't accept it. Complain. Demand. Threaten to go to the regulators. More than likely you'll get the original rate restored.

False Float-Downs

Some lenders will lock in your maximum mortgage interest rate, yet will also give you a float-down if rates fall between the time you apply and the date your loan closes. "Good news," your loan representative tells you, "rates have fallen and we can now close your loan at 7.75 percent instead of 8.0 percent. You're going to save $17.35 a month."

Yes, that's good news. But it may not reflect the full market drop in rates. If market rates really sit at 7.5 percent, by fooling you into accepting 7.75 percent, your loan representative will pocket a nice-sized "overage" commission. Even with float-downs, take care. Make sure you receive the full float-down that you are entitled to.

"Hot" Products/"Hot" Lenders

In highly competitive mortgage markets, mortgage costs such as points, rates, and closing expenses may not vary much among lenders. On occasion, though, some lenders decide to "buy market share" or push a "hot" loan product to rebalance its portfolio of mortgage products. In these cases, if you're in the right place at the right time, you could score a real bargain loan.

Keep your eyes open to various alternatives. I know borrowers who have picked up super-priced ARMs even though they had mentally committed to a fixed-rate product. In other words, mortgage shopping can be compared to going to a restaurant with your appetite set on sirloin steak. Then you learn the lobster-prime rib combo is on special at $17.50. In that situation, why pay $19.50 for sirloin?

APRs and ARMs

When you compare the costs of mortgage loans, you will see the term APR (annual percentage rate). To comply with government truth-in-lending laws, mortgage interest-rate advertising must include this figure. The APR always exceeds the stated interest rate because it supposedly accounts for your total cost of borrowing (interest, fees, points, prepaids, and certain other expenses). Presumably, by comparing APRs among various loan products and lenders, you will be able to select the lowest-cost loan.

Unfortunately, life is not so simple. In the first place, APRs that apply to ARMs make no sense. Under the law, they are calculated as if the ARM interest rate will not change during the life of the loan (except for the scheduled boost up from the teaser rate to the initial contract rate).

Yet, the very idea of an *adjustable* rate mortgage is that the interest rate will change. So, APRs for adjustable-rate mortgages give us mathematically precise, yet irrelevant, figures. True APRs for ARMs cannot be calculated in advance.

In its effort to force lenders to tell the truth about the costs of their mortgage loans, the government misleads borrowers. When comparing ARMs, you cannot rely on the stated APRs. You may find a COFI (Cost of funds index) ARM with an APR of 5.675 percent and a one-year treasury ARM at an APR of 7.25 percent. But since no one knows how these respective ARM indexes will change over time, no one can accurately predict which one represents the lowest-cost loan.

Fixed-Rate APRs

Although it might appear that the APR would apply accurately to fixed-rate mortgages, that is true only in the unlikely event you pay off the loan balance precisely according to schedule over the full life of the loan. If you pay ahead of (or behind) schedule, your actual APR will increase. Similarly, if you sell your house or refinance your mortgage, your actual APR will exceed the APR figure the government requires lenders to calculate.

In mandating APR disclosures, the government addressed a real need: help consumers compare the total costs of mortgage loans. In practice, look beyond the APR. To obtain the best loan at the lowest cost, compare loan products according to your personal financial situation, your tolerance for risk, and the expected period over which you plan to hold your loan.

Summing Up: Loan Costs and Possibilities

To obtain the best loan at the lowest cost, you can't "dial for dollars" and ask lenders, "What's your best rate?" Instead, keep an eye out for the ways that unscrupulous (or inexperienced) loan reps can lead you into paying more than you should. Weigh the pros and cons of a variety of loan types. Negotiate assertively. Most important, work with a trustworthy loan rep who demonstrates savvy, knowledge, competence, patience, and concern. A top loan rep operates with the philosophy, "You'll never come in second by putting the customers first."

A top real estate agent does far more than show houses. Likewise, a top loan rep does far more than give rate quotes and process applications. Put a top loan rep on your side and you'll get the loan that's right for you. (To identify a top loan rep, see the "upfront mortgage broker" pledge at www.mortgageprofessor.com or www.loan-wolf.com. *Every* homebuyer should check these web sites—*before* they apply for a mortgage. I recommend these sites.)

MISTAKE # **91**

Our lender canceled our loan approval because I went into labor early and had to take temporary leave from work.

LESSON: *Don't change your loan status before you close your mortgage. Your lender may revoke your approval.*

Kristi Colburn and her husband, Pat, did all the right things to prepare for buying their home. They saved. They didn't run up large debts. They kept their credit record spotless. They both had worked steadily since graduating from college seven years earlier. And before they started their home search, they received preapproval (not merely a prequalification) of their loan application. (A prequalification tells you how much house you can probably afford according to the lender's standards. With a preapproval, the lender okays your loan subject to underwriter verifications.)

"Everything was going great," says Kristi. "We found a terrific house less than 15 minutes from work. Our offer was accepted and we quickly went into escrow. After years of waiting and months of searching, we were just two weeks from becoming homeowners. Our loan representative told us from now until closing would be smooth sailing. Just paperwork formalities—nothing to be concerned about.

"Instead of smooth sailing, though, during the next two weeks, our sailing ship lost its wind and we hit choppy seas," recalls Kristi. "Eight months along in my pregnancy, I started to feel severe labor pains. It became too difficult for me to work, so I took disability leave. Ten days later I delivered our daughter Jessy."

Gain a Daughter, But Don't Stop Work

"But at the same time we gained a daughter, we lost our loan. The day after I got home from the hospital, the loan representative called and said I needed to go back to my job immediately or the underwriter would withdraw the commitment. The mortgage approval required two incomes, he said. Of course, we knew that and I did intend to return to work—but not for at least two or three months. The loan representative replied that wasn't good enough. He said I had to go back now.

"In trying to find a satisfactory solution, over the next six weeks we went through sheer agony. Our apartment lease expired and we had to move in with Pat's parents. My mom agreed to cosign our note. My employer assured the lender my job was waiting for me anytime I was ready to end my maternity leave. We increased our down payment to 20 percent. The lender switched us from the fixed-rate loan we wanted to an ARM.

"Each time we would make one of these concessions or accept a new demand, the loan representative would reschedule our closing date. Then he would call and cancel until we agreed to something else. It was ridiculous.

"But you won't believe what happened next," Kristi added. "After meeting all the lender's additional requirements and suffering through three cancellations and reschedulings, the loan representative informed us the loan underwriter once again had changed her decision. If we wanted the loan, I would still have to go back to work immediately, receive a paycheck, and then show the lender my paystub.

"At that point, we were frustrated and exhausted. There was nothing we could do. We needed a home and weren't about to start looking for another apartment to rent. I had no choice. I went back to work, got my paystub, and, finally, escrow closed."

Your first reaction to Kristi's ordeal might be that the lender discriminated against Kristi because of her pregnancy and the birth of her daughter. But no matter how absurdly the lender handled Kristi and Pat Colburn's loan processing, it acted within its rights. Whenever a mortgage applicant changes his or her loan status prior to closing, the lender can revoke its loan approval. Since, technically, Kristi's job income had stopped, the lender wasn't required to count it. Without the income, the Colburns no longer qualified.

Many Factors Affect Loan Status

In Kristi's case, her loss of income (even if temporary) triggered the change in the Colburns' loan status. However, all the factors a lender considers in its loan decision will contribute to your loan status:

- Income
- Bills, debts, and expenses
- Length of employment (e.g., don't change jobs without the lender's okay)
- Job security
- Credit score
- Credit record
- Source of downpayment
- Cash reserves
- Net worth
- Type of loan, interest rate, amount of your scheduled payments including property taxes, homeowners' insurance, and mortgage insurance (if any)

After learning that their mortgage had been approved, Phil and Sue Grubbs went out and charged $6,000 of new furniture for their home. When the lender learned of these additional bills through a last-minute credit reverification, the Grubbs lost their mortgage approval. Their additional bills knocked them out of qualifying. Jack Reeves was preapproved for his home loan and then accepted a better job at higher pay. Thinking this was good news, Jack told his loan representative. The loan representative revoked Jack's preapproved commitment. The lender thought new jobs were too insecure. "Come back after a year," the loan officer told Jack.

When it comes to approving and closing loans, lenders show a split personality. Sometimes they will lean over backward to bend the rules to get a borrower qualified. On other occasions they act as if they've locked their common sense in one of their money vaults. So a word to the wise: After you've applied for a loan, don't do anything that might adversely affect your loan status. If you do, your lender may give you the same kind of hassle (or rejection) that hit the Colburns, the Grubbses, and the Reeveses.

Loan Approval versus Loan Commitment

When a loan representative processes your application data through an automated underwriting system, it may signal "approval." But that's not the end of the story. Your loan file will next move to a real live loan underwriter who critically examines the paperwork to make sure every verification and explanation is in order. The automated systems never make the actual loan commitment.

For example, say the system shows you have a 3-bureau average credit score of 730. Thus, it signals approval. But the live loan underwriter notices that your credit record shows a credit card writeoff of $9,346 six years ago. The underwriter may want you to clear that debt before she will *commit* the lender to the loan. When you talk with the loan representative, probe him to learn whether any aspects of your credit profile will likely raise questions from the underwriter.

Better for you to anticipate problems and plan accordingly than to get a nasty surprise six days before your scheduled closing. Never believe that a loan representative's "approval" actually commits the lender to making the loan. It doesn't.

MISTAKE # **92**

My loan fell through because of poor credit. But it wasn't *my* credit that was bad.

LESSON: *Get your credit record and finances in shape before you begin to shop for your home.*

Gwen Davis knew she had excellent credit and had never made a late payment in her life. So she didn't bother reviewing her credit report before she began shopping for a home. As Gwen now realizes, that shortcut proved to be a mistake. It cost her the home she wanted.

"I couldn't believe it," says Gwen. "I was in shock. The loan officer told me the credit report showed I was two months behind on my car loan and that my Visa card had been canceled for nonpayment. 'I don't even have a car loan,' I told him. 'I can show you the title to my car.'"

"The loan officer sympathized but said his hands were tied. If the credit report erred, it would be up to me to straighten it out. Until I could show him a clean record, my application would not be considered.

"My next step," Gwen continued, "was to try to get to the bottom of this. I went to the credit bureau and got a copy of my credit report. Sure enough, the black marks were there for all the world to see. But as I knew, they didn't belong in my file. What had happened was the credit bureau had mingled my record with the record of Gail Davis—my ex-husband's new wife." (As an aside: The credit bureau, Experian, formerly did business under the name TRW. In the lending trade, loan officers often said TRW stood for "The Report's Wrong.")

Beware: Credit Bureaucracy at Work

"At this point, my education concerning the credit bureaucracy was just beginning. I soon learned that to discover a problem is one thing. To fix it is something else. To get those black marks off my record required endless phone calls, a dozen letters, and threats from my attorney. To make matters worse, Gail didn't lift a finger to help. She wasn't eager to see delinquent accounts reappear in her file. All told, it took four months to clear my name. By then, the sellers had already sold their home to other buyers. I really wanted that house, too."

You can prevent Gwen's mistake by contacting your local credit bureau or all of the national credit repositories (Experian, TransUnion, and Equifax). Ask them to provide you with a copy of your credit report. (They may charge a fee.) Then examine the report carefully. If you discover bad credit that doesn't belong to you, tell the credit bureau. Immediately do what's necessary to get it removed. As Gwen Davis found out, that process can sometimes take months.

Make Your Best First Impression

If you find that your credit record accurately shows late payments or other blemishes, these "derogatories" may stop many lenders from approving you for a loan. At a minimum, make sure all your installment accounts are current. Should your record reveal outstanding past-due debts, write-offs, judgments, or tax liens, many lenders will require you to pay them. Most mortgage lenders will not lend money to someone who has not paid legally enforceable obligations (i.e., valid unpaid debts that remain within the applicable statute of limitations). This practice even extends to disputed claims. The lender won't take your word. By whatever means you can, clear these from your record. You will have to negotiate, litigate, or otherwise satisfy the claims. (Sometimes lenders do make exceptions for small amounts, unpaid bills or write-offs that go back more than four or five years, or debts for which the statute of limitations has expired.)

To guard against a turndown, review your credit record, get your finances in the best shape you can, and search for a lender and loan product that matches your situation. To gain approval for home financing, weigh your strengths and weaknesses. Then, before you apply, try to identify the lenders whose qualifying criteria best fit your borrower profile. Prepare to make your best first impression.

MISTAKE # **93**

Our lender turned down our loan application.

LESSON: *Prepare, prepare, prepare.*

"The lender did not approve our loan application. What can we do?" Each year, the number of mortgage turndowns runs into the hundreds of thousands. Sadly, most of these rejections need not have occurred. In a majority of cases, the people who were turned down hadn't done their homework.

Preparation Counts

Many potential homebuyers think they either qualify or don't qualify for financing, as if this were the result of some type of genetic determinism.

They go to a lender, fill out the application forms, then hope for the best. (Of course, a top loan rep would never permit this foolish practice, but most people who are turned down have not sought the counsel of a skilled loan originator. More than likely, they have dealt with a "paper processor.")

Before you apply for a mortgage, evaluate four areas of importance: (1) capacity, (2) collateral, (3) credit, and (4) compensating factors.

Capacity

Nearly every mortgage lender judges whether you bring in enough income to cover your monthly bills, living expenses, and housing costs-to-be (mortgage payments, homeowners' insurance, property taxes, homeowner association fees). *In general,* lenders say your total housing costs shouldn't run any more than 28 percent of your income; your housing costs plus other monthly payments shouldn't exceed 36 percent of your monthly income. These percentages are called qualifying ratios.

However, those ratios are not etched in stone. That's why you need a top loan rep. (Also see Chapter 11.) He or she will go over all of your numbers *prior* to your application. Then he or she will help you arrange your numbers in such a way that loan approval (for the loan program selected) is substantially assured. For example:

1. *Qualifying ratios.* Although 28/36 qualifying ratios are traditional, many automated underwriting programs approve loans with ratios as high as 44/44. FHA and VA frequently approve borrowers with ratios of 33/43—or higher. First-time buyer programs, too, permit high ratios.
2. *Installment debt.* You may make monthly payments on credit-card accounts, car loans, student loans, and maybe alimony or child support. Lenders and loan programs count these debts differently. In addition, you may be able to pay off or consolidate some accounts. These efforts will improve your qualifying ratios. (For more on this topic, see Chapter 11.)
3. *Income.* Even the amount of income you bring in may not prove as simple to count as you think. What if you're self-employed, a commissioned sales rep, or expecting a big raise? What about

part-time work, overtime, or a second job? What if you receive alimony or child support? Can you bring in the income of a co-borrower? Do you expect to houseshare or bring in rental income from tenants? How should your spouse's income be figured?

Although it is easy to fill in the numbers on a form to see if you "qualify," it takes skill, knowledge, and experience to "arrange" your numbers in their best light. Then once you've been made to look as good as you can, a top loan representative can search for the mortgage program (or lender) that will best fit your borrower profile.

Cash Reserves

Many loan programs require cash reserves. Others do not. Nevertheless, in the black box calculations of credit scores and automated underwriting, the greater your cash on hand after closing, the better you look. If it looks like you're running short, sell a car, hold a garage sale, or otherwise increase the amount of cash in your bank account. Cash reserves dampen the lenders concern that a slight financial disturbance will create a storm of problems for you.

Collateral

Sometimes, lenders who want to reject an otherwise creditworthy borrower will use a "lowball" appraisal. To guard against this problem, (1) verify the features and selling prices of a large number of comparable sales, and (2) provide the lender's appraiser with the comp sales data that you (or your real estate agent) have discovered. (See Chapter 4.)

Naturally, too, lenders prefer large down payments (i.e., low loan-to-value ratios) as opposed to low down payments (i.e., high loan-to-value ratios). Should your loan approval look "iffy," try to raise more cash for your down payment. If you're planning to increase the home's value through improvements, tell the lender.

Lenders, too, judge the condition and features of a property. Some lenders may avoid properties that aren't connected to a sewer, have a flat roof, are wired with aluminum writing, include excessive land, or manifest some other out-of-the-ordinary characteristic (such as, perhaps, a retail store on first level with living quarters above).

In the total scheme of things, lenders reject few loans for reasons of inadequate collateral. Even so, do what you can to convince the lender that your property offers solid value.

Credit Record/Credit Score

Automated underwriting typically places the most emphasis on your credit score, not your total record of payments (or nonpayment). If some old writeoffs or judgments show up in your credit records, you can still achieve reasonably high credit scores. (Remember, for most mortgage loans, lenders will run a tri-merged credit report that shows a credit score that's based on your credit records from each of the three major credit repositories.)

However, as noted previously, if your credit record displays some stain or blemish, the loan underwriter who personally reviews your total application file might: (1) ask you for more explanatory information, (2) require you to clear the blemish (such as paying off an old debt), or (3) refuse to issue a commitment. In recent years, the press has greatly publicized the issue of credit scores. But, your credit record still counts.

Naturally, too, your credit record influences your credit score (but recency counts far more than events of four or five years back). Obtain copies of your credit reports long before you plan to apply for a mortgage. Get adverse errors corrected. As to old unpaid bills, check your state's statute of limitations. *Beware: if you start making payments on an old bill, it will not only restart the running date for the statue of limitations, but it also will probably pull down your credit score.*

Before you take any action, talk frankly with a loan pro (and perhaps a good consumer rights attorney). Sometimes you're better off just to let an old debt sit there and fade away. (I'm talking legally and financially, not morally.)

For the latest developments on credit scoring and other credit issues, go to www.creditscoring.com, www.creditaccuracy.com, and ftc.gov. To buy a copy of your scores, see www.myfico.com. Congress has recently passed a law that entitles all consumers to a free copy of their credit reports each year (not free credit scores).

Compensating Factors

Some lenders look for high FICO scores. Others, target borrowers with lower scores. In that case, compensating factors can play a role in the mortgage approval process. What is a compensating factor? It is any evidence that you can provide to support your willingness and ability to make your mortgage payments on time. Here are some examples:

- Low family living expenses
- Energy efficient house
- Low or no costs of commuting
- High net worth (for your age and income)
- Regular pattern of savings
- Low use of credit
- Upward career path
- Rent payments equal to or exceeding your mortgage payments-to-be
- Sterling credit history
- Large cash reserves (or liquid assets)

Also, provide evidence to offset negatives such as write-offs, bankruptcy, foreclosure, or judgments. Lenders forgive isolated instances of trouble—if you convince them that the hardship resulted from some adversity of life such as disability, unemployment, divorce, a spendthrift ex-spouse, real estate market collapse (as happened in Texas, Southern California, and New England), or large, out-of-the-ordinary medical expenses. FHA and VA, especially, have shown forbearance for past instances of *explained* financial difficulties.

Beware of Stacking Risk Factors

Although many lenders look beyond the traditional qualifying rules, they still proceed cautiously when you stack up too many risk factors (e.g., low down payment, credit blemishes, short time on job, high qualifying ratios, no cash reserves, large family with one breadwinner, high installment debt, large number of open credit accounts, payment shock). If your finances push the limit in more than a few risk areas, get together with a homebuyer counselor or loan rep. Then make positive changes wherever possible. Mortgage lenders want to make loans. But they also want to get their money back according to schedule and without hassle.

Lenders also like consistency. They like a pattern of borrower behavior that shows financial responsibility. They want to see long-term prudent borrowing and repayment. Don't wait until the last minute to shape up your financial profile. The longer you show a pattern of responsibility, the better you will look to a mortgage lender.

Summing Up: Qualifying Depends on You

Follow the lessons described in this chapter and work with a trustworthy and skilled loan representative—an upfront mortgage broker. As with most other achievements, a successful loan application requires forethought and planning. Learn the rules. Then learn how to make the rules work for you. Explore many loan possibilities. Provide strong documentation for compensating factors and explanations of "derogs." You'll get the loan you need. (For more on possibility analysis, see Chapter 11. For more extensive suggestions, read my book, *106 Mortgage Secrets All Homebuyers Must Learn—But Lenders Don't Tell*, 2003 [Wiley].)

CHAPTER 9

Become a Satisfied Homeowner

You're about to enjoy the wealth-building and personally enriching experience of home ownership. But before you buy, check these issues. Are you confident this is the home for you? Or are you being pushed into it by others? Do your advisors understand your priorities and possibilities? Are they influencing you according to their own interests and biases?

Review the property's condition and the inspection report. Have you protected yourself against after-closing surprises and unanticipated expenses? Have your real estate agent and mortgage loan representative pulled together all agreements, documents, and verifications that are necessary to effect a smooth closing.

In this chapter we look at some of the common mistakes that homebuyers make as they move into the final stages of homebuying and the early stages of home ownership. Attend to these details and you can count on a homebuying experience that will reward you for years to come.

MISTAKE # **94**

Our friends told us we were getting a great deal.

LESSON: Critically evaluate the advice of friends, relatives, realty agents, and lawyers.

After finding the home he wanted, Steve Carver invited several friends to take a look at the house he had selected. "This house is great," they told him. "You're really getting a good buy." These words of encouragement were exactly what Steve wanted to hear. Although Steve had asked his friends what they thought, he didn't really want their honest opinion. More than anything, he wanted support for the decision he had already made.

Steve had fallen in love with the home's rear deck and canyon views. He didn't want to hear about the small size of the home's bedrooms, its lack of closet and storage space, or the home's needed repairs, which included an aging and leaky roof. Sensing Steve's enthusiasm for the house, his friends steered clear of giving him the advice he really needed. Steve then used the opinions they did offer to calm his anxieties about the home's problems.

Steve bought the house, but the high costs of repairs and cramped living conditions soon dampened his enchantment with his deck and canyon views. Steve admitted that he had made a mistake. Along with being captivated by the home's desirable features, Steve had misinterpreted and misused the advice he had sought.

Like Steve, when you buy a home you'll turn to advice from friends, relatives, your realty agent, and maybe a lawyer. But before you interpret and rely on this advice, answer the following questions.

Advice or Approval?

Do you really want critical counsel? Or do you want someone who agrees with you? There's an old saying among consultants that their clients often want to use advice like a drunk uses a lamppost—for support, not illumination. If support is what you want, your friends will probably oblige. But if that's the case, make sure you recognize this advice for what it is.

Knowledge or Ignorance?

Do those you ask for advice possess the information, experience, and expertise necessary to advise you intelligently? Unless your friends or relatives have recently been shopping for a home in the same neighborhood where you've been looking, they can't tell you whether you're getting a good buy. If your lawyer sister hasn't seen a real estate contract since her Real Property I course in law school, chances are she's not the one who should review your purchase agreement.

You may work with one of the best real estate agents in the city. But if your home tour takes you into neighborhoods or communities where your agent can't find her way without studying a map, it's time to bring in an agent who's more familiar with the area. Whether friend, relative, lawyer, or sales agent, just because someone offers an opinion, it doesn't mean he or she actually knows enough to provide the counsel you need.

Your Preferences or Theirs?

Do your advisors understand your needs and goals? Or are they applying their own preferences or standards? Here's an area where nearly everyone could do better. When we ask for advice, we often don't explain our needs, goals, or the most important things we're trying to achieve. Sometimes we don't even know ourselves. Likewise, when we offer counsel, it's natural for us to shade our advice toward our own biases. We don't clearly see the other person's perspective.

If you ask your brother to tell you what he thinks of that darling three-bedroom ranch in Windsor Heights, he could answer, "No way! I wouldn't even think about living there." Has your brother answered according to your needs? Or does he have some personal bias against ranch-style homes or Windsor Heights? What if your agent tells you Troy Woods is not a good area? Should you accept that advice at face value? Or should you question why the agent holds that view? Maybe the agent doesn't like Troy Woods because he doesn't think much of its schools. But if you don't have kids or you're planning to send your kids to a private school, the reasons for your agent's objections might even work to your advantage. Maybe with less attractive schools, Troy Woods would provide more house for the money. Rather than being helpful, your agent's (or brother's) advice could work against your most important needs.

If people fail to understand what you want, or if they can't put aside their own biases, their advice will not serve you well.

Conflict of Interest?

Do your advisors' interests conflict with yours? Whenever you rely on the advice of other people, think how their interests may conflict with yours. Some unethical realty agents may try to talk you into a home or financing that doesn't meet your needs just so they can gain a commission or a kickback. Your parents may talk against an outlying neighborhood because they'd rather see you live closer to them. Your friends could advise you not to buy a home because they're jealous, or maybe they think that if you move you will drift apart as friends.

People have their own reasons for the advice they offer. They may want to help you make a better decision. But they may have their own agenda, too. When someone says, "This is what you ought to do," take a moment to reflect. Look beyond face value. Think through the actual knowledge, facts, experience, and motives that prompt such advice.

MISTAKE # **95**

The lawyer created more problems than he solved.

LESSON: *Keep the lawyer(s) under control.*

"Although I wasn't in the market to buy a house," says Ramon Williams, "that's exactly what I did. One day I happened to drive by a for-sale-by-owner open house. Just out of curiosity, I went in to look. Sure enough, by the end of the afternoon the owners and I had reached an agreement. But rather than proceed on our own—or bring in a real estate agent—we thought it best to consult a lawyer. Unfortunately, the lawyer we went to created more problems than he solved."

Lawyer Wins, Clients Lose

"First off, instead of formalizing our agreement as we requested, the lawyer sided with the seller," Ramon continues. It turned out they had both played football (in different years) at the same Dallas high school. For at least the first hour of our two-hour office conference, the seller and the lawyer talked Texas football.

"After that, the lawyer offered his unsolicited opinion that the seller was not getting a good price for his home, and then tried to rewrite other terms where we had already reached an agreement. By the time the conference ended, the cordial relations the seller and I had originally developed were quickly moving toward hostility. The seller wanted to revise. I wanted to carry through our original intent.

"The point was that we had a written and signed agreement. We didn't go to the lawyer for advice about what either of us should have done. We only wanted him to make sure the language we used in our agreement actually meant what we had wanted it to mean.

"Eventually, our basic agreement held with just a couple more concessions on my part. Then the seller and I left the meeting by instructing the lawyer to redraft our final agreement in legalese. The contract came back okay, but our surprise came when we got the bill of $1,050. Seven hours of billing at $150 an hour, including the hour wasted on talk of Texas football. At least on this point the seller and I agreed. The bill was outrageous."

Ramon's bad experience with the lawyer who handled his home-buying transaction is not unusual. As evidenced by the proliferation of lawyer jokes, record numbers of complaints to bar associations, and increasing attorney malpractice cases, consumer satisfaction with lawyers has reached an all-time low. In fact, the late Chief Justice of the United States, Warren Burger, complained that half the lawyers he saw practicing before the U.S. Supreme Court were incompetent.

Lawyer Abuses

If you choose to bring a lawyer into your homebuying transaction, guard against three widespread problems: overbilling, underqualification, and gratuitous advice.

When you discuss fees with a lawyer, look beyond the hourly rate. Get a firm estimate of the total bill. In my dealings with lawyers, I've found that some bill eight hours for the same work another lawyer could perform in two. I once hired a lawyer to answer a question. He billed for 12 hours of research and still failed to provide an adequate answer. When I consulted another attorney, I got a sensible answer in less than 30 minutes—no research required.

Verify whether the lawyer routinely handles the type of problems you're asking about. Divorce lawyers may know next to nothing about real estate contracts, escrow, and title insurance. Verify the lawyer's *successful* experience in homebuying transactions.

Beware of gratuitous advice. Most lawyers love to talk and give their opinions regardless of whether they know what they are talking about. I was once in a mortgage closing where in response to a buyer's question the attorney began to explain the mortgage interest figures on the settlement sheet. But rather than admit he didn't know how to calculate mortgage interest, the lawyer tried to bluff his way through. On other occasions, I've listened to lawyers give (unsolicited and incorrect) advice about sale prices, investment returns, zoning ordinances, neighborhood desirability, and a myriad of other topics.

Lawyers should understand the area of the law where you need help. But they also should know what they do not know. Further, they should not give advice that extends beyond their own experience and expertise. Just as important, don't ask lawyers for opinions in areas outside their competence and experience. Few lawyers can resist that temptation.[1]

---

[1] In fact, law articles on malpractice prevention repeatedly tell lawyers to hold their tongues when faced with questions about which they are ignorant. Yet, most do not.

Finally, realize that, nationwide, far more trouble-free homebuying transactions take place without lawyers than with them. In fact, in Maryland so many homebuyers were successfully buying homes without a lawyer that the bar association lobbied for a law that would *force* homebuyers to hire lawyers.

MISTAKE # **96**

We shouldn't have taken escrow allowances for repairs.

LESSON: *When you buy a home that needs extensive repairs, get a substantial price discount.*

When you're looking at a home that needs work, you can require the sellers to credit you with an escrow allowance, bargain for a price discount, or maybe go for a combination of escrow allowance and price discount. Do not, however, accept an escrow allowance or price discount that merely equals the estimated costs of repairs. Ask for substantially more. The chance that you will underestimate is high.

Repairs Often Exceed Estimates

"We knew the house needed work when we bought it," says Kay Schall. "So we got an estimate for repairs before we wrote a contract on the home. In total, everything came to around $13,000. To pay for these repairs, we wrote a clause into our offer where the sellers would credit us $13,000 at closing. But, surprise, surprise, this escrow allowance didn't come close to covering the repairs we had to make. So far we've spent $26,136, with the end still not in sight. We now know what it means to own a money pit."

Kay and her husband made a common mistake. When they accepted an escrow allowance for the estimated cost of repairs, they assumed that the repairs could be completed for the amount of the estimate. For small repairs, the risk of underestimating may not be great. But for more extensive work, no contractor can really tell for sure how much the repairs will cost. Here are five of the unexpected problems the Schalls ran up against:

1. Previous owners of the house had remodeled it without building permits or city inspections. As a result, before permits could be issued for the new work, the old work had to be inspected. That meant opening up walls so the inspector could see whether the earlier construction had been performed according to code. It hadn't. Therefore, the old remodeling had to be redone.
2. The fireplace in the living room had to be completely rebuilt because it had wood instead of metal framing. A second fireplace in the dining room had to be sealed up permanently because of problems with the chimney.
3. A wood patio deck had to be torn out because it was built without proper termite barriers between it and the ground.
4. A tiled exterior entrance to the home had to be jackhammered to oblivion and then rebuilt with poured concrete with steps of a new height and width to comply with the building code.
5. Not only did the roof need to be reshingled, much of the wood had to be replaced, and in an area above the old remodeling, the roof had to be raised a foot.

The Capuanos

When Katie and Joe Capuano bought their rundown clapboard home in Stony Brook, Long Island, they figured the age of the house at 60 years and believed they could restore it with a modest amount of work—much of which Joe could do himself. But once the Capuanos got into the restoration project, it became clear that far more work would be necessary than they had anticipated. "Once I started pulling things out, I realized the house was at least 100 years old," says Joe.

By the time they completed their "modest" restoration, Joe and Katie had spent more than $55,000 to gut the interior of their house, replace a crumbling foundation and wall beams, add on an extension, and install new siding. "At least, now," says Katie, "it's everything we could have wanted."

The Capuanos seem to be taking their unexpected expenses with more aplomb than the Schalls. But the experiences of the Schalls and the Capuanos teach the same lesson: Unless you want to accept the risk of repairs and restoration costs that exceed your estimates, don't accept a dollar-for-dollar escrow allowance or price discount. Instead, build into your figures a reserve for error—or require the sellers to complete your desired repairs and improvements before you close your purchase.

MISTAKE # **97**

We accepted an escrow allowance of $6,000 for termite damage. Our repairs cost $18,347.

LESSON: *All termite inspections are not created equal.*

Before you close your loan, most mortgage lenders will require you or the sellers to provide a termite clearance for the house. Generally, a licensed termite inspector comes out, looks around the house with a flashlight, and, at critical points, pokes into the wood with a knife or screwdriver. If no evidence of termites is found, the inspector issues a clearance certificate and sends it to the escrow agent. But if the inspector finds evidence of infestations, he or she will estimate the cost of treatment and repairs.

Typically, when treatment and repairs are necessary, the sellers either pay for the work or give you an escrow allowance. Which is better? Here you face the same kind of situation as with other kinds of repairs. If the sellers remedy the problem, your risk is reduced. On the other hand, if you accept an escrow credit and get the work done competently for a lesser amount, you come out ahead. The question is, do you want to take a chance?

Ian and Marge Cordall took a chance and lost. They accepted a $6,000 escrow allowance for termite damage and ended up paying $18,347 for treatment and repairs. "We had no idea," says Ian, "that the inspector's estimates weren't guaranteed. By the time our work was fin-ished, the contractor had to tear out the den and completely rebuild it."

This type of unpleasant surprise occurs because all termite inspec-tions are not created equal; and even the best ones can miss serious damage.

Termite Inspectors Only Sample

In performing a pest inspection, an inspector pokes here and there hop-ing to spot problems that might exist. But there's always the possibility the inspector won't hit the right spot, or the damage may be hidden and relatively inaccessible. Either way, actual damage could exceed reported damage. (It's possible that an infested house can receive a clean bill of health.)

Here are four ways to protect yourself:

1. Tag along with the inspector as he tours the house. Did he get under the house and poke around in the crawl space? How about the attic? The foundation? Did he especially check areas where wood (treated or untreated) comes in contact with the ground? How thoroughly has the inspector actually sampled the home for termites?

2. Ask the inspector questions. Find out which areas of the house are most vulnerable to infestation. Note whether any other homes in the neighborhood have experienced a termite problem. Discover whether the house has been treated previously. If so, how exten-sive was the damage? Were there any recurrences?

3. If the inspection company offers a warranty, what does it cover? Will it pay for all damages? Or does it only require the company to treat the home with another dose of pesticides?

4. If the company locates infestation and estimates repair costs, who bears the risk of cost overruns? Is the company merely issuing a good-faith estimate? In that case—unless the firm has been negli-gent in its inspection—you must pay the repairs if additional dam-age is found after work begins. Some exterminators guarantee their estimates. When they miss problems, they bear the costs to correct them.

Never accept a termite inspection, clearance report, or damage estimate without questions. Yes, with some, you can sleep easy knowing you've covered (or limited) your exposure to loss. With others, you just have to hope those pesky little critters have satisfied their appetites somewhere else. Because if they haven't, you'll be the one who's picking up their dinner check.

MISTAKE # **98**

We thought the roof warranty was good for 20 years.

LESSON: Determine exactly what types and amounts of repairs your warranties cover.

"When we bought our house," says Kip Phillips, "the sellers showed us their receipts for a new roof they'd put on four years ago. Plus, they pulled out this engraved certificate that stated in bold print: 20-Year Warranty. With the receipts and the warranty, we didn't think we would have to worry about paying for roof repairs for a long time to come.

"But just 18 months later, the roof started leaking. We learned the shingles were cracking and the entire roof would have to be replaced at a cost of $3,400. At that point, we were glad we had that 20-year warranty, which the owner had transferred to us.

"The next thing we did was to contact the shingle manufacturer's local distributor. 'No problem,' he told us, 'we'll send someone out right away to process your claim.' Faithful to his word, several days later a company representative came out to the house. After inspecting the roof, he agreed the shingles needed to be replaced. He then proceeded to write us a check for $600."

Read the Fine Print

"Six hundred dollars!" we said. "Replacing that roof is going to cost $3,400. How do you expect us to accept a meager $600?"

"Because that's the amount the warranty provides," he said.

"What do you mean?" I asked. "We've got a 20-year warranty."

"True," he said, "but then pointed to the fine print."

"That's when I knew he might as well have said 'Gotcha.' The fine print stated the company was not liable for the costs of taking off the old roof, installing the new roof, or paying for adhesives, wood repair, or any other labor or materials. The warranty covered only the prorated cost of the shingles over a 20-year expected life. In other words, our 20-year roof warranty amounted to nothing more than reimbursement for 70 percent (14/20) of the price of the shingles. To complete the job, we were still going to be out $2,800."

From this experience, Kip Phillips learned an expensive lesson: Don't count on warranties to reimburse you for repairs or replacements unless you've first verified exactly what types of repairs and amounts of protection the warranty offers. Real estate broker Carl Steinmetz says his realty firm stopped dealing in home warranties because "we just had too many cases in which the buyers were upset with the policy coverages. They always thought the policy should have paid for something but didn't."

Not everyone agrees with Carl. California Department of Insurance spokesman John Fogg reports his agency gets fewer complaints about home warranty policies than any other type of insurance. And the real estate brokerage firm Joan M. Sobeck, Inc., thinks so highly of warranties that some of its agents buy the policies as a service to their sellers and buyers. Another broker says, "First-time buyers often don't know much about fixing up a home.... Those folks are really drawn to the protection of a warranty."

How to Inspect a Warranty Agreement

What's the bottom line on home warranties? Read the fine print and look for answers to these eight questions:

1. Does the warranty cover labor, materials, and parts? Or is it limited to certain named items (e.g., roof shingles, furnace combustion chamber, air conditioner compressor)?
2. Will you receive full cost of replacement? Or will the warrantor prorate payment or subtract for depreciation?

3. Must you pay for service calls? Some warranties charge home-owners anywhere from $50 to $200 each time a repairman is called out to the house.

4. If you buy a warranted existing home, what items does the coverage exclude (e.g., roof, foundation, air conditioner, pool equipment, well pump, sprinkler system, plumbing, wiring)?

5. How long will the warranty last? Most overall warranties with existing homes end after one year. New home warranties may cover major structural items for 10 years but limit coverage on appliances, furnace, and air conditioner to just 1 year. (In many instances the manufacturers of these items separately warrant their quality and performance. You'll need to check these separate warranties to determine how you're protected.)

6. Does the warranty cover preexisting conditions? If you buy a home when the pipes are rusty or the furnace is clunking and clanging, the warranty may exempt these items from coverage. Some warranties only guard against unexpected breakdowns or malfunctions—not sure things. Don't count on a warranty to substitute for a thorough inspection of your home by a professional inspector.

7. What is the warranty company's track record for honoring claims? Does it run you through a maze of paperwork and proofs? Or does it enjoy a reputation for quick and fair settlements?

8. Is the warranty company in good financial shape? In the past, some homebuyers have not collected on their claims because the warranty company disappeared or went bankrupt. If you're buying a new home, check to see who stands behind the warranty. Some builders warrant their own work. Others provide protection through independent warranty companies.

Although you want your builder to stand behind his or her work, in most cases it's better to receive your home warranty from a financially strong insurer. Many builders run into tough financial trouble when housing markets head toward a down cycle.

Also, don't be fooled when builders tell you they've been in business 25 years. To gauge financial stability, the real question is how long their present company has been in business. Some builders open a company, run it into bankruptcy, and then start another one. Over a period of 20 or 30 years, fly-by-night builders like these may open and close six or eight different firms. Each time they bankrupt a company, they leave their previous homebuyers without a way to collect the claims they may have for defects in their homes.

During the past 10 years, warranty programs have become popular. And in general, homebuyers, sellers, and builders have benefited from this trend. But as with all types of insurance, read the fine print. Some companies pay fully and promptly. Others build loopholes and escape hatches into their warranty contracts.

MISTAKE # **99**

Our homeowners' insurance didn't cover our losses.

LESSON: *Don't take your homeowners' insurance for granted. Closely check your coverages.*

When fire swept through the Oakland-Berkeley, California, hills, Ron and Betty Bugaj lost their $500,000 home and all their personal belongings. The Bugajes were not alone. In one of the worst residential firestorms in U.S. history, more than 3,300 homeowners suffered total losses. As tragic as the fire was, for many of these families their troubles were just beginning. "The damage we really suffered," says Betty, "was in our negotiations with the insurance company."

Like more than 1,000 other firestorm victims, the Bugajes learned after the fire that their homeowners' insurance policy would pay much less than they expected. To get the amounts they thought they were entitled to, the Bugajes wrangled back and forth with their insurance company for over 10 months. Adding to their hassle was the $75,000 in lawyer bills and consulting fees their negotiations with the insurance company cost them.

In the end, the Bugajes and most of the other firestorm victims did settle with their insurers—but only after the California Department of Insurance, various consumer advocacy groups, and widespread unfavorable publicity pressured the insurance companies to give in. Although to some extent several insurers had tried to lowball their policyholders, most of the settlement problems resulted because homeowners had not purchased the insurance coverage they actually needed (or thought they had).

Review Your Specific Coverages

The important lesson of the Oakland-Berkeley firestorm was not that most insurance companies are bad guys. Rather, it's that far too many homeowners do not know their insurance coverages. They buy a policy and assume (incorrectly) they have the protection they need.

To make sure your policy adequately protects your home and belongings, ask your insurance agent or check your policy and answer the following questions.

What Perils Are Covered?

In insurance language, perils cause losses. Yet, no insurance policy covers every peril. Some policies exclude hurricanes, floods, mudslides, sinkholes, earthquakes, and riots. Sometimes frozen water pipes or roof collapse due to a buildup of snow and ice are not covered. After you learn what perils your basic coverage omits, you can usually buy an endorsement to obtain the extra protection you and your insurance agent believe is wise.

What Property Is Covered?

With tens of millions of Americans now working from home, recognize that business property or sales inventories may not be covered under your homeowners' policy. Nor are your pets, golf cart, or snowmobile. Similarly, if you own any expensive antiques, jewelry, furs, artwork, or a collection of stamps, coins, or baseball cards, find out whether they're covered, and, if so, for how much. More than likely, you'll have to pay extra to secure adequate protection. If you're a writer, store an extra copy of the manuscript you're working on in a safety deposit box. (Dozens of writers in the Oakland-Berkeley fire lost computer disks and partially completed books and articles.) Your homeowners' policy won't pay for the value of your work to date. Even if you've finished the manuscript, the insurer will only reimburse you for the paper, not the work product.

If you live in a co-op, condo, or townhouse, distinguish between property covered by the association's insurance and the property that remains your responsibility. For example, if a water pipe bursts within a wall and causes water and plumbing damages, who pays for what? Check with your board.

How Much Will the Company Pay?

This issue causes the most problems between homeowners and their insurers. That's because ambiguity reigns.

First, your house. You can choose either replacement cost or actual cash value coverage. With a replacement cost policy, the insurer agrees to pay to repair or rebuild your house at today's prices. Under actual cash value coverage, the company subtracts a figure for depreciation from the costs of replacement. Buy replacement cost coverage. Otherwise, the older your house and the greater its wear and tear, the less you collect.

Regardless of which type of coverage you select, here are eight areas where misunderstandings frequently occur (as they did in the Oakland-Berkeley fire storm):

1. How much will you collect if you choose not to rebuild?
2. What happens if government regulations prevent repairs or rebuilding? (For example, some homes now located in coastal areas, floodplains, wetlands, or hillsides cannot be rebuilt because of new safety or environmental regulations.)
3. What if new government regulations (safety codes, environmental laws, building regulations) significantly increase the cost to rebuild your home?
4. In the Oakland fire, many homes devoured by fire were 30 to 70 years old. Legally, owners couldn't rebuild without major code upgrades. Extra regulations added $50,000 or more to the cost of construction. Yet, homeowners' policies often exclude regulatory upgrades. This fact surprised many homeowners when they learned that to rebuild they had to pay large amounts from their own pockets. (A *guaranteed* replacement cost policy is one way to prevent this problem.)

5. How much will your policy reimburse you for your home's unique architectural or historical value? (Usually nothing unless you've requested specific endorsements.)

6. If the insurer needlessly delays settling your claim, can you collect interest payments on the proceeds when the company eventually pays?

7. How high are your policy limits? No matter how much it costs to replace your home, reimbursement won't exceed your policy limits. Make sure you periodically increase the limits of your policy to keep up with the rising costs of new construction. Note, too, that most policies apply lower internal policy limits for certain types of property or perils (e.g., cash, jewelry, stamp collections).

8. If you choose an actual cash value policy, how will the insurer figure depreciation?

Discuss these questions with your insurance agent. Do not wait until after you suffer a loss to understand your coverage.

Give attention to your household furniture and personal belongings. To collect for the contents of your home, choose a guaranteed replacement cost policy. Keep a list and photographic or video inventory of all property. Policies require proof of loss. Photos or videos stored in a safe place can provide the necessary evidence. Without a detailed inventory of your possessions, you will face a difficult time collecting for all you lost—partly because you won't remember.

What Liability Protection Is Offered?

In addition to covering a home and its contents, homeowners' policies protect against liability losses. Liability pays for negligence claims when someone is injured on your property. It may also cover for accidents such as hitting someone with your bicycle or a golf ball.

If you're a member of a homeowners' association, see what type of liability coverage the association carries. In some states, you can be held personally liable (along with each of the homeowners) when someone is negligently injured on the common areas of the property (swimming pool, bike trails, tennis courts, clubhouse, hallways).

Benny Kass, a specialist in condominium and homeowners' association law, warns that too many community associations "are pitifully underinsured and represent a significant risk to association members."

How Much Are the Premiums?

Before you offer to buy a home, determine the cost of insurance protection. During the past 10 years, property insurers have lost billions of dollars from claims such as Florida hurricanes, Texas mold, and California fires and earthquakes. In response, companies have raised premiums and tightened underwriting in areas with high claims potential.

After Florida's recent spate of hurricanes, insurance companies canceled tens of thousands of Florida homeowner policies, and several insurers tried to withdraw completely from writing policies in hurricane areas. In California, insurers have tried to eliminate or severely limit the coverage they offer for earthquake losses. For these and other reasons, prior to buying, check coverages and premiums very closely. In higher risk areas, you may not be able to get the coverage you need at a price you're willing to pay.

MISTAKE # **100**

After we bought, property taxes jumped $2,200 and we got hit with a $1,600 special assessment for new sidewalks.

LESSON: *Before buying, find out how much you must pay for property taxes.*

When Stan and Beth Hill bought their home, the information sheet their Realtor gave them listed property taxes for the most recent year at $2,700. Shortly after the Hills bought, their taxes shot up to $4,900. In addition, the city notified Stan and Beth that it planned new sidewalks for the neighborhood. Their share of these costs would total $1,600, to be added to the Hills' tax bill for the coming year.

Past Taxes Don't Equal Future Taxes

Stan and Beth assumed their future property taxes would cost about the same amount as the sellers had been paying. But in many cities and counties throughout the United States, you can't rely on that assumption.

In most states, county assessors periodically estimate a home's value for the purpose of levying property taxes. This periodic reassessment, though, might occur annually, quadrennially, whenever the assessor's office gets around to it, or sometimes when a property is sold and a new deed (and sales price) is recorded in the county records. In addition, homeowners may be entitled to exemptions (homestead, mortgage, senior citizen). Even when a home is assessed accurately, property taxes can vary when different owners qualify for different types of tax breaks.

In Stan and Beth's case, their property tax surprise arose for two reasons. First, their home had not been reassessed for four years. During that period values in the neighborhood had increased about 35 percent. Second, seven years earlier the previous owners had added an 800-square-foot bedroom suite that enhanced the home's value but had not been noticed by the tax assessor.

As a result, at the courthouse, the home carried a value of only $186,300. But when the Hills' purchase price of $379,000 came through the records office, it triggered an immediate reassessment based upon the home's current market value.

Learn How Property Taxes Are Calculated

To prevent surprise, learn the ins and outs of the property tax system in your area. If the home you buy is underassessed, or if the sellers qualify for more exemptions than you are entitled to, you might face a steep rise in your property tax bill.

To your benefit, by learning the ins and outs of property taxes, you also might discover an *overassessment*. When some homes in the Northeast, California, Florida, Oklahoma, Texas, Arizona, and several other states sold for less than their peak prices of earlier years, savvy owners were able to negotiate their assessments downward. Accordingly, their tax bills fell.

Here are seven property tax questions to ask the tax assessor's office:

1. What is their recorded market value for the home you're buying?
2. What is the current assessed value of the home? (In some tax jurisdictions, the assessed value is stated as a percentage of the home's market value. Therefore, look at both the tax assessor's appraised value and the assessed value before you conclude a home is underassessed or overassessed.)
3. After you buy, will the *assessed* value of the home increase, decrease, or remain about the same?
4. Are you entitled to any exemptions that will reduce your property tax bill?
5. What is the local millage rate? (One mill equals a thousandth of a dollar. A millage rate of say, 17, would mean a property tax of $17 for every $1,000 of assessed value.)
6. Will any improvements you make to the home increase its assessed value? (Some types of improvements will add significantly to assessed value—if the tax assessor learns about them. Built-ins, room additions, a swimming pool, or wall-to-wall carpeting, for example, typically increase a home's assessed value. A new roof, furnace, or hot water heater may not. Every tax assessor's office has its own way of operating. Check the specifics as they may apply to the home you buy.)
7. What amount of taxes can you expect? (To calculate this figure, multiply the millage rate expressed as a decimal by the home's expected assessed value. Seventeen mills, for example, convert to .017. With an assessed value of $100,000, your property taxes would run $1,700 a year.)

Special Assessments

From time to time local governments levy special assessments. These charges pay for new sidewalks, sewers, waste treatment plants, street widenings, or parks. In most cases special assessments will range between $500 and $5,000. On occasion they can go as high as $10,000 to $15,000, or more.

Because special assessments can upset a budget, find out whether any assessements are planned for your neighborhood. Learn of proposed changes before you buy. Better parks may add to your home's value. But street widening may bring more traffic and diminish the value of your home.

MISTAKE # **101**

We didn't know title insurers offered discount policies.

LESSON: *Before you set up escrow, ask whether the sellers have a title policy that can be transferred to you and your lender. It could save you money.*

Before you and your lender release funds to the sellers, a title company (or lawyer) will verify that they actually own the property and that any outstanding liens or claims against the home will be taken care of prior to closing.

Years ago most title searches were performed by lawyers, who would then offer an opinion as to whether title to the home was marketable (free of defects). Although still common in some areas, most lenders and homebuyers no longer use lawyers to assure title. Instead, they wisely buy a title insurance policy.

Obtain Title Insurance

When a lawyer makes a mistake or otherwise misses a defect in the home's title, the only way you can make him or her pay for your loss is to hire another lawyer to sue the first one. That's an expensive, time-consuming, and uncertain challenge. With title insurance, the insurer agrees to pay the expenses necessary to defend your rights in the property against other claims. If unsuccessful in its defense, the company will pay for covered losses.

Like all insurers, title companies write their policies with various exceptions and limitations. If your next-door neighbor's garage sat a foot onto your side of the property line at the time you bought your home, the insurer may exclude that known problem from its coverage. Also, in some states, a basic title policy covers only the lender. Adding your name to the policy may cost slightly more.

Title insurance has proved to be a wise purchase for most homebuyers. It reduces the possibility that you'll be drawn into a long legal battle when some ex-husband of a long-ago owner shows up and claims that his ex-wife forged his name to the deed when she sold the house after their divorce.

Secure an Owner's Endorsement

Title insurers offer two types of coverage: lender's policies and owner's policies. To protect your equity in a property, you (or the sellers) may need to pay an additional premium. Plus, inquire whether you can obtain increasing amounts of protection as your home appreciates in value. Title policies last for as long as you own your home, but many policies limit the amount of coverage to your home's original purchase price.

Determine whether the sellers have a title policy that you can update and transfer to you. If your sellers do have title coverage, by sticking with the same company you might save several hundred dollars. If you can't save money that way, compare insurance premiums among title companies. Because in some states these premiums are set by law, you won't find much difference among companies. But other states encourage competition, and shopping around can pay off.

Stay on Schedule

With home mortgages and loan servicing contracts now being traded among lenders like baseball cards, the paper trail for existing liens and previous mortgage satisfactions sometimes can prove cumbersome to follow. Therefore, to avoid a delay in closing, title checks should proceed as soon as escrow is set up.

On occasion, loan processors busy themselves with credit reports, document verifications, and appraisal and leave the title search and property survey until the last minute. When problems crop up, closing has to be put off, which—at a minimum—disrupts moving plans for both buyers and sellers. Although most title defects and boundary disputes eventually get straightened out, the effort can take several weeks to several months. Good planning and timely processing of the paperwork can free you and the sellers from this type of troublesome situation. (Although realty agents aren't responsible for escrow, top agents monitor progress to keep the closing on schedule.)

MISTAKE # **102**

Our closing was like showdown at the OK Corral.

LESSON: *The best closing is a no-surprise closing.*

Most mortgage closings go smoothly. Yet, occasionally failure to prepare or last-minute changes can create turmoil. "We felt it was a bad sign," says Wendy Kantor, "when the real estate agent telephoned us two days before closing and told us the sellers had decided to take the refrigerator and four window air conditioners with them. These items were included in our purchase price. So the agent said the sellers would give us a credit for their value and we could work out the details at closing.

"But at closing, the sellers only wanted to give us $500. That figure wasn't acceptable. We thought $1,000, maybe even $1,250, was closer to the mark. Besides, we found a $600 mistake in the closing statement and another $1,300 in garbage fees that we hadn't expected. By the time that closing finally settled, it was like showdown at the OK Corral."

Get Everything Settled before Closing

I can empathize with Wendy because I once went through a mortgage closing disaster much like hers—only I was the seller. In my case, several days before closing my agent telephoned and said the buyers had come up short on cash and asked whether I would be willing to carry back $5,000 in seller financing. I said no. I was moving out of town, and I didn't want to worry about collecting $5,000 from a distance of 1,200 miles. If the buyers didn't pay, I could end up spending more than $5,000 in lawyer's bills just to collect.

When we did get into closing, however, the buyers proceeded as if I was going to help them with their financing. As I later learned, "my" agent had set us up. He figured that once we were sitting in closing—both of us with loaded moving vans—we would be forced to work out some kind of compromise. And that's what we did.

But from that experience, I learned the same lesson Wendy Kantor learned: Make sure all details of the transaction are known and agreed to by all parties before closing. To avoid these kinds of last-minute showdowns, many mortgage loans and homebuying transactions are closed through escrow without buyers, sellers, agents, lender, and attorneys all meeting together around a conference table. I've been involved in both types of closings and definitely favor the escrow approach.

Check the Figures and Arithmetic

Even with in absentia escrow closings, carefully check the figures on your closing statement to make sure they're totaled correctly and that the lender hasn't thrown in garbage fees that were not properly disclosed to you in the lender's good-faith Real Estate Settlement and Procedures Act (RESPA) disclosure statement. Stay alert for last-minute tactics to renegotiate amounts in the sellers' favor. Unethical sellers (and buyers) or their lawyers use this technique to extract concessions they otherwise couldn't get. Full preparation and agreement prior to closing helps prevent this gambit.

MISTAKE # **103**

We couldn't believe the way the sellers left the house for us.

LESSON: *Arrange a final walk-through and inspection of the house just prior to settlement—ideally, after the sellers have moved out.*

"We couldn't believe the mess," recalls Derek Chapman. "We walked into the house the day after settlement and discovered the sellers had left piled-up boxes of trash throughout the house, the inside of the oven looked like a grease pit, the carpeting and floors were all tracked up with mud (evidently from their movers), and the dining room chandelier was missing. We also learned the den did not have hardwood floors as we had thought.

"When we first looked at the house," Derek continues, "the sellers had a large area rug in the den so all we saw was the hardwood floors around the edge of the room. Naturally, we assumed the floor under the rug was also finished hardwood. But it wasn't. That part of the floor was unfinished pine. I guess we should have pulled back the rug just to make sure. But it really wasn't anything I had seen before—or would have imagined."

Verify You Receive What You Expect

First, when you inspect a house, get nosy. Pull back rugs and open the cabinets, drawers, and the oven door. Look behind pictures or other wall hangings. Look under the furniture. It's better to discover flaws, stains, cracks, or unfinished floors before you make your offer rather than after.

Second, schedule settlement after the sellers have moved out. Then, before closing, do your final walk-through and inspection. Learn whether the sellers have left the home clean and confirm that they have not taken any personal property, appliances, or fixtures that were supposed to stay with the house. Inspecting a vacant house also gives you another chance to discover any defects that were previously hidden by the sellers' selective placement of furniture, area rugs, or wall hangings.

It's easier to work out problems before the sellers have received their money. This is especially true when the sellers move out of town. Once the sellers are gone with your money, you lose leverage. You might sue, but that might cost you more in time, money, and misery than you could hope to collect. (For some types of claims against the sellers, you might proceed inexpensively in small claims court, but even if your claim wins, you still lose time and effort and you still face collection. Avoid the hassle; inspect closely.)

No Walk-Through? Here's What to Do

If you can't do a final walk-through before the settlement and after the sellers' vacate, put a clause in your purchase offer whereby 10 percent (or so) of the sellers' sales proceeds are escrowed until you've had time to check out the house. (Purchase offers are discussed more extensively in Chapter 12.)

As another tactic, consider putting a compulsory arbitration clause into your purchase agreement. With this kind of clause, you and the sellers use an arbitrator instead of a lawsuit to settle disputes. Lawyers often advise against compulsory arbitration because it cuts down on their fees. For most buyers, though, saving on lawyer's bills and court costs stands as an advantage, not a disadvantage. Through arbitration, you also can settle your disputes much more quickly than with a lawsuit and avoid costly and time-consuming pretrial maneuvers. Arbitration may not be right for everyone, but it's a method of resolving disagreements to consider.

New Homes: Get What You Think You're Paying For

Paul Tate was conducting a preclosing walk-through of his newly built $285,000 split-level ranch home when he discovered that, unlike the model homes he was shown, his home lacked skylights, which were very important to him. "Without skylights," Paul complained to the builder, "the house is way too dark."

The builder sympathized with Paul but pointed out that in their contract, skylights were optional and not included in the basic price. Because Paul hadn't specified he wanted them, the builder didn't put them in. To do so now that the home was complete would cost twice as much as if they had been installed during the construction process.

If you plan to buy a new home that's not yet completed, check two things: Do not assume those gold-plated bathroom fixtures and the marble fireplace in the master bedroom are standard features. Read your purchase contract closely. Look for cost-increasing words such as "optional" and "upgrades." With some houses, the upgrades and options are what transform the frog into Prince Charming.

Keep tabs on the construction as the house is being built. Don't wait until final walk-through to discover the features you wanted aren't the features you're getting. Even when you accurately list your options and upgrades, builders and contractors make mistakes.

If you decide on changes during construction (as you undoubtedly will), make them early and put them *in writing*. The earlier you initiate change orders, the less it will cost you. Memories are too fragile and building sites too hectic to rely on ad hoc talks with your builder, a sales representative, or a contractor.

MISTAKE # **104**

The sellers wouldn't move out of the house.

LESSON: Put a penalty clause in your contract that will force the sellers to either move or pay.

A funny thing happened when first-time buyers Janie Brown and Paul Kelley showed up with a bottle of champagne at their new home in La

Mesa. The sellers refused to move out. But Janie and Paul kept their spirits up, put the champagne back in the refrigerator, and after two weeks of legal process, proceeded to evict the sellers.

Surprising as it may seem, sellers (or tenants) who refuse to move after buyers have closed on a house are not uncommon. Take the case of Chauntann Reid. Chauntann bought a bargain-priced home at a foreclosure sale. After learning the ins and outs of how foreclosure auctions work, Chauntann submitted a successful bid for a two-story brick row house with a garage. This lucky new homeowner, though, soon found out that buying a foreclosed home can be easier than moving into it.

Not only did the prior owner of the home challenge the validity of the foreclosure sale, she filed bankruptcy. Both of these legal actions stalled the eviction proceedings that Chauntann could have used to take possession of the home.

Five months after she became a homeowner, Chauntann and her three children were still living in her sister's home. With legal fees, property tax bills, and sewer charges that Chauntann had to pay to protect her ownership interest in the foreclosed house, she couldn't even afford to move out and rent an apartment.

Be Wary of Tenant-Occupied Houses

Getting a tenant out of a house you've bought can present even more difficulties than removing reluctant sellers. As a matter of law, a tenant's lease takes priority over the possession rights of a new owner. If the tenant's rental agreement with the previous owners still has six months to run, then the tenants have the right to stay in the home for six more months (as long as they pay the rent, of course).

Even when the tenants can't enforce a lease, they may seek the protection of various pro-tenant ordinances. Some cities require property owners to give tenants 60 or 90 days' notice, sometimes longer, before they can be forced to move. If a tenant is pregnant or files for bankruptcy, the law may offer special protection against eviction.

To guard against sellers who won't vacate, put a clause in your purchase contract that obligates the sellers to pay $100 a day (or whatever) for each day they stay beyond the date they're supposed to move out.

That type of penalty generally encourages sellers to quickly find someplace else to live.

Should you buy a home that's occupied by tenants, also note the terms of their rental agreement. (It may not make any difference whether the agreement is oral or written.) Then verify the tenants' intentions and planned moving date. Check with a lawyer or the local landlord-tenant regulatory agency to see if the tenants are protected against eviction by any laws or regulations. Don't think that just because you own the property, you have a right to live there. That's not the way the law works.

New Home Completion Deadlines

If you buy a newly built house, you won't face problems with reluctant tenants. But new homebuyers sometimes experience another kind of problem that keeps them from moving into their home as scheduled. Construction delays. Delays in completing a home can result from bad weather, shortages of building supplies, labor strikes, excessive change orders, or foot dragging by the builder, contractor, or subcontractor.

You want to work cooperatively with your builder. Nevertheless, you still might include a delay penalty in your purchase contract. I know of new homebuyers who have had to wait anywhere from two to six months beyond the completion date they were promised. With a delay that long, require a penalty payment if the builder or his contractors are responsible.

More than likely, though, you'll have to negotiate to get it. Builders don't like penalty clauses. Yet, if you've set a firm move date, your builder should commit to having the home ready for you to move into. If, after a reasonable grace period, the builder can't meet that commitment, he or she should pay the price of your inconvenience and alternative housing arrangements.

CHAPTER 10

The Biggest Mistakes of All

MISTAKE # **105**

We didn't buy. We were afraid of making a mistake.

LESSON: *Educate yourself. Don't let fear block you from home ownership.*

Kyle and Shannon Marks have been shopping for a home for more than two years. Yet, they continue to rent. Every time they get close to an offer, their worries overwhelm their ambition. "You can never be too cautious," says Shannon. "Our home will probably be the biggest investment we ever make. We certainly don't want to make a mistake."

This book has emphasized the need to anticipate and prevent mistakes in homebuying. Homebuying has become more complex, and you must step around roadblocks. Nevertheless, the biggest mistake is to put off becoming a homeowner because you fear you will make a mistake. Educate yourself. Shop the market. Get reliable advice from people more knowledgeable than yourself. Then commit.

You can sit on the fence forever and watch the parade go by. In the words of singer Billy Ray Cyrus, "dreams move on if you wait too long."

What Fears Are Blocking You?

"We could afford the house, but the concerns are, what about the future?" says John Schultz. "What if the roof caves in? Oops, you're repairing the roof. Do you have the money to support that?" he adds.

Luis Arroyo feared paying too much. "At first I was wondering if the property was actually worth what I was paying," says Luis. "I kept asking the Realtor, 'Are you sure I'm not overpaying?' "

Terri Faber is worried about whether to buy a single-family house or a condo. She's not sure whether now is the time to buy, or whether a lender will approve her loan. "Although I've got a good job and savings," says Terri, "who knows what could happen tomorrow? Maybe the bubble will burst. Besides, some of those neighborhoods give me doubts."

Do these fears apply to you? Do you want to own, then back away? You're not alone. "There are people," says Realtor Susan Swift, "who will run you around looking at 150 different houses and keep telling you, and themselves, they are looking for the perfect thing. But they are really afraid."

The Risks of Renting

It is odd that so many renters worry about the risks of home ownership. They do not realize that continuing to rent presents even greater risks. What if interest rates go up? That could cost you tens of thousands of dollars. What if home prices go up? That could cost you tens of thousands of dollars. What if rents go up? That could cost you thousands of dollars. And if you continue to rent, what about the tens (or even hundreds) of thousands of dollars you will lose in home equity?

The costs of repairing a roof, overpaying, or choosing the wrong home or neighborhood pale when compared to the risks and losses of continuing to rent.

Imperfect Home Ownership Beats Perfect Renting

Exercise caution and good judgment. Investigate alternatives. But to get ahead, you must move from the rational and cautious to that leap of faith. To fear mistakes is itself irrational. As decision expert Theodore Rubin points out, no decision is perfect. A successful decision results not from the decision itself. It results from your commitment to make the decision work for you.

"If I compare my house to an imaginary dream house," writes Dr. Rubin, "my house comes off poorly and I destroy my chance of enjoying it. If I compare my house to houses that actually exist, it may come off well in terms of any real specifications a home requires to be comfortable. This is a true luxury, one I can appreciate in reality."

Fear of Commitment

People who fear to buy fear to commit. They say they're holding out for a home that has no flaws, no shortcomings, no drawbacks. But they know such a home doesn't exist.

If you are caught in that trap, steer back onto the right course. Answer three sets of questions:

1. Have you really thought through and ranked your priorities? Have you discovered your most important feelings and values? Are you permitting the opinions and views of others to conflict with your priorities? You can't have it all. You can't satisfy everyone. Focus on what's important to you.

2. Do you compare houses and neighborhoods with an open mind? Have you explored options and possibilities? Have you educated yourself about alternative home finance plans, neighborhoods, types of homes, and price ranges?

   To exercise good judgment, view what the market offers. Put your creativity to work. Don't let wishful thinking push aside market realities. But also don't accept fewer choices than you actually have. Education and creative thinking can go a long way toward reducing your fear, anxiety, frustration, or disappointment.

3. Do you see possibilities and options as problems or opportunities? Fear creates negative thinking. Negative thinking mires you in anxiety and hopelessness. You may think, "We'll never be able to find what we're looking for." Or you tell yourself, "We can't find anything we like that we can afford."

Fear and negative thinking go together to block your ability to create choices, options, or possibilities that could work for you. You may resign yourself to renting—or you could jump into a decision just to get it over with.

When you frame your options in positive terms, you develop self-confidence. As you develop a here's-what-we-can-do attitude, you turn fear into eagerness and excitement. Whereas fear generates avoidance, a positive outlook helps you see opportunity and commit to action. Not only will you make a good decision, through commitment you will make that decision work.

MISTAKE # **106**

We thought it over. We're going to continue renting.

LESSON: Experience proves that continuing to rent is the most costly mistake you can make.

Over the years, hundreds of newspaper and magazine articles have cautioned against buying a home. They persistently try to make the rent vs. buy decision a complex calculation. Financial planners routinely say, "Buy a home as a comfortable place to live, but owning is not for everyone. You'll earn a greater return in stocks."[1]

Biased nonsense. Apart from the fact that naysaying "experts" have been wrong in their warnings against buying for 60 years (see Chapter 3), a review of four powerful reasons shows why home ownership beats renting:

1. Laws favor home ownership.
2. Home ownership produces the safest and surest opportunity to build personal wealth.
3. Over the course of a lifetime, Americans who own will spend far less money on housing than those who rent.
4. Home ownership yields transcendental benefits that far outweigh financial returns.

---

[1] If you're counting on stocks for your retirement (401[k], IRA, Keogh), read my book, *Value Investing in Real Estate*, 2002 (Wiley).

Laws Favor Homeownership

Chapter 2 shows how the tax laws favor home ownership because you can deduct mortgage interest payments from your taxable income. This deduction—which is not available to renters—may save you thousands of dollars a year in income taxes. In addition, once you begin to build home equity, you will never again pay the high nondeductible interest expenses charged on credit cards, auto loans, and other consumer debt.

Why? Because as a homeowner you can arrange a low-interest-rate home equity loan (tax deductible, no less) to cover your essential borrowing needs (new car, kids' college education, starting a new business). Plus, as you sell one home to trade up to another, only profits in excess of $500,000 ($250,000 for singles) will be taxed. You certainly can't buy and sell stocks with this tax benefit.

What happens if at some later time you hit a financial tragedy (e.g., bankruptcy, creditor judgment, lawsuit damages)? Again, home ownership helps protect you from total loss. In nearly every state, homeowners get to exempt part or all of their home equity from loss to creditors, judgments, or bankruptcy. (Even the IRS rarely goes after home equity to collect unpaid income taxes.)

This benefit is called a homestead exemption. In a few states this exemption is as low as $5,000 to $10,000. In others it ranges between $25,000 and $100,000. And in Florida and Texas, 100 percent of your home equity is protected—even if it amounts to $1 million or more. (The new bankruptcy bill continues to protect home equity, but it only applies after several years of ownership. This restriction attempts to prevent debtors on the brink of financial collapse from transferring all of their available assets into homeownership, thus escaping at least partial repayment of the debts.)

Build Personal Wealth

Building wealth through home equity has consistently proven the safest and surest route to a personal net worth of six figures or more. When you combine a decreasing mortgage balance with even modest rates of home appreciation, your wealth multiplies.

Look at the three examples in Table 10.1. These figures reveal how your wealth will grow over time with a beginning down payment of just

Table 10.1 **Building Wealth with Home Equity**[1]

Growing Home Equity at 3% Annual Home Appreciation
Years of Ownership

	10	20	30	40
Appreciated home value	$134,300	$180,600	$242,700	$326,200
Outstanding mortgage balance	77,679	52,299	00	00
Home equity	56,621	128,301	242,700	326,200

Growing Home Equity at 5% Annual Home Appreciation
Years of Ownership

	10	20	30	40
Appreciated home value	$162,870	$265,330	$432,190	$704,000
Outstanding mortgage balance	77,679	52,299	00	00
Home equity	85,191	213,031	432,190	704,000

Growing Home Equity at 7% Annual Home Appreciation
Years of Ownership

	10	20	30	40
Appreciated home value	$196,720	$386,970	$761,230	$1,497,400
Outstanding mortgage balance	77,679	52,299	00	00
Home equity	119,041	334,671	761,230	1,497,400

[1]Assumes a $100,000 purchase price bought with a $10,000 down payment and an original mortgage of $90,000 at 7.25% interest over 30 years. Increase proportionately for higher priced properties.

$10,000 on a home priced at $100,000 and selected appreciation rates of three, five, and seven percent. (For higher-priced homes, proportionately increase these amounts to match your situation.)

Table 10.1 shows that even a three percent average annual rate of appreciation, a beginning home equity of $10,000 will grow to more than $128,301 within 20 years. By retirement age, the homeowner will accumulate equity of $326,200. Plus, remember that these gains in equity and personal wealth will have built up free of local, state, and federal income taxes. (If, say, you place $40,000 down on a $400,000 home, your equity at 3 percent p.a. will grow to $1,304,800.)

Homeowners Spend Less for Housing than Renters

Homeowners not only build more wealth than renters through home equity, they also accumulate higher net worths for another reason: Homeowners spend less for housing than renters. Although the exact cost advantages will differ among towns and cities throughout the United States, over time rents continue to increase as mortgage payments remain the same (or maybe even drop through refinancing). After your mortgage is paid off, your monthly payments fall to zero.

This cost advantage of owning means that as homeowners grow older, they have more money left from their paychecks after paying for housing. So, they'll have more money to invest. Figure 10.1 shows how rents and mortgage payments compare over time. (Again, for higher cost areas, adjust these figures proportionately.)

Based on the monthly mortgage payments and rent levels shown in Figure 10.1, you can see that within 10 years renters will pay far more each month for housing than homeowners. After 20 or 30 years, renters will pay thousands more *per month* than homeowners. If homeowners

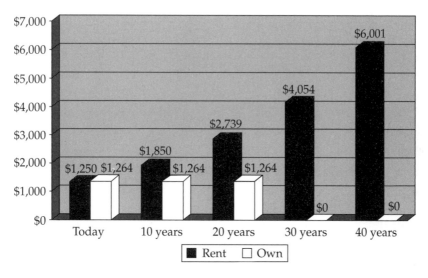

Figure 10.1 Monthly Rents of 1,250 over Time versus Monthly Mortgage Payments.[1]

[1]Mortgage payments are based on a 30-year, fixed-rate mortgage at 6.5% in the amount of $200,000. Rents begin at $1,250 per month and increase 4% per year.

invest an average of only $1,000 a month of these cost savings, say over years 10 through 40, they will accumulate (assuming an annual return of five percent) approximately $675,000. That extra wealth adds to the equity they have built up in their homes.

Housing cost savings that homeowners enjoy as they grow older give them a powerful advantage over renters in their ability to generate personal wealth and create a diversified investment portfolio. But don't just accept these figures or even the results of the aforementioned Harvard study at face value. Test this conclusion for yourself. Compare the wealth position of long-term renters and homeowners you know who have reached their 40s, 50s, or 60s. The net worths of your older friends and relatives who own their own homes greatly exceed the wealth of those who have remained lifelong tenants.

Home Ownership Yields Transcendental Benefits

"Hey, we own this. This home is ours," says Melanie Watts. "We never thought of our home as a money machine—although our equity has steadily built up and our payments are lower now than when we bought 12 years ago. We became homeowners because we wanted the good feelings you get when you own instead of rent. I can't describe it, but it's real.

"After owning our own home, I don't think we could ever feel comfortable again as tenants. In fact, we soon plan to buy rental houses and let our tenants put their money into our retirement fund."

"What I'm saying," Melanie continues, "is that the financial returns of ownership are great. But the most important benefit of owning is ownership itself. There's nothing like knowing a small part of this big old world belongs to you."

"Ownership gives me feelings of security and comfort. When I rented I never felt in control of my life. Now I do. To us, home ownership and ownership of property is a transcendental experience. I'm not into Zen or anything like that. But anyone who rents is missing one of the best feelings they can have. Although we intend to own income properties and will need tenants, I still believe most people who rent are making a big mistake."

History shows Melanie is right. Putting off home ownership remains the most common and most costly mistake of all.

How to Afford the Home You Want

When Jack Holden was asked, "How did your family get started buying real estate?" here's how he answered. "We scraped, borrowed, and leveraged from every resource we had to muster the funds we needed.... For seed money we cashed in savings bonds and borrowed from our insurance policies and credit cards.... The entire family went on an austerity plan to cut back our food, travel, and entertainment expenses. Today we're thankful we made those early sacrifices." Thankful, yes, and also wealthy. Because of their disciplined spending, saving, and investing, the Holdens have built a real estate net worth of $3.5 million, which includes not only their home equity of $600,000, but also nine rental houses and apartment buildings.

As with most first-time homebuyers, the Holdens didn't start out with money. As Jack says, his family scrimped, saved, leveraged, and borrowed every way they could. So what's the mistake to avoid? If you want to own your own home, don't wait until you get the money and then decide to buy. No! First, commit to own. Then figure out how to come up with the money. You can keep wishing and hoping to buy *someday*. Or you can decide to own now and immediately begin to shape up your finances and create a homebuying plan.

Affordability Depends on You

Each year millions of renters make the biggest mistake of all: They continue to rent. These renters believe that they can't afford to own, or in some cases, they believe they can't afford to own the home they want. If you see yourself in either of these situations, you need this chapter.

To a much larger degree than most renters believe, affordability depends on you. Just like the Holdens, you may need to shape up your financial fitness and seek out (or create) a "tailor-made" home finance plan. But if you truly do want to own, you can do it. With home buying, "Where there's a will, there is a way."

To see how you stand financially, your Realtor or mortgage advisor will measure your fiscal fitness. As you have seen, two of these fitness tests are called qualifying ratios: (1) the housing cost ratio, and (2) the total debt ratio. Once the ratios are measured, an advisor can next estimate your borrowing power. If it turns out that you're not as strong as you would like, then you can rely on fiscal fitness and affordability strategies to dramatically boost your chances of owning the home you want.

Housing Cost (Front) Ratio

Many mortgage lenders will say that your total monthly house payments (principal, interest, property taxes, insurance) typically shouldn't exceed, say, 28 to 33 percent of your gross monthly income. According to a lender's reasoning, if you paid a higher percentage of your income toward housing costs, you might not have enough money left to pay for food, clothes, and other bills.

In today's world of automated (computer-programmed) underwriting, qualifying ratios are combined with a multitude of other financial characteristics. Nevertheless, this principle holds: The lower your qualifying ratios, the more likely your mortgage approval will sail through without a snag.

To further illustrate how lenders might apply the housing cost ratio we'll go through an example. To keep it easy, we'll ignore property taxes and insurance. Say your household brings in a gross income of $6,400 a month. If the lender applies a 28 percent housing cost (principal and interest, i.e., P + I) ratio, here's how much you could pay each month for your mortgage:

$$.28 \times \$6{,}400 = 1{,}792 \text{ per month } (P + I)$$

Next, you'll want to see how much money you can borrow if you can afford to repay (according to the lender) $1,792 per month. If the lender's interest rate is eight percent and you want a 30-year, fixed-rate loan, here's how to calculate the amount you can borrow for your mortgage:

$$\frac{\$1,792}{\$7.34} = \$244,142$$

In the above calculation, the $7.34 figure represents the amount of monthly payment (P + I) necessary to pay off $1,000 of borrowed money at eight percent interest, amortized over 30 years. You can find this $7.34 figure in the mortgage repayment table (Table 11.1). Just look in the eight percent row, 30-year column.

To better get the hang of it, here's another example: Say that instead of $6,400, your gross income totals $3,800 per month. If your lender qualifies you with a 28 percent housing cost ratio (principal and interest), you could qualify to pay $1,064 per month for your mortgage.

$$.28 \times \$3,800 = \$1,064 \text{ per month}$$

If you borrowed at eight percent interest with a 30-year payback, you could qualify for a mortgage of $144,959.

$$\frac{\$1,064}{\$7.34} = \$144,959$$

Based on today's current mortgage interest rates (see www.hsh.com), take the appropriate payment factor from Table 11.1 and write out your borrowing power using a 28 percent housing cost ratio and your gross monthly income (GMI):

.28 × (your GMI) = $ _____ (monthly payment)

$ _____ (P + I) = $ _____ (mortgage amount)

$(mo. payment per $1,000)

Table 11.1 **Monthly Mortgage Payment (P + I) for Each $1,000 Borrowed at a Variety of Interest Rates and Terms**

Qualifying Interest Rate	15-year	30-year	40-year
4.0	$7.40	$4.77	$4.17
4.5	7.65	5.07	4.50
5.0	7.91	5.37	4.82
5.5	8.17	5.67	5.16
6.0	8.44	6.00	5.50
6.5	8.71	6.32	5.85
7.0	8.99	6.65	6.21
7.5	9.27	6.99	6.58
8.0	9.56	7.34	6.95
8.5	9.85	7.69	7.33
9.0	10.16	8.05	7.71
9.5	10.45	8.41	8.10
10.0	10.75	8.78	8.50
10.5	11.06	9.15	8.89
11.0	11.37	9.53	9.28
11.5	11.69	9.91	9.68
12.0	12.01	10.29	10.08
12.5	12.33	10.68	10.49

If this mortgage amount is high enough to get you the home you want, great! If not, you have dozens of different ways to boost that figure. Before we get into various fiscal fitness exercises and affordability strategies, here's another type of ratio most lenders will use to help them qualify you for a mortgage. This fitness test is called the total debt (or back) ratio.

Total Debt (Back) Ratio

Whereas a typical *housing cost* ratio is say, .28, lenders typically might use a .36 *total debt* ratio. To illustrate: if your gross income is $2,400 a month, and applying a .36 total debt ratio, according to your lender, your total monthly bills could run up to $864 a month.

$$.36 \times \$2,400 = \$864$$

In this context, the term "bills" doesn't include all of your monthly living expenses. It just includes the payments on your long-term installment debt like car payments, credit cards, department store accounts, and your mortgage payments (to be).

Say your current monthly bills look like this:

Car payment	$142
Visa	68
Sears	45
Best Buy	58
Total	$313

Since your lender says the monthly payments for all of your debts (including mortgage principal, interest, property taxes, and homeowners' insurance, called PITI) can't be more than $864 a month (.36 × your earnings of $2,400), you're left with $551 a month to cover PITI. Assuming your costs for property taxes and homeowners' insurance will run $75 a month, your mortgage payment (principal and interest) can top out at $476 a month. Here are the numbers:

Gross Monthly Income	$2,400	
Total debt ratio	× .36	
Total allowable		
Monthly debt payments	864	
less		
Current installment debt	– 313	
Property taxes and insurance	– 75	
leaves		
Qualifying mortgage payment	$476	(P + I)

Look again at Table 11.1. You can pick out the monthly payment per $1,000 that corresponds to the interest rate and mortgage term lenders now offer—say, 7.5 percent for 30 years—for a figure of $6.99 a month for each $1,000 you borrow. Because you can pay $476 for your monthly principal and interest payment, the mortgage loan underwriters would figure they could loan you $68,097.

$$\frac{\$476}{\$6.99 \text{ per } \$1,000} = \$68,097 \ (68.099 \times 1,000)$$

Gross monthly income $_____

Total debt ratio   × .36

Total allowable debt payments *less*
   total monthly bills   _____

Car payment no. 1   _____

Car payment no. 2   _____

Visa   _____

Master Card   _____

Discover   _____

Department stores   _____

Student loans   _____

Other   _____

Other   _____

Property taxes and insurance
   (estimate)   _____

leaves

Qualifying mortgage payment (P + I) $_____

$_____ (P +I) = $_____ (mortgage payment)

$ payment per $1,000)

Figure 11.1 Your Financial Fitness.

Now, look at the financial fitness form (Figure 11.1). Fill in the blanks for your personal situation and current mortgage interest rates. How does your mortgage amount look? Can you qualify to borrow enough to own the home you want?

If you're like many first-time homebuyers, your numbers won't work out to give you the amount of mortgage you need. Your income may be too low, your debts too high, or perhaps mortgage interest rates are sitting out of sight. How can you overcome these problems?

For starters, look at how Tricia and Herb Renko were able to revamp their qualifying numbers to get approved for the loan they wanted. By following this example, you will see how shaping up your finances and selecting the right home finance plan can dramatically boost your home-buying power.

Tricia and Herb Renko Shape Up Their Financial Fitness

When Tricia and Herb Renko decided to buy a home, they called on loan advisor Steve Bailey. "Steve," Tricia asked, "is there any way that we can buy a house? We're so tired of wasting money on rent. Tell us, Steve, what do we have to do?"

Steve Runs the Numbers

"As a starting point," Steve said, "let's see where you now stand. Then, if necessary, we can work through some other possibilities." Based on their situation at the time, here's how the Renkos' finances looked on paper:

Qualifying the Renkos

Herb's monthly income	$2,050
Tricia's monthly income	1,360
Total gross monthly income	3,410
Total debt ratio	× .36
Total allowable debt payments	$1,228
less total monthly bills	
Car payment no. 1	287
Car payment no. 2	160
Discover card	85
Visa	110
Student loan	138
Property taxes and homeowners' Insurance (estimated)	125
Total monthly bills	$ 905
leaves	
Qualifying mortgage payment	$ 323 (P + I)

At the then market interest rate of 9.5 percent for 30 years, $323 a month would pay off a mortgage loan of $38,407.

$$\frac{\$323 \ (P + I)}{\$8.41 \ (\text{payment per } \$1,000)} = \$38,407 \ (\text{mortgage amount})$$

Because Herb and Tricia were currently paying $850 a month in rent and hoped to buy a home in the $100,000 to $125,000 price range, they were quite disappointed when their loan advisor showed them how their current numbers worked out. They had no idea they were so fiscally out of shape. "But all is not lost," Steve told the Renkos. "We've got lots of possibilities for getting you the home you want.

"Here are three things we can do," Steve pointed out. "First, we'll move you into a 5/25 adjustable-rate mortgage. That will bring down your interest rate. Second, I know of a first-time buyer program that permits a .41 total debt ratio. And third, we've got to figure out how you can get rid of some of your awful monthly bills."

To shape up their finances, the Renkos sold their car. That not only eliminated a $287 per month car payment, it produced $1,200 in cash that the Renkos could use as part of their down payment. Herb and Tricia decided they could get by with just one car until they became homeowners. Next, the couple refinanced and consolidated their Visa, Discover, and student loan balances into one loan with a payment of $185 a month. Tricia also thought that because she had been winning praise in her job she might be in line for a raise. So she asked and received an extra $200 a month.

Here's how the Renkos' new shaped-up numbers worked out:

Total gross monthly income	$3,610
Total debt ratio	× .41
Total allowable debt payments	$1,480
less total monthly bills	
Car payment	160
Consolidated loan	185
Property taxes and homeowners' insurance (estimated)	125
Total monthly bills	$ 470
leaves	
Qualifying mortgage payment	$1,010 (P + I)

Using an 8.5 percent 5/25 ARM, a payment of $1,010 a month will amortize a mortgage of $131,339.

$$\frac{\$1,010}{\$7.69} = \$131,339 \; (131.339 \times 1,000)$$

Back to the Housing Cost Ratio

The first-time buyer program that their loan advisor found for the Renkos applied a .29 housing cost ratio as a separate test of the Renkos' financial fitness. Using this .29 housing cost ratio fitness test, the Renkos qualified for a mortgage payment (PITI) of around $1,047:

$$.29 \; (\text{housing cost ratio}) \times$$
$$\$3,610 \; (\text{their new monthly gross income}) = \$1,047 \; (\text{PITI})$$

If we estimate $125 a month for property taxes and insurance, that leaves the Renkos $922 a month to cover principal and interest ($1,047 less $125):

$$\frac{\$922 \; (\text{P} + \text{I})}{\$7.69 \; (\text{payment per \$1,000})} = \$119.896 \; (\text{mortgage amount})$$

Considering both of these ratio tests, the Renkos' income qualifies them for a mortgage of around $120,000 to $130,000—a figure large enough to get them the home they want.

Mortgage Approval Often Requires a Strategy to Qualify

"If you don't qualify," says mortgage broker Helen Crosby, "then I'm going to see what I can do to make you qualify. I earn my living saying, 'Yes, I think it's doable,' not by saying, 'Oh, you don't fall within Fannie Mae's standard guideline ratios. I guess we'll just have to turn you down.' If I did that," Helen adds, "I wouldn't earn enough to make my own mortgage payments."

As you try to figure out how much home you can afford, it's important for you to work with a Realtor and a loan advisor who are committed to seeing you become a homeowner. You want someone like Steve Bailey and Helen Crosby, who are willing to work and rework your numbers. Never forget that borrowing power depends on how well you and your loan advisor explore possibilities. How much money you can borrow depends on a combination of many factors, such as the following:

1. Your gross monthly income.
2. Your long-term monthly installment debt payments. (Typically, if monthly payments on your car loan or other installment debt end within 6 to 10 months, your lender won't include these payments in calculating your total debt ratio.)
3. The qualifying ratios of a specific lender and loan program. (Remember, different lenders and loan programs set different qualifying ratios. A "not at this time" turndown by one lender may mean you should look for another lender or loan program whose qualifying guidelines better match your level of fiscal fitness. Or you might turn to seller financing.)
4. The type of mortgage you select, its term, and the "qualifying" interest rate. (The qualifying interest rate may be higher or lower than the stated interest rate on your loan.)
5. Other regular monthly costs of home financing or home ownership such as property taxes, homeowners' insurance, and, typically, homeowners' association fees and mortgage insurance.

If you don't currently qualify for the amount of mortgage you want, don't accept no as a final answer. Figure out how you can increase your income, reduce your debt, find a more accommodating lender, or use a loan program that permits higher qualifying ratios. In fact, if you're borderline even after you've completed your fiscal fitness exercises, you still may be able to get your loan approved by emphasizing your *compensating factors.*

Qualifying Ratios and Compensating Factors

When Ursala Chang applied for her mortgage, she was turned down. Her lender's guidelines called for a housing cost ratio of 28 percent. Ursala's ratio was 33 percent. Nevertheless, Ursala didn't give up. She wrote the vice president of mortgage loan operations and explained, "I've got a perfect credit record, no debts, and I can walk to work. So, I don't pay any costs for commuting. Plus, I'm single. My living expenses are far less than they would be if I were supporting a family." By emphasizing these positive compensating factors, Ursala got her loan.

Compensating Factors Make a Difference

Gordon Steinback, an executive at the Mortgage Guarantee Insurance Corporation, says his firm "routinely approves borrowers who don't meet standard underwriting criteria." Yet, as Gordon points out, "regrettably, too many other renters never get beyond the application stage. This happens because these renters don't meet the so-called 'standard' qualifying ratios and are needlessly screened out prematurely by [those] real estate agents or loan officers at the local level [who too quickly try to pigeonhole borrowers as simply qualified or unqualified]. Experience shows, however, that a large percentage of renters fall into a gray area. These borrowers could get approved for a loan if only someone would show them how."

Types of Compensating Factors

What types of compensating factors will lenders consider? Virtually anything positive that reasonably demonstrates you could make your monthly payments responsibly and control your finances. Here are examples:

1. You pay rent that equals or exceeds the after-tax cost of your proposed mortgage payments.
2. You save regularly. You spend less than you earn and use credit sparingly.
3. You are traveling on the fast track in your career or employment. You receive periodic promotions and raises.
4. For your age and occupation, you own a high net worth—cash-value life insurance, 401(k) retirement funds, stocks, bonds, savings account, or other real estate.
5. You have saved more than adequate cash reserves to deal with unexpected financial setbacks.
6. You or your spouse generates extra income through part-time work, a second job, tips, bonuses, or overtime.

7. You owe little or no monthly installment debt. This can work well when your housing cost ratio exceeds its guideline, but your total debt ratio falls within its limits.

8. You've completed a homebuying counseling program that helps homebuyers develop a realistic budget.

9. You're making a large down payment.

10. Your employer provides excellent benefits: auto (a company car or credit for mileage), cash reimbursement for a home office, a superior health and dental insurance plan, or large contributions to your retirement account.

11. You earn an above-average income. People whose earnings exceed, say, $6,000 a month often enjoy the budget flexibility to devote more money to housing than qualifying ratios indicate.

12. Your nonhousing living expenses are lower than average. You would explain that you can afford a higher mortgage because (1) the home is energy efficient; (2) you can walk to work or drive a short commute; (3) you partake of no costly vices (e.g., smoking, drinking); (4) you spend conservatively, backpack for vacations, drive a cream puff 2001 Taurus, and buy clothes at the Goodwill store; (5) you're handy with tools so you can perform your own household maintenance; or (6) your food costs are low because your parents supply you with fresh and home-canned vegetables from their garden.

Put Your Compensating Factors (Letters of Explanation) in Writing

After you've developed a list of reasons why you are willing and able to pay back the mortgage you want, don't just tell the loan representative. Put your explanations in writing. Get supporting letters from your employer, minister, landlord, clients, customers, or anyone else who can vouch for your good character, credit-worthiness, job performance, or personal responsibility. Sometimes, too, it's a good idea to write out a family budget. Show the lender that your monthly income exceeds your monthly spending. Then back up your budget with proof: financial records, cancelled checks, letters, and other compensating factors. With convincing written evidence, you'll be able to break through qualifying guidelines that deter or delay other would-be borrowers.

Credit Record

To qualify for most loan programs—although exceptions exist—mortgage lenders put your credit history under a microscope. If they discover a record of prompt payments, many lenders will stretch their qualifying ratios. In contrast, few lenders will offset a poor current credit record with reduced qualifying ratios. To get a *new* mortgage, in most cases you'll need good credit. But what is good credit?

Maybe not as good as you think. "There are perceptions out there [about credit standards]," says John Hemschoot of Fannie Mae, "that simply have no basis in fact." As Mr. Hemschoot explains, "Generally a credit history that consists of a minor, isolated instance of poor credit or late payments is acceptable—as long as the lapse is satisfactorily explained in writing and the borrower has other credit accounts that have excellent payment records." Rent, though, excepts the rule. A history of late rent payments usually kills mortgage applications.

Whether it's Visa, MasterCard, student loans, car payments, or rent, never carelessly let your payments fall behind. Any payments 30 days late will cause a lender to examine your application more closely. Late payments, when combined with any other problems (e.g., high ratios, low property appraisal, short job history, low down payment), may defer the approval of a new loan until you strengthen your fiscal fitness.

What about Major Setbacks?

If you've suffered major setbacks like foreclosure, eviction, bankruptcy, or multiple and continuous late payments, most lenders will want to see two years of near perfect credit history before they'll consider you for a mortgage. However, recall that these are guidelines. Both FHA and VA have considered former bankrupts after just 12 months. An underwriting guide of Freddie Mac states, "Adverse credit information in and of itself does not mean the borrower is not creditworthy.... Freddie Mac does not specify a minimum time period for re-establishing credit after the occurrence of adverse events."

Freddie (and Fannie) Encourage Lender Flexibility

In its publication *Discover Gold Through Expanding Markets*, Freddie Mac tells mortgage lenders, "Our guidelines do not provide [rigid] rules for creditworthiness. When you evaluate a borrower we want you to weigh the credit record, including any past difficulties, along with other information on the borrower's financial situation to arrive at a well-reasoned conclusion that supports your expectation that the borrower will repay the mortgage...."

Freddie Mac published *Discover Gold Through Expanding Markets* as part of its outreach effort to educate its lenders. "This booklet" says Freddie Mac, "is to ensure that the flexibility you can use when applying our guidelines is widely known.... We provide guidelines for your decision-making that let you assess each borrower.

"Our guidelines," Freddie Mac continues, "provide the flexibility you need to participate in community revitalization ... handle diverse cultural needs such as pooling of funds, financial support from extended families.... We allow gifts or grants ... nontraditional sources of equity such as rent credits and sweat equity.... When you use our guidelines with the flexibility illustrated in this book, you will find that you can serve borrowers of any race, nationality or ethnic background and make more loans in support of your communities...."

Are You a Manageable Credit Risk?

Most important, lenders decide whether you're a manageable credit risk. In its booklet *A Plain & Simple Guide for First-Time Home Buyers,* the Mortgage Bankers Association explains it this way: "If you've had credit problems, prepare to discuss them honestly with your mortgage lenders—and come to your application meeting with a written explanation. Responsible mortgage lenders know there can be legitimate reasons for credit problems ... or other financial difficulties. If you've had a problem that's been corrected, and your payments have been on time for a year or more, your credit will probably be considered satisfactory."

What are some "legitimate" reasons? These include major illness, uninsured medical bills, loss of job, business failure, divorce, or anything that doesn't look like financial irresponsibility.

Write Clear Letters of Explanation

Whether you explain compensating factors or adverse credit history, write clearly and persuasively. State the facts. But also explain those facts in a way that's favorable to your case. Freddie Mac even tells its lenders that in addition to securing explanations, "It is equally important to ensure that a borrower is not disadvantaged by a poorly written or incomplete explanation. We encourage you," says Freddie, "to ensure that the borrower is provided whatever assistance is needed to provide you with complete, accurate information...."

Your Realtor and your loan representative want to get your loan approved. If you could use some help in wording your letters of explanation, ask for it. Sometimes loan reps will draft explanatory notes and simply ask you to sign them. A well-written letter can make the difference between a "not-at-this-time" turndown and a "thumbs up" approval.

Get Copies of Your Credit Reports

Within the United States are hundreds of local credit bureaus and credit agencies. But the great majority of these firms are affiliated with one or more of the three largest credit repositories: (1) equifax.com, (2) transunion.com, and (3) experian.com. Federal law entitles you to a free report each year.

These credit repositories are like large warehouses connected to the information highway. Through the credit data they collect on nearly every adult in the United States, they prepare credit reports by pulling up data from their computer files. Although these three firms are working to merge their data files, at present each company may show a somewhat different credit picture for you. Therefore, before you begin to shop for a home, ask each of these companies to send you a copy of your credit record. Or, more easily, obtain your credit reports and Fico scores at myfico.com. (See next section.)

Once you've received your reports, check them closely for errors. "What's so disturbing," says Allan Fell, director of the Maryland Consumer Credit Commission, "is that we have documented beyond any doubt that the [credit repositories] aren't doing what they say—they're not cleaning up erroneous files when they're asked to by the consumers directly affected by the errors."

Because of this potential for mistake and delays, identify errors as early as possible. When you wait to correct your file until after you've applied for a mortgage, the credit bureau's (or your creditor's) reporting mistakes could put your loan on hold for months. By that time, the house you want may have sold to someone else. Just as important, first impressions count. When a lender pulls your credit report, you want it to look as good as possible. As the saying goes, "You never get a second chance to make a good first impression."

Automated Underwriting and Credit Scoring

Everything this chapter tells you about preparing to qualify stands true. However, two other critical elements of mortgage qualifying enter the picture. They're called automated underwriting and credit scoring.

Objective or Irrational?

Lenders and credit bureaus believe that automated underwriting and credit scoring force greater objectivity. Computer programs treat everyone the same without regard to race, sex, age, ethnicity, or other irrelevant factors. Automated systems eliminate human bias. Nevertheless, critics say that until credit scorers release the exact nature of their methodology, consumers can't learn precisely how to improve their finances and lift their credit scores.

Even worse, some people with excellent credit records score low, and others whose qualifying ratios dramatically exceed 28/36 are approved. At times, automated underwriting seems more irrational than objective. So, what's up?

The lending and credit folks say they can't tell you. If they released this information, they say, borrowers would rig their finances to achieve higher scores. Besides, over a period of years they've spent millions of dollars to finance the development of these statistical programs. Just think how much money they would lose if they opened their black box for everyone to see. Plus, think how much money they're going to make by forcing 100 to 200 million Americans to buy their credit scores every year.

Nevertheless, even though secrecy rules, under pressure, Fair Isaacs now posts credit scoring tips on its website (myfico.com). These tips do not reveal everything you would like to know. But they're a start.

Borrower Gains and Losses

In the overall picture, automated underwriting and credit scoring have helped more consumers than they have harmed. Automation lowers costs, speeds up the approval process, and, as practiced, has actually increased the number of borrowers who qualify for a mortgage and buy a home. Nevertheless, the critics make good points.

As a result, some members of Congress and state legislators are calling for more disclosures. In addition, the powerful lobbying arm of NAR (the National Association of Realtors) has sided with the critics and is also pushing for more disclosure. To follow the latest developments, check out the following web sites: www.myfico.com, www.credit scoring.com, and www.creditaccuracy.com. Plus, you can visit www.ftc. gov, which is the agency responsible for enforcing the Fair Credit Reporting Act and other consumer protection laws.

You Can Raise the Necessary Cash

Q: Would you like to own your own home?

A: Sure, wouldn't everybody?

Q: Then why are you still renting?

A: We don't have enough for a down payment.

Every year the National Association of Realtors, Fannie Mae, Freddie Mac, and other national organizations survey renters about home ownership. And every year a majority of renters answer the same way: "Sure, we'd like to buy a home someday, but we don't have enough money for a down payment." Although it's true that when you buy a home, you will probably need some cash for a down payment, closing costs, and maybe reserves, it's also true that most renters overestimate the actual amount of cash required.

You can buy a $100,000 home with less than $5,000 in cash. You can buy a $250,000 home with no more than $10,000 to $15,000 in cash, sometimes less. (See Mistake #2.)

Even more important, it's not a question of whether you have enough cash *right now.* Instead, the right questions are (1) What's the least amount of cash you need? and (2) How can you raise it? As long as you tell yourself you don't have enough money, you'll never prepare a plan to raise whatever amount you do need. When you *plan* to qualify, you will be able to raise a down payment for some type of loan program within a period of 3 to 12 months.

Fiscal Fitness Exercises

If qualifying looks iffy, and you need to come up with more cash or qualifying income, here are several fiscal fitness exercises that will help you shape up your finances.

1. Save more by cutting your expenses.
2. Save more by increasing your income.
3. Seek a gift, grant, or loan for your down payment.

Save More by Cutting Your Expenses

"We have been wanting to buy our own home for several years," says Paul Silver, "but like a lot of other couples, we didn't have money for a down payment. Yet, we did notice that our friends who bought didn't earn any more than we did. They found the necessary cash; why couldn't we?

"Then it dawned on us," Paul continues. "We were trying to save by default. After we paid our bills each month and covered our living expenses, we said we'd put aside the money left over. Well, guess how much actually went into savings? Seldom anything. In fact, as often as not, by the end of the month, we had added several hundred dollars to our credit card balances. Obviously, after we thought it over we knew that unless we changed our spending habits, we'd still be paying rent with our social security checks.

"So," Paul continues, "here's how we changed our spendthrift ways. To start, I recalled something my grandmother told my parents. 'Pay yourself first,' she always said. 'Write down how much money you want to accumulate by a specific date. Then every week put aside whatever amount is required to reach your goal.'

"So that was our starting point," says Paul. "Rose and I decided we would save $10,000 during the next 10 months. To reach this goal, we adopted one simple rule: Don't spend money for anything (other than bare necessities) that we wanted less than a house. By setting priorities, we found it much easier to pay ourselves first. Every time we considered splurging at an expensive restaurant, taking a weekend trip, or buying some new clothes, we asked ourselves, 'Is this more important than owning our own home?"

"We ruled out the answer, 'just this time won't hurt.' While my mother was on a diet, she gained 25 pounds repeating that excuse. 'Just this time' always leads to trouble. Once we committed to home ownership, we didn't punish ourselves by longing for things we didn't need. We just kept our goal in sight.

"And I mean literally in sight," Paul continued, "We took photographs of homes we liked and stuck them up all over our apartment. With these ever-present reminders of our soon-to-be achieved reward, even the major slashes we made to our spending didn't feel like sacrifices. Anyway, this approach worked for us. Eleven and a half months after we made up our minds to own, we closed on our first home."

Do you find yourself short of cash? Then take the Silvers' approach. Pay yourself first. Then, to maximize savings, itemize and list your current spending. (See Mistake #3.) Give yourself a Draconian line-item veto. Slash out all but necessities. Prioritize. Eliminate all purchases that you value less than home ownership. For spending that remains, shift to lower cost stores, products, and services.

Try the following suggestions:

1. *Never say budget.* No one likes to budget. It sounds like work. Instead, think priorities. Think reward. The quality of your life improves as you allocate your money according to your highest values. If you truly want to own your own home, put your money where your heart is.

2. *Stop paying rent.* For most people who don't own their own homes, rent is the biggest money waster. Can you figure out how to eliminate or reduce your rent payments? Can you switch to a lower cost apartment? Can you houseshare? Can you find a housesitting job for the next 3 to 12 months? Can you move in with your parents or stay rent-free with relatives or friends? Bank your rent money for 6 to 12 months and you'll never pay rent again.

3. *Cut your food bills in half.* Eliminate eating out. Brown bag your lunches. Buy unbranded foods in bulk. Prepare your food in large quantities and freeze portions in meal-sized servings. Forget those $3 microwave lunches and dinners. Locate a discount grocery like Aldi's Canned Foods, Big Lots, or Drug Emporium. Shop at

the new food warehouses that have opened in many cities. Food prices in discount stores run 20 to 50 percent less than big name supermarkets. Collect and use as many coupons as you can find. When you see bargain-priced items that you use regularly, buy them in quantity.

4. *Cut up your credit cards.* Credit cards make spending too easy. Put yourself on a cash diet. Nothing curbs spending more than having to count out real cash. Besides, credit card bills zap strength from your borrowing power. Even worse, by the time you pay off your credit card balances at 18 percent interest, you will have paid back two dollars for every dollar you originally charged—and that's in after-tax take-home dollars. Once you consider that you take home only 60 to 80 percent of what you earn, you have to earn more than two dollars to pay back every dollar you charge to your credit cards.

5. *Don't put the car before the house.* If you own a car that's worth nearly as much as a down payment on a house, sell it. Get rid of those cash-draining car payments. If your car is mostly paid for, there's a good part of the money you need to move up to home ownership. If you think about buying a more expensive car, don't! Until you can afford your own home, drive the least expensive, dependable car you can find. For too many renters, a car is the enemy of their house.

6. *Eliminate costly vices.* How much do you spend each year on cigarettes, beer, liquor, and drinks at restaurants, clubs, or bars? Add them up. These costly vices range upwards of $2,000 to $5,000 per year or more. Eliminate these wasteful habits. You magnify your power to save money.

7. *Buy clothes from thrift shops.* Even if you're an up-and-coming investment banker on Wall Street, don't spend your hard-earned after-tax dollars on new, expensive clothing. How about an $1,800 Armani suit for $695, or an Armani silk tie priced at $40? Both of these (and many comparable bargains) were available at GENTLY Owned in Atlanta. These fashion items were new, bought at close out. For recycled clothing, savings can be much higher. In her newspaper column "Dress for Less," Candy

Barrie writes, "I'm a big fan of these [consignment and thrift] shops for the fashion bargains you can find there.... Get on down and you'll discover we're not just talking about 20, 30, or 40 percent discounts. Sometimes you can get your clothes for 90 to 95 percent off retail. Some wealthy people don't give their expensive clothes away, so they place them in consignment and thrift shops."

Want to save money? Follow Candy's advice: Locate all the recycled and closeout clothing stores in your area or a nearby big city. Whatever your tastes and price range, you'll find that you can slash your clothing expenses by 50 percent or more.

8. *Wait to buy new furniture and appliances.* As with cars and clothing, most renters spend too much too soon for furniture and appliances. Even worse, instead of paying cash, they charge it. They chain themselves to several years of payments at high interest rates. (Or, increasingly, they are hooked into those "no payments, no interest for six months" promotions that make credit purchases tough to pass up.) Do yourself a favor: resist this temptation. Like cars and clothing, furniture and appliances depreciate in price faster than they depreciate in condition. As a result, you can find second-hand bargains. I have bought many beautiful older pieces of high-quality furniture for less than the cheap particleboard stuff that most lower-priced furniture stores sell. Although used appliances can pose some risk, you can reduce this risk when you buy appliances with transferable extended warranties (or buy a home warranty plan that covers appliances).

Whether you buy clothing, cars, furniture, or appliances, let someone else suffer the depreciation. Pay only for the use of a product. The less money you waste on depreciating assets, the faster you can build wealth through home ownership.

Save More, Increase Your Income

Increasing your income not only improves your qualifying ratios, it helps you accumulate savings. Use the following techniques to bring in more income:

1. Ask for a raise, promotion, or transfer to a higher-paying department. Most employers want their employees to own their own homes. Let your manager know how he or she can help.

2. Work overtime or take on a second job.

3. Find a higher paying job in your own field. Although lenders prefer to see two years of job stability, if you accept a new job where you have proven skills, an upward career move is usually considered a plus. On the other hand, if you've been selling shoes for six years, no lender would look favorably on your quitting your job to start selling cars—even if you earn more money. In that case, most mortgage lenders would want to see one or more years of steady earnings in auto sales before they would approve you for a new mortgage.

4. Put your spouse or kids to work. Today it often takes two incomes to afford a home. If they're working already, make saving for a down payment a family affair. Even income from a part-time job helps.

5. Not married? Buy with a friend. Nationwide, more than 250,000 homes a year are bought by alternative types of households. (This figure doesn't include singles who buy alone or POSSLQs—a census term meaning persons of the opposite sex in shared living quarters.) See *The New York Times* (June 20, 2005) "Shared Ownership Grows to Combat High Housing Prices."

6. Take in housemates, create an accessory apartment, or buy a duplex, triplex, or other multiple-unit building. Part of the rent you collect counts toward your qualifying income.

7. Earn more or cut spending through barter. Do you have skills or knowledge that you can swap for other goods or services?

8. If you work in commissioned or incentive employment (tips, bonuses, piecework), think of ways you can work smarter and more effectively.

In the long-standing best seller, *The Magic of Getting What You Want,* Dr. David Schwartz points out that the other side of spending is earning. Although reduced spending keeps more money in your pocket, you gain even more when you figure out ways to increase your income. What are you going to do to earn more?

Caveat: You or your spouse generally can't boost your *qualifying* income by starting to work overtime or taking on a second job just several months before you apply for a mortgage. Lenders usually like to see an earnings history of one or two years. They want you to show that your income has proven steady and foreseeable.

Even when lenders won't include extra or indefinite income directly in your qualifying ratios, all is not lost. In those instances, lenders may count your extra income as a compensating factor. Treated in this manner, the income permits a lender to qualify you using ratios that exceed its typical guidelines. Either way, the extra income boosts your borrowing power.

Seek a Gift, Grant, or Loan for Your Down Payment

Would your parents, other relatives, or employer give or loan you some or all of the cash you need for a down payment and closing costs? At least 20 percent of all first-time homebuyers use this technique to raise money. When Joan and Theo Clapp got married, they told their friends and relatives, "Please, no china sets, Crockpots, or espresso machines." But if their friends and relatives wanted to help, a cash gift to the Clapps' "house account" was truly appreciated.

Besides the help of family or friends, some first-time homebuyers obtain down payment grants from government agencies or not-for-profit housing groups. This trend is growing. In addition to assistance from grants, some cities and states will loan homebuyers all or part of the money they need for a down payment or closing costs. "Public notice," says the ad in the *Los Angeles Times*, "the city of Los Angeles will loan you up to $50,000 toward the purchase of your new home. No monthly payments required. Loan may never have to be repaid." Other sources of loans (or gifts) for down payments include OWC (owner will carry) sellers, shared equity investors, homebuilders, and mortgage companies.

CHAPTER 12

Draft Your Offer

When you and your realty agent (or lawyer) draft your purchase offer, aim for three objectives: (1) a win-win agreement, (2) a legally enforceable agreement, and (3) a clear and comprehensive agreement that diminishes ambiguity, confusion, and conflict. Because Chapter 7 shows how to negotiate win-win, this chapter highlights legality and clarity.

A Legally Enforceable Agreement

Generally, a legally enforceable real estate purchase agreement must meet the following criteria:

1. In writing
2. Includes the names and signatures of all parties
3. No counter offer changes
4. Delivered to the other parties
5. Clauses clear and without material mistake
6. No material fraud or misrepresentation

In Writing

Usually courts will not enforce oral agreements for the sale of real estate. Therefore, until you put your offer in writing, it has no legal effect. Likewise, a seller who orally promises to sell at a specific price (or specific terms) cannot be compelled to honor that promise.

Along these same lines, courts generally follow the parole evidence rule. This means that to effect a change, addition, or deletion to a valid written contract, you need to get that change in writing. For example, say your written contract sets June 1 as the date of closing, but you learn that you need more time. The sellers say, "No problem; July 1 will work just fine for us."

Don't rely on this oral promise (or any others the sellers might make). Courts seldom permit oral modifications to trump the written word. If you want to hold the sellers to their promises, write such promises out and leave no doubt.

Includes the Names and Signatures of All Parties

Most often homes are jointly owned by husband and wife, relatives, partners, or friends. Without the signatures of *all* owners, a court will not compel a sale—even though one of the owners told you, "No problem, Mary will sign when she gets back in town." Don't count on it. Sometimes joint sellers can't agree among themselves. Until all sellers sign, you have no enforceable contract.

No Counter Offer Changes

When you submit an offer to the sellers, they must accept it exactly as written. If they change any terms or clauses, as a matter of law, they have rejected your offer and are proposing a counteroffer (a new contract). Likewise, if you change any part of their counteroffer, you, too, make a counter-counteroffer.

In other words, if you or the sellers reject and counter, you face the risk of losing the deal altogether. You can't counter-counteroffer, face a seller rejection, and then say, "Okay, then, we'll go ahead and accept the seller's last counteroffer." In that situation, the sellers are under no legal obligation to revive their counteroffer. They may. Or, they may not.

This accept or reject dilemma generates an element of risk. Say you're willing to pay $485,000 for a home that's listed at $499,000. You open negotiations at $470,000. The sellers counteroffer at $479,000. Do you comeback with a bid of $475,000? Think carefully. If you do, the sellers may say no—and further refuse to accept even $479,000. I would advise you to accept the $479,000 price. Don't push. Don't risk losing a good price in the hope of getting a better one.

Hardball negotiators would probably urge you to counter their $479,000. In the end, it's your call. Just realize that leaving something on the table best serves the philosophy of win-win negotiating. If you try to pull all of the chips into your pile, other players may walk away from the game—or kick sand in your face later in the deal if they get the chance.

Delivered to the Other Parties

In and of itself a signed offer or counteroffer does not create an enforceable contract. Generally, your signed agreement must be delivered (or, at the least, communicated) to the other parties. Say you offer to buy a house. The sellers sign the contract later that day, but then have second thoughts. They tell no one and simply leave the contract sitting on their dining room table.

Meanwhile, you discover that a house you wanted more has come back on the market. You submit an offer. The sellers sign it right away and say to you, "We've got a deal."

You next call the first sellers and say, "Cancel the offer. We've bought something else." By now, though, the first sellers have decided that they do want to go through with the deal. Can they force you to buy? Probably not. As a rule, you are free to withdraw an offer any time before the sellers notify you that they have signed the contract.

Of course, this rule works both ways. If you want to enforce the sellers' counteroffer, you must do more than sign it. You must communicate your acceptance. Until notified, they, too, are free to change their minds and withdraw.

Clauses Clear and without Material Mistake

As a minimum, courts require enforceable contracts to clearly specify the property to be conveyed, the price, and the terms. On occasion, parties to a sales contract write something like, "buyer agrees to pay $225,000 on terms mutually agreeable to buyers and sellers." On other occasions, the sales contract may read, "buyer agrees to pay $289,500 for the property known as the McDill farmhouse and adjoining acreage."

Should a dispute later arise between the parties of either of these purported contracts, the courts would be reluctant to step in and order a sale. These types of clauses leave too much to the imagination. A court typically will not rewrite your contract to correct a property description or clarify the terms of the owner-finance clause. Likewise, courts may not enforce a contract that includes a mistake that runs counter to the true intent of the parties (e.g., the real estate agent mistakenly writes a price of $289,500 when the agreed price was actually $259,800).

No Material Fraud or Misrepresentation

In an effort to persuade prospective buyers, sellers often assert, "We've never had any problems with the roof," "This is a wonderful neighborhood for kids," or maybe, "Oh yes, this addition to the house meets all the building and safety codes." In instances where you justifiably rely on such statements, you have a right to expect the truth.

If after signing a sales contract you learn that the sellers' statements were false, you can legally refuse to go through with the agreement. Likewise, if you have already closed on the house, you can ask the courts to rescind the contract or award you damages, or some combination of both. Generally, courts will not hold a party to a contract induced by false statements that were material to the contract.

Buyers, Too, Must Speak the Truth

Although misrepresentations usually come from the mouths of sellers, buyers can also mislead. Say you're trying to talk the sellers into an OWC arrangement by claiming, "My job's perfectly secure; in fact, I'm in line for a big raise and promotion." If the sellers accept your claims as true and therefore carry back financing, they can rescind if later they learn that you were not telling the truth—that you knew all along that your whole department was about to be downsized right out of the company.

Parole Evidence Rule Doesn't Apply

Under the parole evidence rule, courts won't *change* the terms of a written contract based upon oral testimony. However, in cases of fraud or misrepresentation, courts do not merely alter your agreement. They refuse to enforce the agreement. And when deciding such issues, courts will accept into evidence, "he said/she said" types of oral testimony. In cases of fraud, a signed contract does not end the matter.

A Clear and Comprehensive Agreement

The *ideal* purchase contract not only satisfies the minimum requirements of enforceability, it also sets out the full scope of the parties' agreement. Such a contract anticipates everything, leaves no room for subjective interpretation, and treats each party fairly. Of course, no ideal contract has ever been written, or ever will be written.

Nevertheless, to work toward this goal, attend to the following details.

The Myth of the Standard Contract

Today, few sales contracts are drafted from scratch. Instead, most realty agents, lawyers, and by-owner sellers use a fill-in-the-blank form. No matter what someone may tell you, though, these forms do not represent *standard* contracts. Various "standard" forms differ in many ways. In my files are real estate contract forms of one and a half pages, and others of eight pages plus addendums and riders.

Before you prepare an offer, obtain the forms typically used in your area by Realtors and lawyers. Read though it (them). Compare its terms to those discussed in this chapter. For more in-depth treatment, read through Mark Warda's *How to Negotiate Real Estate Contracts*, 2000 (Sourcebooks). With this knowledge, you'll gain the ability to ask your realty agent more probing questions and hopefully write a contract that guides you and the sellers through a smooth and cooperative transaction.

Property Description

When you buy a home, your purchase agreement will likely include four types of property: (1) site, (2) buildings, (3) fixtures, and (4) personal property. Make sure you receive exactly what you're bargaining for in each category.

1. *Site.* Include not only the legal description (e.g., plot plan), but also site dimensions, size, and boundaries. You might note the

plantings, too. It's a good idea to actually walk the site boundaries. Many times, buyers learn after a sale that their site isn't what they thought it was. Sometimes, sellers even dig up flowers and shrubs and take them to their new home. The same for fencing, mailboxes, lampposts, and so on.

2. *Buildings.* Do you believe the outdoor storage shed goes with the property? Do you believe the house was designed by a famous architect? Do you believe the house is of a particular age, square footage, construction materials, or energy efficiency? Then put these items into the property description.

3. *Fixtures.* Fixtures include all personal property permanently attached or adapted for use with a home—for example, light fixtures, chandeliers, garage door opener, sinks, cabinetry, mailboxes, ceiling fans, built-in window or wall AC units, wall-to-wall carpeting, and storm windows. Two types of problems can arise: Sometimes sellers simply unbolt the fixtures and take them; and second, sometimes an item that appears permanently attached really isn't. So, list all fixtures (or at least all that may wander off.)

4. *Personal Property.* Confusion over personal property accounts for a large number of buyer–seller disputes. Personal property includes items such as area rugs, furniture, appliances, blinds, draperies, doormats, and lawn equipment. If you expect the sellers to include these or other similar items in the sale, list them in the contract, along with serial numbers and descriptions where applicable.

Many realty agents will think I'm paranoid. But I know of transactions where sellers have dug up their tulip bulbs, substituted old, cheap appliances for new, expensive ones, removed a Tiffany chandelier, unbolted a large over-the-mantel mirror, replaced Hunter ceiling fans with cheap imitations, and disassembled a storage shed and packed it up with their other household belongings.

As to site size, site boundaries, and building size, mistakes occur frequently. Take measurements. Compare a physical site inspection to the survey. A moment of prevention beats two years of litigation. When you write it out, you reduce doubt. Learn of any misunderstandings before you buy not after you move in.

Earnest Money

Often called a good faith deposit, earnest money tells the seller that you're a serious buyer. How serious? That depends (from the seller's perspective) on how much you deposit. Large amounts (5 to 10 percent of the purchase price) speak louder than small deposits (1/2 to 1 percent).

Required Minimum

Contrary to popular belief, legally valid offers do not require a deposit of a certain amount—nor, in fact, any deposit at all. Also, some buyers choose to pay their deposits in stages: a small amount attached to the offer and a larger amount when the sellers accept. (Never offer a post-dated check as your deposit. It destroys your credibility.)

Don't Give the Sellers Your Deposit

If you offer to buy from a FSBO (for sale by owner), do not hand your earnest money directly to the sellers unless it's such a small amount that you don't mind the risk of loss. Instead, open an escrow or trust account. Title insurers provide this service. When your offer goes through a realty agent, she will place these funds into her company's trust account.

What Happens to the Money?

If the sale closes, your earnest money will count toward your down payment and settlement expenses. If, in spite of good faith efforts on your part, the sale falls through, ask for a return of the deposit. As long as the sellers sign a release, the trust account will issue you a check. If the sellers won't sign a release—absent success in informal negotiations—you'll probably need to arbitrate or litigate the dispute.

Contingencies

Most buyers condition their offers with one or more contingencies. Common contingencies apply to (1) the buyers' ability to obtain financing, and (2) a professionally prepared physical inspection of the property. In addition, some buyers include contingencies for attorney approval, the sale of an existing home, or perhaps even the receipt of a tax return check.

You can include whatever contingencies you like. Just realize, the more escape hatches (or "weasel clauses") you write into your offer, the less likely the sellers will accept it. A no strings attached offer (i.e., no contingencies) always looks better than one entangled with a myriad of ifs, ands, or buts.

The Financing Contingency

To strengthen your offer, show the sellers a mortgage preapproval letter, a copy of your (excellent) credit report, or perhaps your FICO score of 740. Convince the sellers that your financing is a sure thing.

However, for your protection, do not use a financing contingency clause that says something like, "buyer to obtain a mortgage on terms generally prevailing." Instead, specifically write the type of loan, loan-to-value ratio, maximum interest rate, and maximum fees and points that you are willing to accept. With the plethora of mortgage plans available today, a vague financing contingency opens the door to potential disputes.

Likewise, specifically define the phrase, "buyer shall in good faith diligently pursue a mortgage commitment." Does this mean you must apply to 3 lenders, 10 lenders, or 30 lenders? How many mortgage rejections must you suffer before you are entitled to a return of your deposit? Remember, lenders may accept a borrower's credit, yet turn down a loan because of poor property condition, a low appraisal, an environmental hazard, or numerous other reasons.

Also, during the time you are applying for a loan, interest rates could jump. So, for all of these reasons, define the meaning of "good faith efforts."

Physical Inspection Contingency

Here's another contract clause that often lacks specificity. For example, one such form reads as follows:

> If it is the opinion of such inspector that the property contains serious structural, mechanical, or other defects, then BUYER shall have the option to revoke this offer....

Notice, first, that under this clause, the property need not actually suffer defects. All you need to escape from this contract is to find some inspector who will opine defects. Moreover, the nature of the defects pertinent to items structural or mechanical ostensibly needs to be serious. But what does "serious" mean? Five hundred dollars, five thousand dollars, or what?

Also, the "other defects" term need not meet the "serious" test, whatever serious may mean. Moreover, the contract grants the buyer the right to withdraw without even giving the seller the option to remedy or repair.

As a seller, I would never accept such a vague and biased clause. But as a committed buyer, you, too, should reject it. For starters, place a dollar threshold that must be exceeded before you can revoke the offer. And grant the sellers the right to fix whatever is wrong—regardless of cost—as long as it can be completed satisfactorily within a time frame that fits your schedule.

Types of Inspection Experts

For most home inspections, an all-purpose, professionally certified home inspector can do a good job for you. But if the house presents specialized legal or physical hazards, write your contingency to allow for inspections by one or more of the following specialists:

- Surveyor: Site size and boundaries.
- Lawyer: Compliance with (or applicability of) zoning, health, building safety, rent control, and other government laws and regulations.
- Site (or soils) engineer: Earthquake, mudslide, and flooding potential, foundation problems, etc.
- Environmentalist: Radon, asbestos, mold, formaldehyde, lead paint, soil contamination, and water quality.
- Component specialist: Roofing, electrical, HVAC, plumbing, and waste disposal (e.g., septic system).
- Pest control: Termites, roaches, and other types of infestation.

Except for surveys and pest control, an all-purpose inspector should satisfy your inspection needs.[1] Yet, with certain hazard-prone areas, complex (or expensive) houses, or for peace of mind, you might include

---

[1] Of course, for larger investment properties, most buyers (myself included) use a team of due diligence specialists.

specialist inspection contingencies. Usually, buyers pay the inspection expense. In some cases, where problems are suspected, try to shift this cost to the sellers.

Attorney Approval Contingencies

If a buyer submits an offer to me with an attorney approval contingency, I say, "Go talk to your lawyer all you want. Then come back when you're ready to make a real offer." As far as I'm concerned, dealing with someone who needs a lawyer to hold their hand is not only a waste of time, it's an invitation for continuing hassles.

In a few states, buyers do use attorney approval contingency clauses. But unless it's an unavoidable practice, avoid them. If necessary, talk to a lawyer first, not after you make an offer. Smart sellers reject such contracts. Generally known as "weasel clauses," these contingencies permit buyers to tie up a property, yet weasel out of the contract at a later date without penalty if it so pleases them. "Sorry, my lawyer has advised me not to go through with this purchase."

Humbug! Go waste the time of someone else.

Other Types of Contingencies

As noted, legally you can place any "if, and, or but" that you want into your purchase offer. But every contingency weakens you as a buyer in the eyes of the sellers. Contingencies diminish your ability to negotiate effectively and to extract seller concessions of substantial value.

However, if you are buying a property with OWC financing, a lease-option, or a mortgage assumption, I do suggest an appraisal contingency. With easy finance deals, first-time homebuyers (and investors) too often overpay for their properties. As when buying a car, they focus on the amount of the down payment and their monthly payments, not the price. Avoid this mistake. Get an appraisal and closely review it (see Chapter 4).

Assignments

Typically, you may legally assign (transfer) your purchase contract to another buyer should you choose to. However, to reduce uncertainty, you could explicitly include such a clause with your offer. Here are three reasons this tactic can benefit you:

1. You buy into a fast-rising market. Prior to closing, you find that you can "flip" your contract for $25,000 in cash. Since you believe the market is now overheated, you decide to pocket a quick profit and avoid the risk of loss in a market collapse.
2. You experience a change in circumstances: A job relocation, a death in the family, or maybe you see another home you greatly prefer. By assigning your contract, you recoup your earnest money deposit that you otherwise may have forfeited.
3. You buy with a lease-option or lease-purchase agreement. Closing is scheduled within 18 months. To earn a profit, you assign the contract (i.e., the right to purchase at a preset price) to another buyer.

Although most homebuyers seldom use an assignment clause, when the need does arise, it proves quite valuable. And because it doesn't harm the sellers—except perhaps in an OWC sale, they might want to qualify the new buyers—sellers have no good reason to oppose it. (However, to discourage speculators, some homebuilders do restrict or deny the right of their buyers to flip their purchase agreement to other buyers.)

Prorations (Apportionments)

Property taxes, improvement bonds, sewer and water charges, homeowners' association fees, and county assessments are assessed against properties, not persons. Accordingly, a purchase contract usually prorates these expenses between the sellers and the buyers as of an agreed upon date (usually closing). Sellers remain liable for charges levied up to the named date. Buyers assume liabilities for the days remaining in the billing period.

Calculating Prorations

To calculate prorations, the math requires nothing more than simple division: Divide the respective number of seller/buyer days into the total amount of each bill. The catch, though, is to make sure you and the sellers identify every bill that needs to be apportioned, and that the amounts are accurate for the time periods in question.

For example, if a closing is scheduled for March 15, 2006, and property taxes are payable for the calendar year 2005 by March 31, 2006, the sellers should pay taxes for all of 2005 and for the first 74 days of 2006. Yet, since the 2006 property taxes have not yet been billed, you don't know for sure how much they will amount to.

Decide ahead of Time

Your realty agent should know various possible ways to deal with this and related apportionment problems. Just don't leave it until closing to find out. Decide at the time you are preparing your purchase contract. I've seen verbal fights break out during settlement over matters that involved less than $100. Ideally, get the sellers or your realty agent to prepare a list of all expense items subject to proration, along with their total amounts and the amounts of contribution required of the sellers.

Backup Offers

If you dilute your purchase offer with contingencies, you might sweeten the deal for the sellers with a backup clause. This clause permits the sellers to continue showing their property and accept other offers. Then, if your contingencies don't clear, the sellers can step right into another agreement.

In an even stronger version of this clause, the sellers are permitted to accept an alternative offer. Then they give you, say, 24 or 48 hours to either fish or cut bait. You either remove your contingencies or you lose the house. (In this situation, you should receive a return of your earnest money deposit.) Backup offers fairly address concerns about a weak offer. Otherwise, the sellers could waste 30 to 90 days of valuable marketing time waiting to see if you're really going to buy.

Time Is of the Essence

Generally, buyers and sellers want a home sale to progress according to schedule. So most purchase offers specify that "time is of the essence." This clause means a party breaches the contract if they fail to strictly meet agreed deadlines.

Sellers, for example, want buyers to quickly clear their contingencies. Accordingly, buyers often agree to complete their inspections and arrange financing within periods of, say, 10 days and 30 days, respectively. (Indeed, you can often soften the adverse effect of contingencies by attaching a short fuse to them. A 24-hour attorney approval contingency or a 10-day financing contingency may get a signature when longer periods would fail.) Buyers, in turn, want sellers to quickly make any agreed-upon repairs and deliver clear title as scheduled. The parties, of course, negotiate the specific number of days allowed for each of these deadlines. But once they are written into the contract, the "time is of the essence" clause requires parties to perform accordingly.

Risk of Damage

The sellers should deliver the property to you on schedule and in the condition agreed to in your contract. To effect this result, bind the sellers through a clause in your contract.

Same Condition Clause

Some purchase offers include language similar to the following:

> Sellers agree to deliver possession of the real estate in the same condition as it is at the date of this contract, except for ordinary wear and tear.

This clause includes two potential sources of confusion. First, if your contract calls for inspections and repairs, then you don't want the same condition. You want the improved condition. Make sure this clause does not conflict with a repair clause. Second, unless closing extends more than, say, six months beyond the contract date, eliminate the wear and tear exception.

You do not want to take possession of a house with newly broken screens, soiled carpets from careless movers, or a greasy stove and oven. Yet, sellers can reasonably argue that each of these defects is nothing more than "normal wear and tear."

Spell Out the Condition You Want

Rather than merely specifying "same condition subject to wear and tear," your offer could define standards of upkeep, cleanliness, repair, maintenance, and yard care. Some sellers cease most (or all) upkeep and maintenance once they believe they've made a sale. Some sellers will leave their trash, debris, and unwanted items that didn't fit into their moving van.

Most sellers, will not abuse their property or stick you with their mess. But, when you clarify the standards that you expect the sellers to meet, you remove a big source of potential dispute.

Casualty Damage

On occasion, a home under contract suffers damage from fire, flood, ice storm, earthquake, or other disaster. If your home-to-be suffers such damage, you would want a clause in your agreement that requires the sellers to repair the damage or compensate you. For damages in excess of, say, $10,000, $20,000, or some higher figure, you may want the right to simply cancel the sale and take back your earnest money deposit.

Final Walk-Through

You can fill your contract with all types of protective covenants. But if you don't discover the sellers' nonperformance until after they've deposited their sales proceeds and have taken off for Toledo, you've still got problems. So, put a final walk-through clause in your agreement. Shortly prior to disbursement (and preferably after the sellers have vacated), perform an inspection of the property.

Verify its condition. Verify cleanliness. Verify that all bargained-for fixtures and personal property remain in the home. If for some reason you can't verify prior to disbursement, seek a 5 or 10 percent holdback of funds until you've completed your walk-through.

"As Is" Condition

Sometimes contracts include an "as is" clause. In the days of caveat emptor (let the buyer beware), this clause diminished seller liability for property defects. "As is" waved a red flag to buyers. It signaled that the seller did not guarantee the condition of the property. "As is" meant "buy at your own risk."

Today, sellers may still attempt to use this clause. But many statutes and court decisions now require "as is" sellers to disclose code violations and property defects to their buyers. Nevertheless, when you see such a clause, strike it. Insist that the sellers provide a list of all property and neighborhood defects, code violations, and disturbances. (Except in some cases, "as is" sellers offer their properties at a steep discount. On those occasions, you must decide whether the reward justifies the risk.)

Because in *most* residential sales "as is" doesn't serve the purpose that many out-of-date sellers believe it does, resolving this issue up front wards off later confusion and conflict. Without early clarification, you might later say to the seller, "You should have told me. I'm suing." And the seller will respond, "That was your responsibility to investigate. I told you 'as is.' That risk was yours to discover. You can't blame me now."

Get full disclosures into your agreement. Protect yourself against being drawn into the blame game.

Proceeds from Condemnation (Eminent Domain)

On occasion—I've experienced this only once, as a seller—the government or a public utility will use its power of eminent domain to acquire certain rights to part of your property (e.g., road widening, sidewalks, sewer lines, utility poles). In exchange, they pay for what they take. Now, what happens if this condemnation occurs after you contract to buy a property, but before you've received title? Who gets the eminent domain money? You or the sellers?

An Example

In my case, here's what happened. After I had entered an agreement to sell my house, a representative from the local electric utility knocked on my door and said that the company wanted to secure one of its poles with a guide cable that would be anchored on my lot. If I would grant them permission to go ahead with this work, they would pay me $2,000. Since my sales contract was silent on this issue, I replied, "Fine, write me a check." And that's what they did. (Had I refused to grant permission for the work, the company would have proceeded anyway and I would have been required to initiate legal proceedings to obtain a larger award—which was not likely.)

Buyers' Rights

As is typical in sales contracts, I promised to deliver a marketable title to the buyers. As a rule, utility easements do not cloud title. Therefore, I was able to keep up my end of the bargain. Legally, was I obligated to give the $2,000 to the buyers? No. At the time, it was still my property to do with as I pleased as long as I didn't violate the terms of our purchase agreement. The moral: If you want the eminent domain money, say so in your contract.

I should add that negotiations for this sale did not follow win-win principles. The buyers were represented by two contentious law firms, one local, one in their current hometown. The lawyers pushed as hard as they could to "win" at my expense. So I was quite happy to claim payback—which is exactly how win-lose negotiations typically turn out.

Date of Possession

Typically, sellers deliver possession of their property at settlement. Sometimes, though, the sellers may want to stay on for a while (say, to await completion of a new house they are building). Or, buyers may want to move in prior to closing. Either way, remember that in a win-win negotiation, possession and closing can be scheduled in a way that best satisfies both buyers and sellers.

Lease Agreement

If you or the sellers decide to rent the home to the other party, enter into a complete and well thought-out rental agreement. (See Chapter 11 in my forthcoming book, *Investing In Real Estate, 5th Edition, 2006,* [Wiley].) Don't simply tack a line onto your sales contract that says something like, "Sellers to deliver house by 9:00 A.M., June 1, 2006, and to pay rent of $1,800 per month for the period March 1, 2006, through May 31, 2006." In other words, deal with the rental period with a written lease, not merely an ad hoc statement.

Penalty Clause

If taking possession by a particular date is important to you, place a penalty clause in your purchase offer. Usually these penalties are written as a certain amount per day. The penalty amount is generally high enough to serve two purposes: (1) to cover whatever expenses and inconvenience seller delays cause you, and (2) to impose a cost on the sellers that's large enough to get them motivated to vacate on time. A penalty clause agreed to up front in purchase negotiations will ward off the conflict and debate that otherwise could come up later on.

Keys, Warranties, Et Cetera

Before you close the sale, ask the sellers to leave you all of the keys, lock combinations, garage door remotes, warranties, receipts, guarantees, instruction booklets, and any other items that you will need. The sellers should label everything. Don't accept a shoebox full of assorted papers or a large key ring of unmarked keys.

To insure that the sellers perform, place an appropriately worded clause in your purchase agreement. I can testify from experience that without a contract clause, some sellers will put this off until the last minute. Then, they'll tell you they've lost or inadvertently packed some of these items. To avoid this problem, list everything the sellers should provide and start clearing items long before they have boxed up their belongings.

Quality of Title

Real estate is subject to liens, encumbrances, encroachments, easements, right-of-ways, and other claims that can interfere with an owner's use and peaceful enjoyment of a property. So, your purchase offer should refer to the quality of title and the type of deed that the sellers will provide you. You want clear title subject only to various named exceptions (such as a utility easement or the lien of your mortgage lender).

Preliminary Title Report

Typically, after you have a signed agreement, your lender will order a preliminary title report. At this point, inquire about the quality of title. Sometimes legal specialists "approve" title quality without explicitly mentioning to you that a neighbor's garage sits two feet onto your property line, or that a road widening easement could take 20 feet off the front of your lot.

Because methods of verifying and conveying good title vary throughout the country, familiarize yourself with the procedures used in your area. Ask about the limitations (sources of error or omissions) that can disappoint buyers. Learn the property rights that you'll receive. And also note what exceptions might apply.

Title Insurance

Before closing a loan, most mortgage lenders require buyers to furnish a title insurance policy. Title policies protect against potential (but currently unknown) clouds. Such clouds might include a long-forgotten pipeline easement, a previously forged deed, or a misfiled mortgage lien. A title policy itself does not guarantee clear title. Instead, it guarantees to pay for (or defend against) claims in the future. In fact, title insurers usually do not cover known title defects.

So, don't confuse a title report with title insurance. It is the title report that you (or legal council) should look at. Then, determine whether you're satisfied with the quality of title the seller is providing.

Who Pays?

As you move from contract to closing, someone must pay for the numerous expenses (title insurance, loan fees, appraisal, deed stamps, survey inspections, etc.). The question your purchase agreement should answer is who? In many instances, local custom prevails. But custom need not dictate. You can negotiate "who pays" just as you can negotiate a sales price and possession date.

So, before you write an offer, talk with your realty agent and loan advisor. Decide whether you wish to follow custom, shift more costs to the sellers, or in some cases, assume more expenses yourself (as might occur when a seller agrees to discount the price). Or, if you are cash short, you might shift more closing costs to the sellers and, in exchange, agree to a higher price.

(Note: From an income tax standpoint, you should pay all costs associated with borrowing money. That's because you are permitted to deduct these expenses, but the sellers are not. Talk with a tax professional to learn whether this general principle fits your specific tax situation.)

Notices and Extensions

From the time you and the sellers sign your sales agreement up through closing, each of you must comply with various contract deadlines. Since these deadlines affect the dates of closing and possession, sales contracts typically require the respective parties to notify each other as progress occurs. It's not enough to merely comply with deadlines. You also must notify the sellers as various steps are completed. (In most instances, the sellers' real estate agent should stay updated and keep the sellers informed.)

Should you delay, immediately inform the sellers. Obtain from the sellers a written okay to extend the deadline. Otherwise, you risk losing your earnest money deposit. Be aware that to grant an extension (especially in hot markets), the sellers may try to extract a penalty fee or some other concession from you. If the sellers delay, you enjoy a similar negotiating advantage—especially when the sellers want to avoid putting their home back on the market should you choose to exercise your right to withdraw. (For example, the sellers often must provide a marketable title by some specified date prior to closing.)

Dispute Resolution

When you and the sellers cooperate, you should be able to informally work out any snags that arise on the way to closing. For those instances that do explode into a dispute that you can't (or won't) settle amicably, your contract should spell out a procedure to resolve such conflict.

Historically, buyers and sellers who are unable to informally resolve their differences have filed lawsuits. Today, many agreements require (or encourage) parties to use an alternative dispute resolution (ADR) procedure such as mediation or arbitration. Given the high costs, entangled process, lengthy delays, and roulette-like results of lawsuits, I favor ADR clauses.

Others disagree. They say you shouldn't give up your right to have a jury decide the matter. Who's correct probably depends on how the various approaches will work in your area with respect to your case. Weigh the pros and cons of placing an ADR clause in your purchase offer. (Be wary of your lawyer's advice on this issue. Remember, lawyers make more money from litigation than mediation. As a result, self-interest drives many lawyers to unduly criticize ADR.)

Attorney Fees and Costs

Apart from settlement expenses, purchase contracts frequently allocate the costs and fees of settling disputes. For example, one such contract states:

> The prevailing party in any legal proceeding brought under with respect to the transaction described in this contract is entitled to recover from the non-prevailing party all costs of such proceeding and reasonable [sic] attorney fees.

Generally, this type of clause can be referred to as "loser pays." While superficially, the clause seems straightforward, such is not the case.

Who Is the "Prevailing" Party?

In many legal disputes, opposing parties hurl various charges and countercharges at each other. As the litigation proceeds, the parties may settle, drop, or give up some of these claims. So, by judgment day, either in court or at an ADR meeting, one party may have scored wins *and* losses. In addition, say you claim $8,000 in damages for the undisclosed oil contamination caused by a leaking underground oil tank. In pretrial negotiations, the sellers offer to settle for $5,000.

You refuse and win a court award of $6,000. So, you won, right? Not necessarily. In some states, because your "win" didn't exceed the seller's settlement offer by more than 25 percent, it is you who "lost." You pay costs and fees. Absurd, maybe. But that's the law.

"Reasonable" Fees and Costs

When referring to attorney fees and court or ADR costs, the term "reasonable" seems bizarre. Even in a relatively minor dispute of $5,000 or $10,000, total legal fees and costs can easily top $15,000 or $20,000. Worse, even if you've got a slam-dunk case on the issues, you could still lose due to judicial error, attorney error, a technicality, or just plain bad luck.

So, even when you believe the other side will lose, don't be too sure. If a jury can find O.J. Simpson "not guilty," likewise, your judge or jury might find "no liability" for the sellers.

Implications

In discussing the downside of "loser pays," I emphasize two points: (1) The high costs of dispute settlement mean that you should strive to nurture a cooperative relationship with the sellers, and (2) it reinforces the need for you and your realty agent (or attorney) to draft a clear, unambiguous written agreement.

Sloppy Drafting: An Example

To illustrate the all-too-frequent practice of sloppy drafting, closely read these two actual contingency clauses:

1. Contingent on seller paying up to and no more than $3,000 of buyer's closing costs and/or prepaids + escrows. This includes FHA mandatory fees.

2. Contingent on acceptable home inspection within 10 days of acceptance.

The two clauses above are reprinted exactly as they were written in an offer prepared by a real estate agent and submitted to me for review at the time I was writing this chapter. By now, I hope you see the ambiguities in each of these clauses.

Consider contingency number one. Are mortgage points included within the sellers' obligations? What about title insurance, an up-front mortgage insurance premium, and the home inspection expense? What is included within "FHA mandatory fees"? The answer to each of these questions is open to debate because no two people will necessarily agree on the definition of "closing costs," "prepaids," "escrows," or "mandatory fees." A complete list of specific items would have clarified these potential sources of dispute.

With respect to contingency number two, as a seller, I would reject it. Why? Because it fails to objectively define "acceptable." In reality, the clause gives the buyer a free pass to walk away from the contract. Of course, when you're the buyer a similarly written clause greatly favors you. And if it's part of a "standard" printed sales contract, the seller may not even notice that it gives you an easy, no cost out.

Summing Up

Closely read your purchase agreement. Eliminate ambiguities and sources of confusion. Ask yourself, "Do I fully understand the meaning and implications of each and every clause? Will others interpret each clause in the same way that I do? Does the written agreement express the full agreement that I (we) and the sellers have negotiated?"

Too many buyers and sellers accept the so-called standard contract forms and the fill-in-the-blank (sloppy or otherwise) terminology of their realty agents or lawyers. But, with the information presented in this chapter, you need not act so passively. Question your contract critically. Make suggestions. Working together, you and your agent (or lawyer) can draft an agreement that will guide you through a no-hassle, dispute-free purchase.

Internet Appendix

hroughout, our discussions refer you to a variety of web sites that expand upon the topics covered. For convenience, I have arranged these web sites by category and have listed them here. For an overall information and referral site, see garyeldred.com.

With hundreds of thousands of real estate- and mortgage-related web sites, the following list only samples some of the more popular sites. If you've got the time and the will to sort through the data overload that the web now offers, you can certainly make a more informed homebuying and borrowing decision.

Yet, beware. Many sites do not provide accurate data, nor does the data necessarily relate to your specific need. For example, neighborhood data and school data are plagued with inconsistencies, omissions, errors, and ill-defined measures. I performed an analysis for the neighborhood where I was raised and was truly baffled by some of the wildly incorrect information that appeared. Do not accept web-based data as the last word. Check and verify all information. The web does not reduce your need to walk and talk the neighborhood; visit schools, shops, parks, and other facilities; physically view comp properties; and drive areas where you might like to look for For Sale signs.

City and Neighborhood Data

stats.bls.gov

usacitylink.com

venus.census.gov

www.census.gov

www.crime.org

www.ojp.usdoj.gov.bjs

Comp Sales

www.dataquick.com

www.latimes.com

www.propertyview.com

www.[your tax appraiser/assessor web site]

Credit Information

www.creditaccuracy.com

www.credit411.com

www.creditscoring.com

www.econsumer.equifax.com

www.experian.com

www.ftc.gov

www.myfico.com

www.qspace.com

www.transunion.com

Financial Calculators and Spreadsheets

www.hsh.com

www.loan-wolf.com

www.moneyweb.com

www.mortgage-minder.com

Foreclosures and Repos

www.all-foreclosure.com

www.bankhomes.net

www.bankofamerica.com

www.bankreo.com

www.brucebates.com

www.fanniemae.com

www.4close.com

www.homesteps.com

www.hud.gov

www.premierereo.com

www.treas.gov

www.va.gov

Home Improvement

www.askthebuilder.com

www.bhglive.com

www.hardware.com

www.hometime.com

www.housenet.com

www.michaelholigan.com

Home Inspection

www.ashi.org

www.creia.com

Homes for Sale

www.buyowner.com

www.cyberhomes.com

www.fsbo.com

www.houseandhome.msn.com

www.homes.com

www.homeseekers.com

www.ipix.com

www.owners.com

www.realtor.com

Insurance Information

www.cpcu.com   www.statefarm.com   www.insure.com

Law Information

www.lectlaw.com

www.lexis.com

www.municode.com

www.nolo.com

Mortgage Applications

www.eloan.com

www.fhatoday.com

www.interest.com

www.loanweb.com

www.mortgageauction.com

www.mortgage101.com

www.mortgagequotes.com

Mortgage Information

www.hsh.com   www.loan-wolf.com   www.mortgageprofessor.com

Mortgage Providers (Underwriters)

www.fanniemae.com

www.homesteps.com

www.hud.gov

www.va.gov

Real Estate Information

www.arello.org

www.garyeldred.com

www.inman.com/bruss

www.ired.com

www.johntreed.com

www.ourfamilyplace.com

www.realtor.com

www.rebooksandseminars.com

www.stoprentingnow.com

www.trumpuniversity.com

School Data

www.schoolmatch.com   www.schoolreport.com   www.2001beyond.com

Index

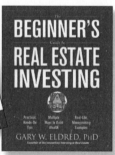

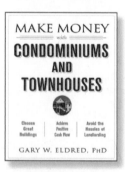
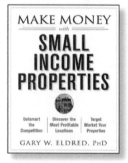